United States
Department of
Agriculture

Forest Service

Pacific Northwest
Research Station

Resource Bulletin
PNW-RB-255
March 2008

Production, Prices, Employment, and Trade in Northwest Forest Industries, All Quarters 2006

Debra D. Warren

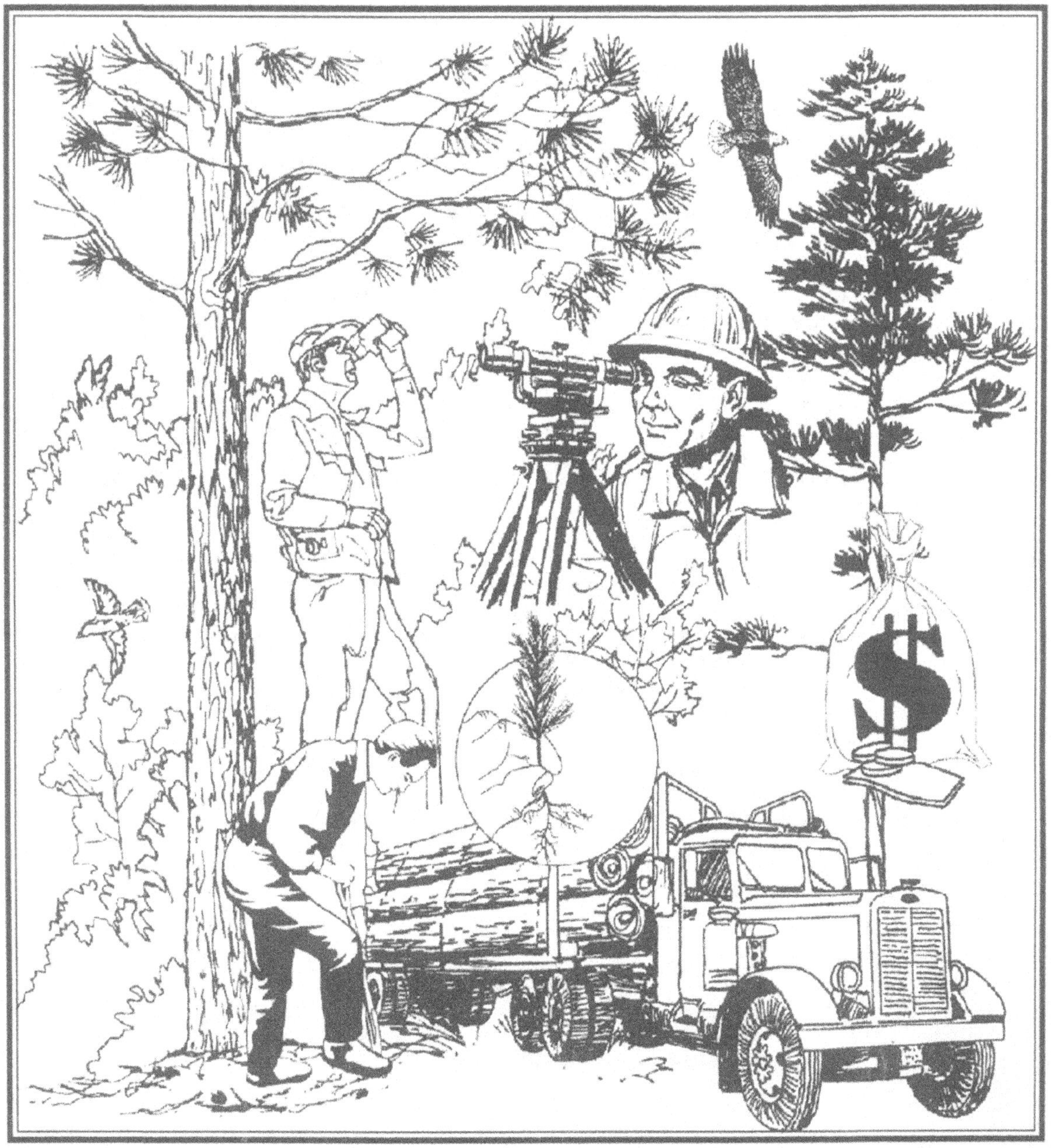

ABSTRACT

Warren, Debra D. 2008. Production, prices, employment, and trade in Northwest forest industries, all quarters of 2006. Resour. Bull. PNW RB 255. Portland, OR: U.S. Department of Agriculture, Forest Service, Pacific Northwest Research Station. 163 p.

Provides current information on lumber and plywood production and prices; employment in the forest industries; international trade in logs, lumber, and plywood; volume and average prices of stumpage sold by public agencies; and other related items.

Keywords: Forestry business economics, lumber prices, plywood prices, timber volume, stumpage prices, employment (forest products industries), marketing (forest products), imports and exports (forest products).

PREFACE

Due to temporary unavailability of trade data, this report was delayed. In the interest of efficiency and timeliness, all four quarters of 2006 are being published in one book. This report presents current information on the timber situation in Alaska, Washington, Oregon, California, Montana, Idaho, and British Columbia, including data on lumber and plywood production and prices; timber harvest; employment in forest products industries; international trade in logs, pulpwood, chips, lumber, and plywood; log prices in the Pacific Northwest; volume and average prices of stumpage sold by public agencies; and other related items.

Cooperation in supplying data has been received from the following sources: U.S. Department of Agriculture, Forest Service, Forest Inventory and Economics Research Staff in Washington, DC; Washington State Department of Natural Resources and Employment Security Department; Oregon State Department of Forestry and Department of Employment; California State Department of Employment and Department of Conservation; Montana State Forester and State Employment Service; Idaho State Department of Public Lands and Department of Employment; Alaska State Department of Labor and Department of Natural Resources of the Division of Lands; U.S. Department of Commerce; U.S. Department of the Interior, Bureau of Land Management and Bureau of Indian Affairs; British Columbia Department of Industrial Development, Trade, and Commerce; and a number of private industry associations, firms, and individuals. A special "thank you" goes to Judy Mikowski at the PNW Research Station for her assistance in the Washington and Oregon employment tables (25 and 26), the Western Wood Products Association tables (9 13), and all of the graphs.

The valuation definition used in the export statistics is the value at the seaport or border port of exportation. It is based on the selling price (or cost if not sold) and includes inland freight, insurance, and other charges to the port of exportation. Seattle Customs District includes all coastal and inland ports in the State of Washington, except Longview and Vancouver. Columbia Snake Customs District includes all Oregon ports and Longview and Vancouver, Washington. Anchorage Customs District is the State of Alaska. San Francisco Customs District includes Monterey and all ports north of Monterey, California.

The statistical data are from secondary sources and are brought together to make such information more readily available. Sources are indicated for each table and can be contacted directly for means used in data collection.

Readers are cautioned that unit values should not be interpreted as accurate indicators of prices. Unit values for individual trade flows, especially those involving small volumes, frequently vary widely within a year, across origins or destinations, and through time.

AUTHOR

DEBRA D. WARREN is an economist, Pacific Northwest Research Station, Suite 400, 620 SW Main, Portland, OR. The mailing address is P.O. Box 3890, Portland, OR 97208 3890. The phone number is 503/808 2001, and the FAX number is 503/808 2033. This report is also available online in portable document format (pdf) at the following address: http://www.fs.fed.us/pnw/pubs/rb255.pdf.

Tables Included in This Series of Reports
and Frequency of Updates

Tables Included in This Series of Reports (continued)

Tables Included in This Series of Reports (continued)

NOTE: The old Tables 44 and 45 (volume and value of log exports from British Columbia) are being discontinued due to lack of availability of data. The tables that follow have been renumbered.

Tables Included in This Series of Reports (continued)

Tables Included in This Series of Reports (continued)

Tables Included in This Series of Reports (continued)

Tables Included in This Series of Reports (continued)

Tables Included in This Series of Reports (continued)

Figures Included in This Series of Reports
and Frequency of Updates

Conversion Factors Used in This Report

For logs: 4.53 cubic meters equals 1 thousand board feet

For lumber: 2.36 cubic meters equals 1 thousand board feet

For veneer: 92.9 square meters equals 1 thousand square feet

For plywood: .885 cubic meters equals 1 thousand square feet (3/8 inch basis)

For chips and pulpwood: .907 metric tons equals 1 short ton

**Western Lumber
Production and
Prices**

- Softwood lumber production

A total of 17.6 billion board feet of softwood lumber was produced
in the Western United States in 2006, and the total U.S. figure was
38.0 billion board feet (table 1). Total softwood lumber production
in the fourth quarter of 2006 was 8.3 billion board feet, and 46.0
percent of that was produced in the West.

- Wholesale lumber prices

Average wholesale prices decreased in 2006 for all of the selected
lumber products (table 7). Year-end 2006 prices averaged a 8.3-
percent decrease from year-end 2005, across all five selected
lumber products.

**Plywood Production
and Prices**

- Plywood production in 2006

United States softwood structural panel board production in 2006,
at 28,383 million square feet (3/8-inch basis), increased 3.2 percent
from 2005. Monthly figures are no longer available (table 1).

Wholesale prices of selected plywood products decreased from
2005 to 2006. Year-end 2006 prices averaged a 7.3-percent
decrease (table 8) from year-end 2005 prices.

**Employment in
Forest Products
Industries**

- Employment numbers for 2006

The number of persons employed in the lumber and wood products
industries decreased in 2006 in Oregon and Washington (table 21).
Once again, third quarter 2006 employment numbers were higher
than the other quarters.

In Oregon, there were 10.5 direct jobs per million board feet of
timber harvested in 2006 (using the harvest figures from table 16).
In Washington, there were 12.2 direct jobs per million board feet
of timber harvested in 2006.

Log, Pulp, and Chip Exports

- Washington and Oregon log exports

Log exports from Washington and Oregon ports totaled 534.3 million board feet in 2006, as compared to 535.2 million board feet in 2005. In 2006, Washington Customs District exported 204.2 million board feet of logs to all countries, and Oregon Customs District exported 330.1 (table 27).

- Log export prices for Washington and Oregon

Softwood log exports from Washington and Oregon ports averaged $838.25 (per thousand board feet) in 2006, up from the 2005 average of $819.04. The fourth quarter 2006 values for both states averaged $799.47 (table 29), down from $845.28 in the third quarter of 2006.

- Log exports from California and Alaska

San Francisco Customs District exported 75 thousand board feet of logs in 2006, compared with 140 mbf in 2005 (table 30). The Anchorage Customs District exported 254.1 million board feet of logs in 2006, compared with 216.0 in 2005 (table 31).

- Pulp volumes in the Pacific Northwest

There were decreases in the pulp export volumes of 2006 in three of the four customs districts (table 46).

- Average value of pulp exports

All the customs districts showed an increase in the average value for both grades of pulp exports from 2005 to 2006, except the Anchorage Customs District which had no pulp exports in 2006 (table 47).

- Chip exports

All four customs districts reflected a decrease in the volume of chips exported in 2006. The average value of chips increased only in the Columbia-Snake Customs District (table 48).

Lumber, Plywood,

- Lumber export volumes from the Northwest

and Veneer

Both the Columbia-Snake and the Seattle Customs Districts had an increase in the volume of lumber exports from 152.1 million board feet in 2005 to 171.3 in 2006 (table 50). Southern California lumber export volumes decreased in 2006 (table 53). Northern California lumber exports decreased 4.6 percent in 2006 (table 54). Alaska decreased lumber export volumes to 2.2 million board feet in 2006 (table 55).

- Average value of lumber exports

In the Seattle and Columbia-Snake Customs Districts, the average value of lumber exports increased from $759.06 (pcr thousand board feet) in 2005 to $796.29 in 2006 (table 52). Southern California lumber export prices rose in 2006 (table 53). Northern California (table 54) lumber export prices increased from $738.25 in 2005 to $848.97 in 2006. Alaska lumber prices (table 55) increased sharply from $561.77 in 2005 to $1,005.35 in 2006.

- Oregon and Washington lumber imports

The Seattle Customs District imported 4.5 billion board feet of lumber in 2006, mostly from Canada (table 68). The Columbia-Snake Customs District imported 79.1 million board feet in 2006, compared with 80.8 million in 2005 (table 70).

- Softwood plywood exports

The volume of softwood plywood exports from both the Seattle and the Columbia-Snake Customs Districts decreased in 2006, but the average values of softwood plywood exports increased in 2006 (table 72).

- Softwood veneer exports

In 2006, softwood veneer export volumes decreased in both the Seattle and Columbia-Snake Customs Districts (table 74). The prices rose in Washington, but dropped for softwood veneer in Oregon.

**Timber Sold by
Forest Service
Regions**

- Sold volume in Northern Region

Not all ownership numbers are available, but the amount of timber sold on National Forest lands in Montana and northern Idaho decreased 58.0 percent from 2005 to 2006 (table 75).

- Sold volume in northern California

In 2006, the volume of timber sold on USDA Forest Service lands in northern California decreased 36.3 percent from the 2005 total (table 83).

- Sold volume in Washington and Oregon

Oregon and Washington showed a decrease of 56.9 percent in the amount of timber sold on USDA Forest Service lands from 2005 to 2006 (table 89).

- Sold volume in Alaska

In 2006, the volume of timber sold on National Forest lands in Alaska was 46.7 million board feet, compared to 81.8 million board feet in 2005 (table 95). Average values decreased from $14.67 in 2005 to $11.18 in 2006 (table 96).

TABLES AND FIGURES

Table 1—U.S. softwood lumber and structural panel board production, 1995-2006

Year	U.S. softwood lumber production				U.S. softwood structural panel board production
	Total softwood lumber	Western region[a]	Southern pine region	Other softwoods	
	Million board feet				*Million feet, 3/8 inch basis*
1995	31,915	15,665	14,731	1,519	26,766
1996	33,812	16,811	15,163	1,838	27,787
1997	34,720	16,818	16,013	1,889	27,151
1998	34,740	16,782	16,057	1,901	29,128
1999	36,534	17,744	16,642	2,150	29,034
2000	35,884	17,154	16,619	2,111	29,381
2001	34,206	16,765	15,428	2,013	27,653
2002	35,832	17,039	16,685	2,108	28,626
2003	35,879	17,146	16,624	2,110	28,321
2004	38,314	18,762	17,306	2,246	28,936
2005	40,336	19,400	18,564	2,371	29,315
2006:					
January	3,512	1,631	1,674	207	NA
February	3,216	1,474	1,572	170	NA
March	3,550	1,671	1,692	188	NA
Total, 1st quarter	10,278	4,776	4,938	565	NA
April	3,294	1,475	1,645	174	NA
May	3,360	1,580	1,602	178	NA
June	3,485	1,612	1,689	184	NA
Total, 2d quarter	10,139	4,667	4,936	536	NA
July	3,195	1,455	1,571	169	NA
August	3,246	1,570	1,504	172	NA
September	2,877	1,367	1,358	152	NA
Total, 3d quarter	9,318	4,392	4,433	493	NA
October	3,154	1,460	1,528	167	NA
November	2,601	1,208	1,256	137	NA
December	2,514	1,132	1,249	133	NA
Total, 4th quarter	8,269	3,800	4,033	437	NA
2006 total	38,004	17,635	18,340	2,031	28,383

NA = not available.

[a] Includes western, inland, and California redwood regions.

Note: As of November 2004, monthly statistics were no longer available from the American Plywood Association. This is the final issue for the last column.

Source: Western Wood Products Association, Portland, Oregon, and American Plywood Association, Tacoma, Washington.

Table 2—Lumber production in Northwest States, 1996-2006

(In million board feet)

Year	Washington	Oregon	California[a]	Montana	Idaho
1996	3,917	5,374	3,257	1,170	1,802
1997[b]	3,851	5,589	3,432	1,234	1,859
1998	3,913	5,486	3,188	1,304	1,908
1999	4,224	6,056	3,216	1,345	1,975
2000	4,384	5,927	3,173	1,177	1,896
2001	4,257	6,056	2,731	1,080	1,833
2002	4,625	6,177	2,634	1,143	1,906
2003	4,898	6,532	2,654	1,078	1,949
2004	5,455	7,126	2,763	985	1,964
2005	5,729	7,433	2,688	1,001	2,026
2006	5,130	7,032	2,590	917	1,846

[a] Includes 1 mill in Nevada.

[b] Beginning in 1997, Oregon and Washington figures reflect the elimination of hardwood production.

Source: Western Wood Products Association, Portland, Oregon.

Table 3—Softwood lumber production in the inland region, by species, 1996-2006[a]

(m llion board feet)

Year	A l softwoods	Ponderosa p ne	daho wh te p ne	Sugar p ne	Doug as-f r and arch	Hem-f r[b]	Enge mann spruce	Lodgepo e p ne	Other softwoods
1996	7 079	2 146	33	122	1 825	1 597	335	612	409
1997	7 382	2 077	31	138	2 055	1 708	334	652	387
1998	7 297	1 832	33	102	2 136	1 766	344	722	362
1999	7 576	1 803	36	122	2 138	1 891	430	765	391
2000	7 076	1 737	36	110	2 101	1 761	345	582	404
2001	6 563	1 555	32	133	1 991	1 665	273	600	314
2002	6 760	1 550	36	109	2 047	1 761	260	645	352
2003	6 717	1 522	23	105	2 054	1 912	242	544	315
2004	6 777	1 599	25	99	2 065	1 957	225	465	343
2005	6 687	1 546	33	87	2 165	1 818	281	363	394
2006	6 227	1 397	c	c	1 952	1 767	259	336	517

[a] nc udes eastern Wash ngton eastern Oregon Ca forn a (except redwood reg on) Nevada daho Montana Wyom ng Utah Co orado Ar zona New Mex co and a port on of South Dakota

[b] Western hem ock and wh te f r

[c] Th s spec es was added to the "Other softwoods" category

Source Western Wood Products Assoc at on Port and Oregon

Table 4—Lumber production in the coast region, by species, 1996-2006[a]

(million board feet)

Year	All species	Douglas-fir	Hem-fir[b]	Western redcedar	Incense-cedar	Pine	Other softwoods	Hardwoods
1996	7 745	4 478	2 090	509	31	167	63	407
1997	7 772	4 632	2 362	506	35	177	60	0
1998	7 799	4 674	2 426	432	19	186	62	0
1999	8 625	5 246	2 642	494	22	173	48	0
2000	8 781	5 363	2 683	515	15	144	61	0
2001	8 765	5 425	2 729	409	20	119	63	0
2002	9 243	5 814	2 812	388	17	148	64	0
2003	9 904	6 232	3 002	420	12	140	92	0
2004	10 919	6 827	3 435	431	23	104	99	0
2005	11 598	7 401	3 562	452	21	82	80	0
2006	10 732	6 821	3 346	371	c	c	193	0

[a] Includes western Washington and western Oregon

[b] Western hemlock and white fir combined

[c] This species was added to the "Other softwoods" category

Source: Western Wood Products Association, Portland, Oregon

Table 5—Softwood structural panel board production in the United States, by State, 1996-2006[a]

(In million square feet, 3/8 inch basis)

Year	Total	Oregon	Washington	Oklahoma, New York, Colorado, and Tennessee	Montana and Idaho[b]	Southern States[c]	Northern States[d]
1996	28,495	3,773	1,045	1,180	1,262	18,747	3,668
1997	28,497	3,471	986	1,162	1,024	18,367	3,487
1998	29,003	3,492	978	1,323	980	18,496	3,733
1999	29,428	3,510	1,152	1,385	1,031	18,463	3,887
2000	29,441	3,696	989	1,558	918	18,446	3,834
2001	27,653	3,348	836	1,818	562	17,164	3,925
2002	28,626	3,058	1,133	1,905	553	17,833	4,144
2003	28,321	3,214	969	1,907	438	17,571	4,222
2004	28,936	3,143	1,063	2,305	444	17,786	4,196
2005	29,315	3,033	1,092	2,757	408	17,819	4,206
2006	28,383	2,668	963	2,405	363	18,233	3,751

[a] Structural panel board includes plywood, waferboard, and oriented strand board (OSB).

[b] Since 2001, these figures are Montana only. Idaho has been combined with the previous column "Oklahoma, New York, Colorado, and Tennessee" since 2001.

[c] Southern states include Alabama, Arkansas, Florida, Georgia, Louisiana, Maryland, Mississippi, North Carolina, South Carolina, Texas, Virginia, and West Virginia.

[d] Northern states include Maine, Michigan, Minnesota, New Hampshire, and Wisconsin.

Source: American Plywood Association.

Table 6—Softwood lumber and plywood production in British Columbia, 1996-2006

Year	Softwood lumber production			Softwood plywood production
	Total	Coast	Interior	
	Million board feet			Million ft², 3/8 inch basis
1996	13,845	3,387	10,458	1,671
1997	13,376	3,032	10,344	1,668
1998	12,814	2,684	10,130	1,574
1999	13,490	2,809	10,681	1,739
2000	13,627	2,851	10,776	1,737
2001	13,770	3,141	10,629	1,770
2002	15,112	3,096	12,015	1,893
2003	15,292	3,302	11,990	1,958
2004	16,898	2,664	14,234	NA
2005	17,381	2,500	14,881	NA
2006	17,394	2,332	15,062	NA

NA = not available.

Source: Statistics Canada, Ottawa, Canada, and Council of Forest Industries.

Table 7—Wholesale prices of selected lumber products, 1995-2006

(In dollars per thousand board feet)

Year	Douglas fir std. and btr., 2 by 4 RL, 8/20', KD, net, f.o.b. mill	Ponderosa pine boards, no. 3, 1 by 12 RL, KD, net, f.o.b. mill	Ponderosa pine, no. 2 shop, 6/4 RWRL, S2S, net, f.o.b. mill	Fir larch std. and btr., 2 by 4 RL, 8/20', KD, net, f.o.b. mill	Spruce pine fir std. and btr., 2 by 4 RL, 8/20', KD, net, f.o.b. mill
1995	332.49	468.38	970.40	325.92	250.88
1996	421.77	461.58	919.19	420.28	350.80
1997	417.49	545.96	1,008.33	408.08	354.47
1998	339.98	384.92	879.90	340.07	288.31
1999	409.33	464.06	903.33	406.37	342.99
2000	340.33	364.71	876.02	341.37	257.58
2001	333.72	346.92	921.09	333.07	250.33
2002	328.18	331.87	953.88	326.68	236.35
2003	347.25	360.98	866.75	345.73	261.23
2004	458.67	471.46	1,051.58	461.57	386.72
2005	405.66	392.46	923.98	408.49	346.85
2006:					
January	423.75	390.00	891.25	421.75	347.50
February	425.50	397.50	900.00	435.00	335.75
March	419.00	405.00	900.00	431.00	322.60
Average, 1st quarter	422.75	397.50	897.08	429.25	335.28
April	405.00	406.25	911.25	417.75	327.00
May	397.50	434.75	925.00	406.25	316.00
June	371.00	430.40	925.00	374.60	294.40
Average, 2d quarter	391.17	423.80	920.42	399.53	312.47
July	355.00	402.50	925.00	355.50	288.00
August	315.00	427.50	920.00	324.25	268.25
September	298.00	457.00	914.00	303.60	265.60
Average, 3d quarter	322.67	429.00	919.67	327.78	273.95
October	258.75	378.75	910.00	276.50	234.00
November	265.00	333.75	910.00	272.25	237.25
December	283.00	319.00	910.00	292.20	245.60
Average, 4th quarter	268.92	343.83	910.00	280.32	238.95
2006 average	351.38	398.53	911.79	359.22	290.16
Year end 2006 change, in percent					
From: Year end 2005	13.38	1.55	1.32	12.05	16.34

Source: Random Lengths Publications, Inc.

11

Table 8—Wholesale prices of selected softwood plywood products, 1995-2006

(In dollars per thousand square feet)

Year	Sheathing, western exterior, 3/8 inch, CD, net f.o.b. mill	Sheathing, southern (west)[a] exterior, 3/8 inch, CD, net f.o.b. mill	Sanded, western interior, 1/4 inch, AD, net f.o.b. mill
1995	256.93	241.71	337.56
1996	230.08	200.75	339.23
1997	240.38	212.81	363.52
1998	235.69	225.83	359.69
1999	282.72	259.75	401.20
2000	227.67	213.37	347.50
2001	224.26	216.58	342.53
2002	221.82	203.83	329.59
2003	271.71	269.69	358.81
2004	374.80	346.92	526.69
2005	321.25	297.62	462.50
2006:			
January	319.75	276.25	470.00
February	314.00	270.00	481.25
March	310.40	273.60	485.00
Average, 1st quarter	314.72	273.28	478.75
April	310.00	276.25	485.00
May	303.00	257.75	485.00
June	304.80	258.80	485.00
Average, 2d quarter	305.93	264.27	485.00
July	302.25	242.50	478.75
August	303.50	226.75	475.00
September	299.20	218.00	470.00
Average, 3d quarter	301.65	229.08	474.58
October	282.50	202.75	463.75
November	278.25	211.75	457.50
December	275.00	216.20	455.00
Average, 4th quarter	278.58	210.23	458.75
2006 average	300.22	244.22	474.27
	Year end 2006 change, in percent		
From: Year end 2005	6.55	17.94	2.54

[a] Texas, Louisiana, and Arkansas.

Source: Random Lengths Publications, Inc.

Table 9—Percentage of total volume and f.o.b. mill prices for Douglas-fir lumber, coast mills, 1995-2006[a]

(Volume in thousand board feet; price in dollars per thousand board feet)

Year	C selects Percent	C selects Price	D selects and shop Percent	D selects and shop Price	Structural items Percent	Structural items Price	Heavy framing Percent	Heavy framing Price	Light framing Percent	Light framing Price	Utility Percent	Utility Price	Economy Percent	Economy Price	Total volume all grades
1995	0.1	1 172	0.7	699	12.2	448	21.9	442	57.2	330	4.9	224	3.0	142	2 436 390
1996	0	--	.7	668	10.1	519	21.8	485	60.1	392	3.5	261	3.8	134	2 385 259
1997	0	--	.4	711	9.1	530	23.2	499	59.9	397	3.4	274	4.0	164	2 345 066
1998	0	--	.4	655	9.2	421	24.1	383	59.0	325	3.6	266	3.7	143	2 327 074
1999	0	--	.2	676	8.6	463	23.6	467	60.3	390	3.7	268	3.6	137	2 498 118
2000	0	--	.2	631	7.5	425	22.1	412	62.6	339	3.8	220	3.8	125	2 733 326
2001	0	--	.1	598	7.0	389	23.3	382	62.8	319	3.7	201	3.2	111	2 612 460
2002	0	--	.1	666	8.6	361	23.5	367	61.4	309	3.3	201	3.0	119	2 798 254
2003	0	--	.3	622	9.5	376	23.7	400	60.1	318	3.5	203	3.0	110	2 803 404
2004	0	--	.2	661	10.5	467	22.9	496	59.5	421	3.4	291	3.5	168	2 748 988
2005	0	--	.1	649	8.5	430	18.8	457	65.6	381	3.6	281	3.4	153	4 116 884
2006															
1st quarter	0	--	.1	725	7.7	447	20.4	490	66.3	373	2.3	246	3.3	151	929 840
2d quarter	0	--	.1	721	9.8	415	19.6	486	64.5	347	2.7	243	3.2	151	893 710
3d quarter	0	--	.1	881	7.5	292	21.2	464	64.8	320	3.1	209	3.4	129	779 167
4th quarter	0	--	.1	756	7.8	351	21.7	422	63.8	273	3.3	170	3.3	116	762 182
2006 average	0	--	.1	759	8.2	384	20.7	467	64.9	332	2.8	216	3.3	138	3 364 899

[a] Figures are a volume-weighted average of green and dry surfaced and rough grades.

Source: Data are compiled by Western Wood Products Association from copies of invoices submitted to the Association by mills accounting for about 65 to 70 percent of the region's production and individual groupings from Pacific Northwest Research Station.

13

Table 10—Percentage of total volume for ponderosa pine lumber, inland mills, 1995-2006[a]

(in thousand board feet)

Year	4/4 selects and 1 shop					5/4 and thicker moulding and shops					4/4 commons and 8/4 std & btr				Low value		Total volume all grades
	C and btr 6-12 in	D 12 in	C and btr D 4 in 6-10 in	D 4 in	1 shop	Mdg and btr	1 shop	2 shop	3 shop	Shopout	2 com 12 in	2 com 4-10 in	3 com 6-12 in 8/4 dim	3 com 4 com 4-12 in	No 3 and ut	5 com and econ	
1995	0.3	0.1	0.2	0.4	1.5	3.8	1.3	10.2	21.0	15.0	4.0	11.9	22.1	5.8	13	11	1 519 049
1996	0.3	0.1	0.2	0.4	1.5	3.3	1.2	9.4	20.8	17.7	3.5	12.1	21.2	6.2	11	11	1 421 090
1997	0.2	0.1	0.2	0.4	1.5	2.4	1.0	7.8	19.6	16.0	4.0	14.6	23.5	6.7	10	12	1 304 349
1998	0.2	0	0.2	0.5	1.1	2.7	1.1	8.3	21.2	15.0	3.9	14.8	22.8	6.5	8	10	1 281 067
1999	0.2	0	0.1	0.4	1.2	2.4	0.9	8.3	21.9	15.3	4.0	14.0	23.2	6.1	10	9	1 277 164
2000	0.2	0	0.1	0.4	1.1	2.4	0.7	7.4	20.3	12.6	4.5	15.6	25.9	6.6	11	9	1 159 786
2001	0.2	0	0.2	0.4	1.2	1.8	0.7	7.0	19.0	11.4	4.1	16.0	28.7	7.3	11	10	1 070 041
2002	0.2	0	0.1	0.5	1.2	1.6	0.7	7.0	18.7	9.6	4.5	17.2	29.0	7.9	9	10	983 261
2003	0.2	0	0.2	0.5	1.1	1.9	0.5	5.6	17.4	5.8	5.2	19.9	31.1	7.7	16	14	886 501
2004	0.2	0	0.2	0.5	1.2	1.8	0.6	6.1	19.2	7.3	4.6	18.2	30.1	7.0	13	15	964 783
2005	0.2	0	0.2	0.4	1.2	1.4	0.7	7.3	21.7	6.8	4.6	16.0	30.0	6.5	15	15	996 126
2006																	
1st quarter	0.3	0	0.2	0.4	1.1	1.3	0.8	7.7	22.6	7.5	4.1	15.8	28.8	6.5	12	16	224 054
2d quarter	0.2	0	0.2	0.4	1.0	1.4	0.6	7.6	23.3	7.3	4.0	17.8	27.6	6.8	6	11	223 718
3d quarter	0.3	0	0.2	0.3	1.0	1.4	0.6	6.8	21.7	7.4	4.0	17.2	30.7	6.6	7	12	239 529
4th quarter	0.2	0	0.2	0.3	1.1	1.5	0.6	6.6	20.4	9.1	3.8	17.4	29.2	7.7	7	12	204 809
2006 average	0.3	0	0.2	0.4	1.1	1.4	0.7	7.3	22.4	7.9	4.0	17.3	28.1	7.0	8	13	879 498

[a] Figures are a volume-weighted average of green and dry surfaced and rough grades

Source: Data are compiled by Western Wood Products Association from copies of invoices submitted to the association by mills accounting for about 80 percent of the region's production individual groupings from Pacific Northwest Research Station

Table 11—F.O.B. mill prices for ponderosa pine lumber, inland mills, 1995-2006

(In dollars per thousand board feet)

Year	4/4 selects and 1 shop					5/4 and thicker moulding and shops					4/4 commons and 8/4 std. & btr.				Low value	
	C and btr. 6-12 n.	D 12 n.	C and btr. D 6-10 n. 4 n.	D 4 n.	1 shop	Mdg. and btr.	1 shop	2 shop	3 shop	Shopout	2 com. 12 n.	2 com. 4-10 n.	3 com. 6-12 n. 8/4 d m.	3 com. 4 n. 4-12 n.	No. 3 and ut.	5 com. and econ.
1995	1 887	1 982	1 095	737	550	1 491	1 089	972	661	410	695	507	367	251	215	158
1996	1 569	1 251	1 071	802	585	1 381	1 005	899	692	427	683	544	361	250	224	141
1997	2 123	1 571	1 366	906	672	1 659	1 141	1 024	766	482	825	602	427	302	248	169
1998	2 116	1 608	1 202	711	462	1 480	1 006	892	615	414	685	515	337	278	213	155
1999	2 129	1 615	1 266	796	562	1 579	1 036	913	695	458	808	548	385	275	219	143
2000	1 908	1 480	1 106	705	506	1 428	1 024	893	611	376	676	494	328	242	187	136
2001	1 691	1 440	1 000	687	484	1 677	1 047	922	602	325	684	453	283	201	164	110
2002	2 076	1 500	1 059	618	436	1 710	1 092	954	620	355	720	492	294	228	167	126
2003	1 651	1 291	786	650	453	1 393	1 015	883	483	261	569	468	300	236	157	120
2004	1 701	1 513	935	676	612	1 624	1 173	1 049	687	378	756	537	381	316	243	179
2005	1 765	1 665	1 037	688	574	1 426	1 076	961	552	325	637	510	344	318	222	169
2006																
1st quarter	1 609	1 658	1 052	686	574	1 394	1 072	960	642	399	594	570	370	333	207	167
2d quarter	1 531	1 595	976	651	593	1 481	1 085	973	653	400	653	529	373	320	213	170
3d quarter	1 440	1 631	972	690	582	1 536	1 086	972	599	374	603	491	267	297	183	150
4th quarter	1 469	1 622	945	671	556	1 304	1 084	965	472	250	776	485	290	214	156	127
2006 average	1 518	1 628	988	674	576	1 431	1 081	968	597	353	651	518	339	290	193	154

Source: Data are compiled by Western Wood Products Association from copies of invoices submitted to the association by mills accounting for about 80 percent of the region's production. Individual groupings from Pacific Northwest Research Station.

15

Table 12—Percentage of total volume and f.o.b. mill prices for hem-fir lumber, inland mills, 1995-2006[a]

(Volume in thousand board feet; price in dollars per thousand board feet)

Year	Moulding		Shop		Structural items		Heavy framing		Light framing		Utility		Economy		Total volume all grades
	Percent	Price	Percent	Price	Percent	Price	Percent	Price	Percent	Price	Percent	Price	Percent	Price	
1995	0.8	1 133	3.9	602	3.8	407	29.1	399	48.1	325	10.1	244	4.3	140	1 103 315
1996	0.8	1 149	4.2	584	3.5	454	25.6	431	53.7	392	7.4	241	4.9	140	1 087 999
1997	0.8	955	3.6	641	3.4	489	30.0	479	50.1	396	7.5	262	4.7	174	1 176 948
1998	0.6	956	2.8	495	4.3	371	26.2	335	54.9	332	6.9	224	4.3	150	1 237 282
1999	0.6	1 064	2.1	603	5.2	448	28.0	440	53.3	379	6.8	238	4.1	142	1 362 760
2000	0.6	1 026	2.1	562	5.6	387	26.8	352	54.6	323	6.0	206	4.3	135	1 260 807
2001	0.5	732	1.6	438	6.4	347	25.7	311	55.5	302	5.8	189	4.5	115	1 165 610
2002	0.3	858	2.0	537	6.6	351	22.7	313	58.3	299	5.2	191	4.9	124	1 138 731
2003	0.3	986	1.1	454	7.7	337	23.9	289	56.4	285	5.5	174	5.1	117	1 272 949
2004	0.3	1 111	1.1	689	8.3	449	23.7	396	56.3	401	5.5	247	4.9	184	1 399 551
2005	0.1	885	0.4	637	9.3	419	22.4	387	56.3	367	6.0	231	5.5	165	1 247 061
2006															
1st quarter	0.1	948	0.4	599	9.3	397	22.1	355	58.0	366	5.2	227	4.9	163	322 178
2d quarter	0.1	998	0.5	642	9.3	412	22.9	362	59.3	350	5.4	234	2.5	177	287 930
3d quarter	0.1	1 021	0.6	614	9.3	406	24.1	342	54.0	308	5.6	195	6.4	151	290 472
4th quarter	0.1	1 076	0.6	568	10.3	348	24.2	283	53.6	272	6.0	155	5.1	119	286 379
2006 average	0.1	1 012	0.5	603	9.6	390	23.3	335	56.3	327	5.5	202	4.8	150	1 186 959

[a] Figures are a volume-weighted average of green and dry surfaced and rough grades

Source: Data are compiled by Western Wood Products Association from copies of invoices submitted to the Association by mills accounting for about 80 percent of the region's product on individual groupings from Pacific Northwest Research Station

Table 13—Percentage of total volume and f.o.b. mill prices for hem-fir lumber, coast mills, 1995-2006[a]

(Volume in thousand board feet; price in dollars per thousand board feet)

	C selects		D selects and shop		Structural items		Heavy framing		Light framing		Utility		Economy		Total volume, all grades
	Percent	Price	Percent	Price	Percent	Price	Percent	Price	Percent	Price	Percent	Price	Percent	Price	
1995	0	—	0.5	590	3.7	357	22.9	397	59.1	312	7.6	209	6.2	154	1 001 187
1996	0	—	.5	593	3.4	424	20.5	436	61.2	376	7.4	243	7.0	148	1 177 493
1997	0	—	.4	560	2.5	451	20.0	469	62.1	375	7.9	263	7.2	176	1 395 881
1998	0	—	.2	499	2.3	371	21.3	343	62.8	314	7.9	227	5.5	153	1 345 836
1999	0	—	.1	568	2.0	436	19.6	438	65.8	359	7.3	255	5.1	144	1 504 206
2000	0	—	.2	521	2.0	375	19.5	357	65.7	300	7.4	209	5.3	134	1 543 582
2001	0	—	.1	395	2.6	343	20.3	305	66.3	280	6.0	187	4.8	124	1 567 009
2002	0	—	.1	448	2.5	341	19.1	309	66.8	280	5.8	187	5.7	132	1 637 829
2003	0	—	.2	466	3.5	326	20.0	299	65.2	277	5.2	173	5.9	123	1 713 922
2004	0	—	.1	527	2.8	430	19.7	398	67.9	383	3.5	233	5.9	184	1 803 795
2005	0	—	.1	465	1.8	399	17.0	387	70.5	356	4.0	235	6.7	172	2 031 168
2006															
1st quarter	0	—	0	—	2.1	388	17.6	371	68.8	364	4.8	223	6.8	172	475 554
2d quarter	0	—	0	—	2.3	367	17.3	371	69.8	343	4.6	232	5.9	168	480 484
3d quarter	0	—	0	—	2.5	337	18.7	338	66.9	292	5.4	185	6.4	140	438 580
4th quarter	0	—	0	—	2.3	310	20.1	283	66.2	262	5.0	157	6.4	120	363 668
2006 average	0	—	0	—	2.3	352	18.3	343	68.0	320	4.9	201	6.4	152	1 758 286

[a] Figures are a volume-weighted average of green and dry surfaced and rough grades

Source: Data are compiled by Western Wood Products Association from copies of invoices submitted to the Association by mills accounting for approximately 65 to 70 percent of the region's production on individual groupings from Pacific Northwest Research Station

Table 14—Weighted average f.o.b. mill prices for coast and inland lumber, 1995-2006

(In dollars per thousand board feet)

Year	Coast			Inland		
	Douglas fir	Hem fir	Weighted average	Ponderosa pine	Hem fir	Weighted average
1995	361	317	348	580	351	483
1996	413	365	397	568	395	493
1997	420	373	403	627	417	527
1998	340	306	328	536	327	433
1999	402	357	385	579	389	487
2000	350	298	331	504	328	420
2001	328	274	308	468	297	379
2002	318	274	302	490	298	387
2003	334	269	309	432	279	342
2004	430	370	406	551	390	456
2005:						
1st quarter	404	397	401	531	390	453
2d quarter	388	349	376	498	383	440
3d quarter	383	320	362	422	336	376
4th quarter	379	319	358	492	330	395
2005 average	388	346	374	495	359	419
2006:						
1st quarter	393	346	377	541	372	442
2d quarter	372	333	358	544	350	435
3d quarter	340	286	320	479	312	388
4th quarter	304	253	287	440	270	341
2006 average	354	310	338	510	319	401

Note: Weighted averages are based on the volume of all grades combined.

Source: Western Wood Products Association.

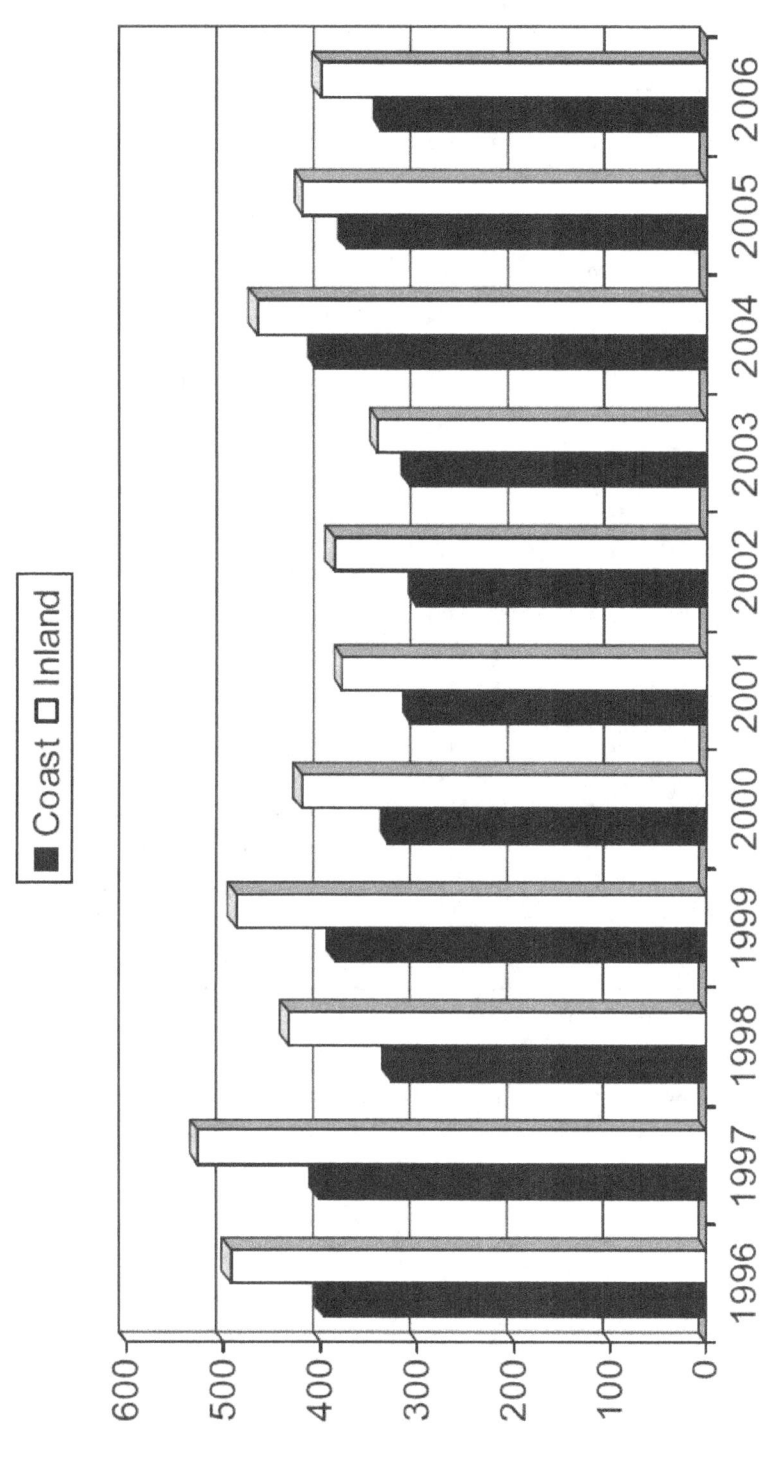

Figure 1—Weighted average f.o.b. mill prices for coast and inland lumber, 1996-2006, in dollars per thousand board feet

Table 15—Average prices for domestic and exported alder, western region, 1995-2006

(Prices in dollars per thousand board feet, f.o.b. mill)

Year and quarter	Domestic alder		Exported alder	
	1 by 4 green pallet stock	4/4 select and better	Logs	Lumber
1995	260.00	1,210.00	536.43	1,098.04
1996	NA	NA	513.97	1,139.34
1997	NA	NA	669.27	1,127.64
1998	NA	NA	978.17	1,007.67
1999	NA	NA	668.05	1,026.34
2000	NA	NA	1,268.19	958.74
2001	NA	NA	1,523.69	881.48
2002	NA	NA	1,488.35	839.24
2003	NA	NA	1,463.33	862.47
2004	NA	NA	1,567.08	820.17
2005:				
1st quarter	NA	NA	1,636.08	909.30
2d quarter	NA	NA	1,536.08	940.87
3d quarter	NA	NA	1,300.79	966.74
4th quarter	NA	NA	1,414.63	921.58
2005 average	NA	NA	1,486.05	934.77
2006:				
1st quarter	NA	NA	905.93	909.74
2d quarter	NA	NA	1,696.60	947.55
3d quarter	NA	NA	1,743.32	955.25
4th quarter	NA	NA	1,794.58	939.15
2006 average	NA	NA	1,429.11	936.88

NA = no longer available.

Source: Weekly Hardwood Review and U.S. Department of Commerce.

Table 16—Washington and Oregon timber harvest by ownership, 1996-2006

(In million board feet, Scribner scale)

State and year	Private	State	National Forest	Bureau of Land Management	Bureau of Indian Affairs	Other public	Total
Washington:							
1996	3,274	600	182	a	270	40	4,366
1997	3,139	645	166	a	226	44	4,221
1998	3,044	546	111	a	275	46	4,022
1999	3,246	662	117	a	334	24	4,383
2000	3,131	559	81	a	334	24	4,130
2001	2,818	496	68	a	324	11	3,716
2002	2,722	457	72	a	319	12	3,582
2003	2,697	567	80	a	161	34	3,539
2004	2,754	588	R96	NA	NA	52	3,489
2005	2,609	594	R81	NA	NA	32	3,316
2006	2,528	404	75	NA	NA	59	3,066
Oregon:							
1996	3,018	115	401	289	71	29	3,923
1997	3,133	176	523	136	79	35	4,081
1998	2,840	141	333	122	71	25	3,532
1999	3,014	246	233	150	68	49	3,759
2000	3,167	255	245	83	62	42	3,854
2001	2,905	268	135	38	63	30	3,440
2002	3,319	269	166	55	71	42	3,922
2003	3,313	293	203	78	63	52	4,002
2004	3,606	291	337	96	79	42	4,451
2005	3,495	341	275	121	61	61	4,355
2006	3,596	296	216	131	56	34	4,328

R = revised.

NA = not available.

a Less than 1 million board feet.

Source: Washington Department of Natural Resources and Oregon Department of Forestry.

Table 17—British Columbia log production, 1996-2006

(In thousand cubic meters)

Year	Coast[a]	Interior[b]	Total
1996	22,865	52,348	75,213
1997	22,337	46,291	68,628
1998	19,013	45,954	64,967
1999	23,721	52,277	75,998
2000	24,996	51,992	76,988
2001	21,546	50,672	72,212
2002	22,203	51,315	73,518
2003	16,474	45,451	61,925
2004	27,789	64,571	92,361
2005	22,099	61,037	83,136
2006	NA	NA	NA

NA = not available.

[a] Comprises the Vancouver Forest District and half of Prince Rupert Forest District.

[b] Comprises Cariboo, Kamloops, Nelson, and Prince George Forest Districts and half of Prince Rupert Forest District.

Source: Council of Forest Industries annual report, "British Columbia Forest Industry Statistical Tables."

Table 18—Montana and Idaho timber harvest by ownership, 1996-2006

(In million board feet, Scribner scale)

State and year	Private	State	Bureau of Indian Affairs	Bureau of Land Management	National Forest	Total
Montana:						
1996	612.3	25.2	28.9	3.0	209.0	878.4
1997	624.7	27.9	29.4	10.7	208.9	901.6
1998	587.5	30.5	23.4	2.8	201.0	845.1
1999	624.1	38.1	32.0	3.6	156.2	853.9
2000	574.3	35.9	24.2	.8	120.4	755.6
2001	555.6	43.1	9.0	7.6	110.0	725.4
2002	550.4	45.8	15.8	1.8	159.5	773.1
2003	469.6	34.7	42.7	1.4	149.1	697.6
2004	517.9	59.5	49.2	5.6	134.7	766.9
2005	429.2	54.3	11.2	7.2	161.6	663.4
2006	438.2	47.9	26.7	4.1	102.1	618.9
Idaho:						
1996	822.4	228.9	13.3	11.4	338.3	1,414.4
1997	878.7	180.9	17.2	8.4	283.2	1,368.5
1998	753.3	258.0	12.9	8.3	239.8	1,272.2
1999	888.0	269.3	4.8	2.5	172.0	1,336.6
2000	792.2	239.3	11.7	2.6	166.7	1,212.6
2001	726.4	209.6	10.8	5.4	102.3	1,054.6
2002	760.9	191.0	4.2	8.8	136.6	1,101.5
2003	720.5	138.1	6.6	4.7	123.2	993.2
2004	849.9	163.5	3.2	5.5	143.3	1,165.4
2005	804.4	178.9	7.1	6.9	161.5	1,158.7
2006	773.9	188.5	5.4	9.6	89.2	1,066.7

Source: Region 1, USDA Forest Service.

Table 19—Alaska timber harvest by ownership, 1996-2006

(In thousand board feet, Scribner scale)

Year	State	Private	Bureau of Indian Affairs	Bureau of Land Management			National Forest			Total
				Free use	Cut	Total	Tongass	Chugach	Total	
1996	R15,100	R537,700	R0	1,959	126	2,085	94,748	3,182	97,930	R652,815
1997	R14,100	R620,600	0	501	5	506	122,107	2,527	124,634	R759,840
1998	R12,600	388,800	0	224	21	245	120,491	1,038	121,529	R523,174
1999	12,800	378,900	0	128	212	340	153,229	356	153,585	545,625
2000	61,700	216,900	0	NA	NA	NA	119,318	163	119,481	NA
2001	55,300	191,100	R0	NA	NA	NA	44,077	335	44,411	NA
2002	R57,700	R184,700	0	NA	NA	NA	31,898	198	32,096	NA
2003	R49,700	R137,900	0	NA	NA	NA	48,107	15	48,122	NA
2004	R28,200	R120,200	0	NA	NA	NA	49,180	17	49,197	NA
2005	R46,200	R120,200	0	NA	NA	NA	46,583	61	46,645	NA
2006	45,300	74,300	0	NA	NA	NA	40,045	24	40,069	NA

R = revised.

NA = not available.

Source: Respective agencies.

Table 20—California timber harvest by ownership, 1996-2006

(In million board feet, Scribner scale)

Year	Private	State	Bureau of Indian Affairs	Bureau of Land Management	National Forest[a]	Total
1996	1,985	55	13	12	458	2,523
1997	2,042	48	15	5	548	2,658
1998	1,836	30	16	1	453	2,336
1999	1,903	26	15	1	433	2,378
2000	1,701	16	19	8	368	2,112
2001	1,476	3	NA	NA	262	NA
2002	1,521	4	NA	NA	299	NA
2003	1,509	NA	NA	NA	284	NA
2004	1,593	NA	NA	NA	264	NA
2005	1,496	NA	NA	NA	381	NA
2006	1,430	NA	NA	NA	338	NA

NA = not available.

[a] Includes sawtimber, poles, posts, fuelwood, cull logs, and other miscellaneous convertible products.

Source: Respective agencies.

Table 21—Employment in forest products industries in Washington and Oregon, 1996-2006

(In thousands of persons)

Year	Washington and Oregon			Washington			Oregon		
	Total	Lumber and wood products	Paper and allied products	Total	Lumber and wood products	Paper and allied products	Total	Lumber and wood products	Paper and allied products
1996	111.6	86.0	25.6	52.3	35.5	16.9	59.3	50.6	8.7
1997	112.0	87.3	24.7	51.7	35.4	16.3	60.3	51.9	8.4
1998	110.4	85.9	24.5	51.9	35.6	16.3	58.5	50.3	8.2
1999	107.0	83.0	24.0	49.8	34.0	15.7	57.3	49.0	8.3
2000	105.9	82.4	23.5	49.0	33.4	15.6	56.9	49.0	7.9
2001	99.9	77.5	22.4	46.4	31.5	14.9	53.5	46.0	7.5
2002	98.7	78.2	20.5	45.5	32.3	13.2	53.2	45.9	7.3
2003	R102.6	R82.5	R20.1	R36.8	23.5	R13.3	45.7	38.9	6.8
2004	R101.3	R81.6	R19.7	R35.7	23.0	R12.7	45.9	38.9	7.0
2005	R103.1	R84.3	R18.8	R37.5	25.3	R12.2	46.8	40.2	6.6
2006:									
January	81.7	63.4	18.3	36.7	24.9	11.8	45.0	38.5	6.5
February	82.5	64.2	18.3	36.8	24.9	11.9	45.7	39.3	6.4
March	82.6	64.0	18.4	36.6	24.7	11.9	45.8	39.3	6.5
Average, 1st quarter	82.2	63.8	18.3	36.7	24.8	11.9	45.5	39.0	6.5
April	83.3	65.0	18.3	37.8	26.0	11.8	45.5	39.0	6.5
May	83.6	65.4	18.2	37.6	25.9	11.7	46.0	39.5	6.5
June	83.5	64.6	18.9	37.5	25.2	12.3	46.0	39.4	6.6
Average, 2d quarter	83.4	65.0	18.4	37.6	25.7	11.9	45.8	39.3	6.5
July	84.7	66.0	18.7	37.7	25.6	12.1	47.0	40.4	6.6
August	84.4	65.8	18.6	37.4	25.4	12.0	47.0	40.4	6.6
September	83.7	65.4	18.3	37.3	25.5	11.8	46.4	39.9	6.5
Average, 3d quarter	84.3	65.7	18.6	37.5	25.5	12.0	46.8	40.2	6.6
October	82.1	63.9	18.2	37.4	25.7	11.7	44.7	38.2	6.5
November	81.1	62.9	18.2	37.1	25.4	11.7	43.7	37.2	6.5
December	80.6	62.4	18.2	37.0	25.3	11.7	43.6	37.1	6.5
Average, 4th quarter	81.3	63.1	18.2	37.2	25.5	11.7	44.0	37.5	6.5
2006 average	82.8	64.4	18.4	37.3	25.4	11.9	45.5	39.0	6.5

R = revised.

Note: "Lumber and wood products" category was changed in 2003 and now includes logging and wood product manufacturing.

Source: State employment agencies. Includes both covered and noncovered employment.

Figure 2—Employment in forest products industry, Washington and Oregon, 1996-2006, in thousands of persons

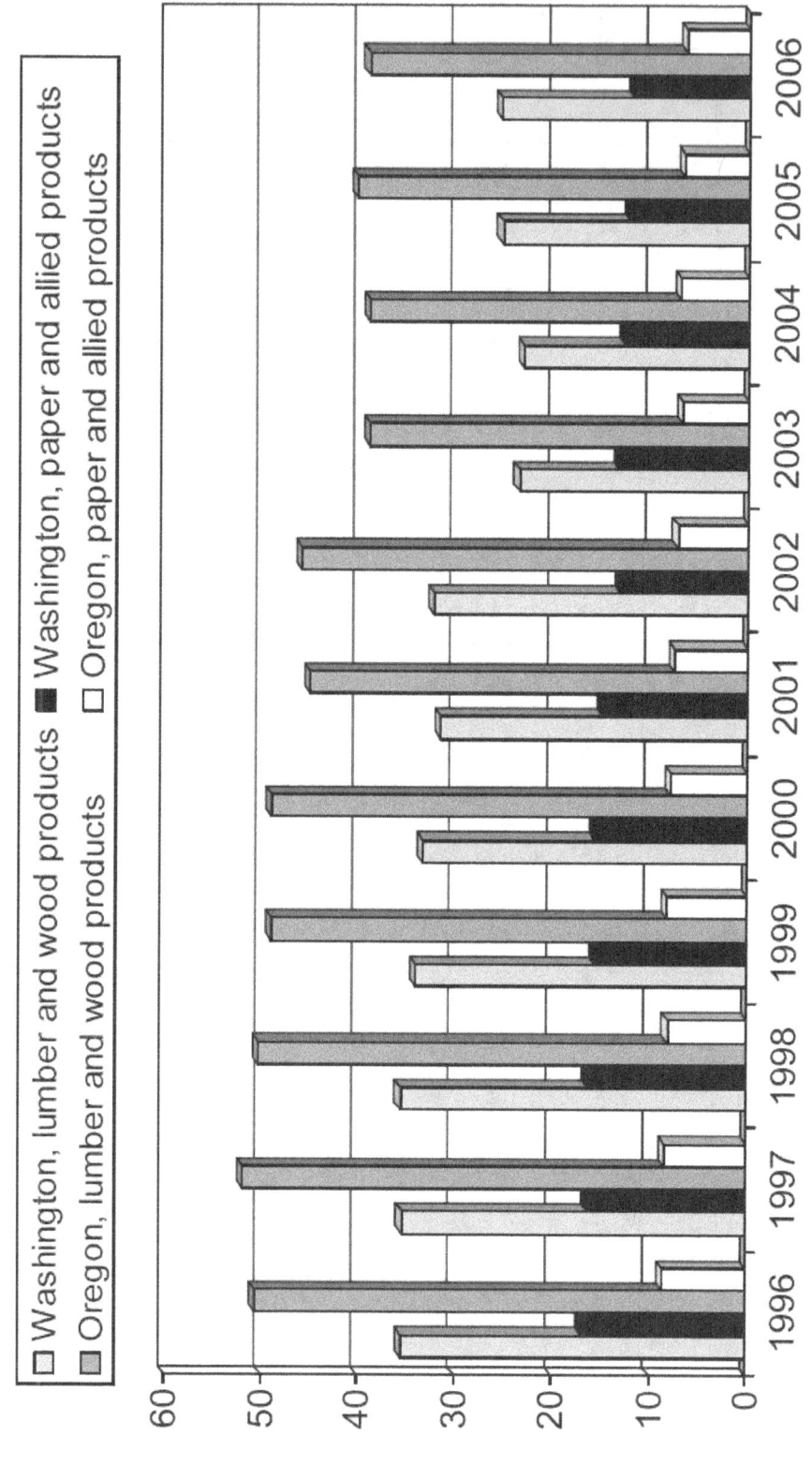

Table 22—Total nonagricultural employment and employment in forest products industries in Washington and Oregon, 1996-2006

(In thousands of persons)

Year	Washington and Oregon		Washington		Oregon	
	Total	Forest industries	Total	Forest industries	Total	Forest industries
1996	3,888.6	111.6	2,411.8	52.3	1,476.8	59.3
1997	4,034.9	112.0	2,512.0	51.7	1,522.9	60.3
1998	4,070.8	110.4	2,514.2	51.9	1,556.6	58.5
1999	4,215.0	107.0	2,642.6	49.8	1,572.4	57.3
2000	4,320.1	105.9	2,716.8	49.0	1,603.3	56.9
2001	4,294.0	99.9	2,697.8	46.4	1,596.1	53.5
2002	4,236.5	98.7	2,656.9	45.5	1,579.6	53.2
2003	4,221.9	69.2	2,659.9	23.5	1,562.0	45.7
2004	4,315.7	68.9	2,707.3	23.0	1,591.1	45.9
2005	4,414.2	72.0	2,765.1	25.3	1,649.1	46.8
2006:						
January	4,442.1	81.7	2,778.1	36.7	1,664.0	45.0
February	4,477.7	82.5	2,798.8	36.8	1,678.9	45.7
March	4,514.1	82.6	2,823.3	36.6	1,690.8	45.8
Average, 1st quarter	4,478.0	82.2	2,800.1	36.7	1,677.9	45.5
April	4,545.2	83.3	2,845.2	37.8	1,700.0	45.5
May	4,586.5	83.6	2,870.4	37.6	1,716.1	46.0
June	4,616.5	83.5	2,891.0	37.5	1,725.5	46.0
Average, 2d quarter	4,582.7	83.4	2,868.9	37.6	1,713.9	45.8
July	4,586.3	84.7	2,876.2	37.7	1,710.1	47.0
August	4,588.8	84.4	2,873.3	37.4	1,715.5	47.0
September	4,618.0	83.7	2,897.9	37.3	1,720.1	46.4
Average, 3d quarter	4,597.7	84.3	2,882.5	37.5	1,715.2	46.8
October	4,610.1	82.1	2,878.6	37.4	1,731.5	44.7
November	4,611.6	80.8	2,882.3	37.1	1,729.3	43.7
December	4,621.9	80.6	2,899.6	37.0	1,722.3	43.6
Average, 4th quarter	4,614.5	81.2	2,886.8	37.2	1,727.7	44.0
2006 average	4,568.2	82.8	2,859.6	37.3	1,708.5	45.5

Note: Starting in 2003, some categories were lost under the new North American Industry Classification System (NAICS).

Source: State employment agencies. Includes both covered and noncovered employment. Data are based on place of employment.

Table 23—Employment in forest products industries in California and Alaska, 1996-2006

(In thousands of persons)

Year	California			Alaska		
	Total	Lumber and wood products	Paper and allied products	Total	Lumber and wood products	Paper and allied products
1996	92.5	52.6	39.8	2.5	2.0	.5
1997	97.1	56.5	40.6	2.1	1.9	.2
1998	98.2	58.3	40.0	1.7	1.6	.1
1999	100.5	61.3	39.2	1.7	1.7	a
2000	100.1	61.6	38.5	1.5	1.5	a
2001	98.1	60.7	37.4	1.1	1.1	a
2002	75.0	43.5	31.5	1.1	1.1	a
2003	72.4	42.3	30.1	0.8	0.8	a
2004	82.3	41.7	40.6	0.8	0.8	a
2005	83.3	41.3	42.0	0.8	0.8	a
2006:						
January	84.0	39.4	44.6	0.5	0.5	a
February	84.3	39.6	44.7	0.6	0.6	a
March	84.7	39.7	45.0	0.7	0.7	a
Average, 1st quarter	84.3	39.6	44.8	0.6	0.6	a
April	83.3	38.9	44.4	0.7	0.7	a
May	84.4	39.9	44.5	0.8	0.8	a
June	84.9	40.1	44.8	0.8	0.8	a
Average, 2d quarter	84.2	39.6	44.6	0.8	0.8	a
July	85.6	41.0	44.6	0.9	0.9	a
August	85.2	40.8	44.4	0.9	0.9	a
September	84.6	40.2	44.4	0.9	0.9	a
Average, 3d quarter	85.2	40.7	44.5	0.9	0.9	a
October	83.7	39.7	44.0	0.8	0.8	a
November	83.1	39.1	44.0	0.7	0.7	a
December	82.2	38.4	43.8	0.6	0.6	a
Average, 4th quarter	83.0	39.1	43.9	0.7	0.7	a
2006 average	84.2	39.8	44.5	0.7	0.7	a
	2006 change in employment					
From: Year end 2005	0.9	(1.5)	2.5	(0.1)	(0.1)	a

Note: In 2002, there was a change in reporting from the Standard Industry Classification (SIC) system to the North American Industry Classification System (NAICS).

a Less than 10 persons.

Source: State employment agencies. Data are based on place of residence.

Table 24—Employment in forest products industries in Montana and Idaho, 1996-2006

(In thousands of persons)

| Year | Montana | | Idaho | | |
	Lumber and wood products	Paper and allied products	Total	Lumber and wood products	Paper and allied products
1996	7.0	a	17.0	15.0	2.0
1997	7.1	a	15.7	13.6	2.1
1998	7.1	a	15.7	13.5	2.3
1999	7.2	a	15.7	13.4	2.3
2000	7.2	a	14.6	12.4	2.2
2001	6.7	a	13.2	11.0	2.2
2002	6.5	a	12.8	10.7	2.1
2003	5.9	a	10.7	9.0	1.7
2004	5.8	0.5	NA	NA	NA
2005	5.7	a	11.2	9.6	1.6
2006:					
January	5.7	a	11.1	9.6	1.5
February	5.7	a	11.1	9.5	1.6
March	5.6	a	11.3	9.7	1.6
Average, 1st quarter	5.7	a	11.2	9.6	1.6
April	5.5	a	11.0	9.4	1.6
May	5.6	a	11.0	9.4	1.6
June	5.9	a	11.4	9.9	1.5
Average, 2d quarter	5.7	a	11.2	9.6	1.6
July	5.9	a	12.1	10.5	1.6
August	5.8	a	12.2	10.5	1.7
September	5.7	a	11.9	10.3	1.6
Average, 3d quarter	5.8	a	12.0	10.4	1.6
October	5.7	a	11.7	10.1	1.6
November	5.6	a	11.7	10.1	1.6
December	5.6	a	NA	10.2	NA
Average, 4th quarter	5.6	a	NA	10.1	NA
2006 average	5.7	a	11.5	9.9	1.6
2006 change in employment					
From: Year end 2005	0.0	a	0.3	0.3	0.0

NA = not available.

Note: "Lumber and wood products" and "Paper and allied products" columns for Idaho may not add to "Total" because of rounding.

[a] Withheld to avoid disclosing figures for individual companies, but permission was granted to publish an annual number as of 2004.

Source: State employment agencies. Data are based on place of residence.

Table 25—Employment, wages, unemployment and population for the State of Oregon, by county

(Employment and population in number of people, wages in dollars per week, unemployment in percent)

County	Average annual covered employment			Average weekly wages			Unemployment	Population
	Total	NAICS 321[a]	NAICS 113[b]	Total	NAICS 321[a]	NAICS 113[b]		
Baker								
2002	5,090	0	47	479.15	0	486.41	9.0	16,496
2003	5,040	0	31	497.72	0	448.99	9.5	16,375
2004	5,066	0	0	505.36	0	0	9.1	16,470
2005	5,171	D	D	519.46	D	D	7.5	16,287
2006	5,349	D	D	520.68	D	D	6.6	16,243
Benton								
2002	34,116	480	206	707.03	738.19	647.53	5.2	78,618
2003	34,012	478	262	716.14	753.90	691.99	5.7	79,335
2004	34,516	433	300	716.28	768.18	709.88	5.4	79,357
2005	34,886	405	300	755.37	803.25	692.73	4.8	78,640
2006	35,168	384	310	778.37	805.24	699.76	4.7	79,061
Clackamas								
2002	133,957	1,075	163	660.23	589.33	577.76	6.9	351,815
2003	131,779	1,093	171	682.43	605.36	572.70	7.5	357,453
2004	137,870	1,256	168	703.15	668.04	601.05	6.8	363,276
2005	143,625	1,241	D	726.52	676.13	D	5.4	368,470
2006	146,876	1,212	149	753.73	701.67	607.93	4.8	374,230
Clatsop								
2002	14,999	236	248	505.55	763.06	710.89	7.0	35,791
2003	15,421	247	247	515.59	826.79	694.89	7.5	35,820
2004	15,729	268	252	533.33	835.52	731.15	6.9	36,340
2005	16,295	276	272	544.62	845.68	793.99	5.7	36,798
2006	16,556	288	272	565.12	541.38	809.15	5.0	37,315
Columbia								
2002	9,873	487	289	587.09	732.99	683.38	9.4	45,313
2003	9,689	441	241	595.57	731.52	688.00	10.3	46,261
2004	9,977	456	236	605.46	760.63	711.74	9.2	46,971
2005	10,320	447	237	614.54	807.27	742.66	7.3	48,065
2006	10,686	462	242	619.49	743.79	735.91	5.8	49,163
Coos								
2002	20,873	868	700	514.05	719.65	704.97	8.8	62,670
2003	22,303	876	665	509.90	762.47	702.48	9.1	63,019
2004	22,257	922	636	524.62	784.76	742.27	9.1	63,739
2005	23,533	902	648	527.31	779.79	795.93	7.3	64,711
2006	23,696	884	636	539.35	783.35	818.56	6.9	64,820
Crook								
2002	6,005	1,084	129	541.18	525.03	643.05	9.2	19,999
2003	5,903	1,007	127	564.83	563.54	705.84	9.5	20,600
2004	6,310	1,071	134	591.91	591.79	766.81	8.2	21,424
2005	6,685	1,149	135	608.97	600.94	858.54	6.7	22,067
2006	6,972	1,109	105	629.20	587.90	731.78	6.0	22,941
Curry								
2002	6,240	486	103	458.52	791.95	472.67	7.8	21,294
2003	6,464	470	111	458.05	814.19	507.75	8.1	21,813
2004	6,761	478	103	475.09	849.46	583.55	7.3	22,100
2005	7,047	468	104	499.10	899.98	577.28	6.5	22,427
2006	7,019	481	107	517.45	904.25	612.22	7.0	22,358
Deschutes								
2002	53,057	1,920	165	543.33	557.25	707.88	7.6	125,258
2003	54,651	1,794	155	559.82	597.20	792.00	7.6	129,492
2004	58,487	1,790	120	578.47	647.34	710.58	6.7	134,479
2005	63,037	1,834	95	605.43	660.42	739.69	5.5	141,382
2006	67,638	1,892	99	640.95	679.39	721.47	4.6	149,140

Table 25—Employment, wages, unemployment and population for the State of Oregon, by county (continued)

(Employment and population in number of people, wages in dollars per week, unemployment in percent)

County	Average annual covered employment			Average weekly wages			Unemployment	Population
	Total	NAICS 321[a]	NAICS 113[b]	Total	NAICS 321[a]	NAICS 113[b]		
Douglas								
2002	37,419	4,524	1,032	547.01	733.00	703.14	8.9	100,921
2003	37,067	4,393	1,006	559.31	755.86	671.74	9.8	102,332
2004	37,900	4,331	992	578.55	827.57	684.74	9.4	103,152
2005	38,947	4,198	1,021	591.53	830.49	659.99	8.1	104,202
2006	39,589	4,008	904	603.87	807.21	651.10	7.6	105,117
Gilliam								
2002	753	0	0	485.17	0	0	6.5	1,842
2003	732	0	0	507.57	0	0	6.9	1,778
2004	765	0	0	533.93	0	0	6.2	1,817
2005	770	0	0	534.96	0	0	5.8	1,794
2006	768	0	0	600.30	0	0	5.0	1,775
Grant								
2002	2,697	213	97	496.30	657.06	493.10	9.5	7,480
2003	2,699	0	109	487.20	0	468.85	10.6	7,454
2004	2,775	217	136	503.14	694.40	529.93	10.2	7,380
2005	2,671	204	132	522.14	677.58	601.92	9.9	7,297
2006	2,653	200	142	551.61	710.47	619.61	8.4	7,250
Harney								
2002	2,565	0	0	474.02	0	0	9.8	7,339
2003	2,463	0	0	493.10	0	0	11.1	7,184
2004	2,490	0	0	512.76	0	0	9.9	7,132
2005	2,552	D	D	524.74	D	D	9.1	6,898
2006	2,526	D	D	547.48	D	D	8.2	6,888
Hood River								
2002	10,480	132	0	434.61	503.46	0	8.3	20,805
2003	10,412	118	68	438.66	483.19	383.24	8.6	20,760
2004	10,920	130	0	448.17	504.02	0	7.5	21,155
2005	11,241	163	D	461.09	545.01	D	6.4	21,284
2006	11,700	187	D	487.32	589.84	D	5.5	21,533
Jackson								
2002	74,688	2,596	626	540.34	642.83	871.67	7.4	186,430
2003	76,578	2,355	743	553.47	652.03	854.30	7.6	190,077
2004	79,373	2,392	772	572.62	682.64	866.28	7.1	192,992
2005	82,372	2,340	773	586.57	683.33	850.51	6.0	195,322
2006	83,537	2,278	810	609.17	701.23	907.48	5.8	197,071
Jefferson								
2002	5,582	0	34	499.93	0	549.28	6.8	19,768
2003	6,304	0	0	518.36	0	0	7.1	19,667
2004	6,488	0	0	531.74	0	0	6.6	19,868
2005	6,653	D	D	546.39	D	D	6.1	20,100
2006	6,618	D	D	572.54	D	D	5.7	20,352
Josephine								
2002	21,823	885	273	487.45	562.17	651.99	8.7	77,496
2003	22,377	683	292	500.82	562.10	752.25	8.9	79,030
2004	23,303	649	346	522.74	610.10	816.21	8.2	79,920
2005	24,691	715	318	532.84	605.75	872.45	6.9	80,761
2006	25,434	744	247	547.27	597.36	984.30	6.7	81,688
Klamath								
2002	22,469	1,378	220	533.75	696.58	723.27	9.0	64,363
2003	21,905	1,346	224	556.95	733.32	714.56	9.8	64,769
2004	22,224	1,419	226	568.64	829.08	720.14	9.5	65,098
2005	23,409	1,478	213	573.02	810.93	745.52	7.6	66,192
2006	23,939	1,479	203	597.90	834.48	747.08	6.8	66,438

Table 25—Employment, wages, unemployment and population for the State of Oregon, by county (continued)

(Employment and population in number of people, wages in dollars per week, unemployment in percent)

County	Average annual covered employment			Average weekly wages			Unemployment	Population
	Total	NAICS 321[a]	NAICS 113[b]	Total	NAICS 321[a]	NAICS 113[b]		
Lake								
2002	2,287	236	29	478.59	587.44	636.08	8.8	7,444
2003	2,306	251	27	488.79	570.12	652.35	9.6	7,440
2004	2,335	278	26	520.98	692.37	659.17	9.9	7,382
2005	2,402	253	D	532.25	625.26	D	8.5	7,313
2006	2,534	277	D	556.97	606.85	D	7.6	7,473
Lane								
2002	137,969	5,023	932	565.89	722.01	630.65	7.1	326,666
2003	136,533	4,698	851	582.90	757.55	620.99	8.0	330,527
2004	139,599	4,711	808	602.65	817.25	650.50	7.4	331,594
2005	145,269	4,916	782	621.18	818.90	945.34	6.1	335,180
2006	148,824	4,717	741	639.11	795.28	660.69	5.5	337,870
Lincoln								
2002	16,664	51	138	470.17	518.99	595.72	8.1	44,644
2003	16,597	62	146	483.61	560.97	671.99	9.0	44,667
2004	17,162	0	149	500.25	0	634.11	8.3	45,277
2005	17,862	63	131	515.66	617.62	698.96	6.7	45,994
2006	18,162	70	129	536.10	605.11	746.28	6.1	46,199
Linn								
2002	39,644	2,234	539	578.80	716.68	786.97	9.0	104,941
2003	38,632	2,175	474	589.36	763.17	722.42	10.1	106,121
2004	39,200	2,300	492	603.86	769.72	732.73	9.3	107,410
2005	41,440	2,342	481	613.57	769.34	738.40	7.4	108,914
2006	42,345	2,320	460	643.97	792.10	757.33	6.6	111,489
Malheur								
2002	12,660	0	0	464.69	0	0	9.1	31,248
2003	12,427	0	0	481.25	0	0	9.9	31,239
2004	12,596	0	0	492.04	0	0	10.1	31,425
2005	12,656	D	0	498.64	D	0	8.8	31,330
2006	12,483	0	0	523.31	0	0	6.5	31,247
Marion								
2002	127,320	1,845	0	569.71	575.27	0	7.3	293,155
2003	128,073	1,680	0	582.48	598.99	0	8.0	296,995
2004	129,975	1,938	0	595.87	617.60	0	7.6	301,841
2005	135,107	2,206	D	611.95	635.67	D	6.4	305,265
2006	137,862	2,308	D	640.81	645.23	D	5.7	311,304
Morrow								
2002	3,494	0	41	545.65	0	713.60	7.6	11,585
2003	3,752	0	39	557.25	0	674.82	8.1	11,627
2004	3,690	0	40	583.92	0	701.50	8.2	11,681
2005	3,903	0	56	592.39	0	877.15	7.5	11,666
2006	3,908	D	35	626.49	D	810.25	6.8	11,753
Multnomah								
2002	428,919	679	0	735.36	564.81	0	8.1	677,626
2003	419,917	650	0	748.28	608.73	0	8.6	677,813
2004	420,325	643	0	773.08	587.66	0	7.6	672,161
2005	428,250	612	15	793.15	633.77	261.83	6.2	672,906
2006	439,464	632	15	827.15	649.88	292.34	5.2	681,454
Polk								
2002	16,145	376	179	498.74	706.61	669.69	6.2	64,657
2003	16,224	394	212	499.18	743.51	605.47	6.7	65,995
2004	16,611	354	216	511.04	764.66	654.81	6.6	67,565
2005	17,286	359	229	521.94	740.98	702.66	5.5	70,295
2006	18,261	343	246	544.29	761.72	717.75	5.1	73,296

Table 25—Employment, wages, unemployment and population for the State of Oregon, by county (continued)

(Employment and population in number of people, wages in dollars per week, unemployment in percent)

County	Average annual covered employment			Average weekly wages			Unemployment	Population
	Total	NAICS 321[a]	NAICS 113[b]	Total	NAICS 321[a]	NAICS 113[b]		
Sherman								
2002	636	0	0	475.37	0	0	10.1	1,784
2003	630	0	0	502.63	0	0	10.9	1,754
2004	605	0	0	538.79	0	0	9.7	1,712
2005	643	0	0	562.16	0	0	7.2	1,749
2006	644	0	0	602.82	0	0	6.2	1,699
Tillamook								
2002	8,094	413	244	488.50	746.09	654.26	6.6	24,613
2003	8,034	412	255	510.11	832.28	687.98	7.3	24,590
2004	8,242	439	264	533.18	871.30	696.55	7.1	24,922
2005	8,566	453	277	541.94	888.33	729.37	6.0	25,277
2006	8,749	455	253	560.11	939.05	751.50	5.6	25,380
Umatilla								
2002	29,205	484	52	531.84	581.90	574.55	7.9	71,428
2003	29,112	464	40	545.21	614.31	634.95	8.3	72,008
2004	29,052	543	0	564.29	632.07	0	8.2	73,436
2005	28,975	543	D	570.52	654.77	D	7.9	73,878
2006	29,153	520	D	587.25	657.19	D	6.8	72,928
Union								
2002	9,632	660	0	500.64	674.78	0	6.5	24,484
2003	9,580	736	0	521.69	783.38	0	7.4	24,561
2004	9,546	730	0	536.22	859.88	0	7.4	24,406
2005	9,518	689	107	545.20	808.28	828.92	6.9	24,540
2006	9,785	696	113	560.74	833.56	681.42	6.0	24,345
Wallowa								
2002	2,331	0	57	493.64	0	604.13	8.5	7,025
2003	2,254	0	64	446.69	0	583.00	9.8	7,082
2004	2,266	0	67	457.85	0	644.51	9.1	6,976
2005	2,369	D	71	477.93	D	660.40	7.6	7,014
2006	2,442	D	72	484.20	D	711.28	6.8	6,875
Wasco								
2002	10,463	113	0	484.94	767.39	0	9.1	23,667
2003	9,619	122	48	491.66	686.49	654.19	9.8	23,591
2004	9,800	0	55	498.00	0	688.03	8.9	23,669
2005	10,066	D	D	513.58	D	D	7.1	23,593
2006	10,640	D	D	546.08	D	D	5.6	23,712
Washington								
2002	221,543	1,617	112	807.01	796.09	641.44	6.9	473,263
2003	219,257	1,614	164	830.79	768.01	668.03	7.4	479,496
2004	224,216	1,630	192	879.94	797.07	669.37	6.3	488,253
2005	235,074	1,681	160	899.70	842.63	689.88	5.2	499,794
2006	245,983	1,665	145	925.76	868.38	725.98	4.5	514,269
Wheeler								
2002	310	0	0	394.42	0	0	7.6	1,532
2003	309	0	0	409.21	0	0	7.5	1,505
2004	284	0	0	441.00	0	0	7.9	1,483
2005	289	0	D	447.96	0	D	6.4	1,455
2006	271	0	D	432.81	0	D	6.8	1,404
Yamhill								
2002	28,051	796	214	552.30	706.95	600.57	7.4	88,055
2003	28,652	842	184	573.29	741.27	609.68	8.2	89,384
2004	29,577	885	206	586.69	766.51	634.75	7.4	90,723
2005	31,081	953	191	603.79	757.41	670.31	6.1	92,196
2006	32,222	1,007	178	630.39	748.79	675.44	5.2	94,678

Table 25—Employment, wages, unemployment and population for the State of Oregon, by county (continued)

(Employment and population in number of people, wages in dollars per week, unemployment in percent)

County	Average annual covered employment			Average weekly wages			Unemployment	Population
	Total	NAICS 321[a]	NAICS 113[b]	Total	NAICS 321[a]	NAICS 113[b]		
Oregon								
2002	1,573,083	32,405	7,984	647.78	670.87	707.90	7.6	3,521,515
2003	1,563,282	31,111	7,984	662.62	700.90	713.75	8.1	3,559,596
2004	1,595,683	32,089	8,104	685.01	740.77	729.04	7.4	3,594,586
2005	1,652,874	32,639	7,925	703.65	744.83	758.75	6.1	3,641,056
2006	1,700,407	32,320	7,624	731.87	746.77	772.13	5.4	3,700,758

Note: D = data is not shown to avoid disclosure of data for individual employers.

[a] NAICS 321 = North America Industry Classification System for lumber and wood products.

[b] NAICS 113 = North America Industry Classification System for forestry services and logging.

Source: Employment and Wage for covered employment and weekly wages data are from Web site

http://www.qualityinfo.org/olmisj.

Unemployment rates are from U.S. Department of Agriculture, Economic Research Service. Web site

http//:www.ers.usda.gov/Data/Unemployment.

U.S. Department of Commerce, Bureau of the Census, population estimates are from Web site http//:www.ers.usda.gov/Data/Population.

Table 26—Employment, wages, unemployment and population for the State of Washington, by county

(Employment and population in number of people, wages in dollars per week, unemployment in percent)

County	Average annual covered employment			Average weekly wages			Unemployment	Population
	Total	NAICS 321[a]	NAICS 113[b]	Total	NAICS 321[a]	NAICS 113[b]		
Adams								
2002	7,001	D	0	439.54	D	0	9.2	16,434
2003	6,953	0	0	459.45	0	0	8.9	16,602
2004	6,890	D	0	477.09	D	0	7.9	16,596
2005	6,894	D	0	507.10	D	0	7.0	16,803
2006	6,898	D	0	531.12	D	0	6.5	16,887
Asotin								
2002	5,149	D	D	466.31	D	D	7.3	20,453
2003	5,348	D	5	471.66	D	193.35	7.6	20,625
2004	5,346	D	6	484.01	D	400.96	6.6	20,831
2005	5,373	D	D	505.40	D	D	6.2	21,178
2006	5,520	D	D	532.29	D	D	4.8	21,247
Benton								
2002	66,203	0	0	737.20	0	0	6.3	150,366
2003	68,130	0	0	755.79	0	0	6.8	153,660
2004	69,424	0	0	786.84	0	0	5.9	155,991
2005	69,968	0	0	807.88	0	0	5.7	157,950
2006	69,284	0	0	810.38	0	0	5.7	159,463
Chelan								
2002	34,938	160	77	506.90	625.73	491.42	8.7	67,050
2003	35,125	135	77	517.08	662.38	469.79	8.5	67,973
2004	36,598	151	70	517.77	648.49	547.67	6.9	68,987
2005	37,500	174	65	535.36	649.62	534.93	5.9	69,791
2006	38,848	164	53	557.85	745.27	585.73	5.2	71,034
Clallam								
2002	20,480	492	347	500.58	559.37	651.95	8.5	66,302
2003	20,751	466	358	518.64	585.97	656.00	8.3	66,892
2004	21,586	452	399	536.06	651.19	692.78	6.9	67,867
2005	22,548	631	391	554.47	737.64	720.15	6.1	69,689
2006	23,054	674	392	579.30	760.55	757.27	5.9	70,400
Clark								
2002	114,062	732	84	650.66	578.84	953.55	9.1	370,236
2003	115,870	710	99	661.55	616.36	895.79	9.4	379,577
2004	120,634	766	111	680.20	674.10	938.62	7.5	392,403
2005	125,552	806	D	705.19	750.71	D	6.2	403,766
2006	129,862	830	158	730.78	731.10	764.68	5.8	412,938
Columbia								
2002	1,473	D	D	468.05	D	D	10.1	4,103
2003	1,465	D	D	476.19	D	D	9.4	4,093
2004	1,427	D	D	513.72	D	D	8.0	4,187
2005	1,403	D	D	531.37	D	D	7.7	4,129
2006	1,219	D	D	564.18	D	D	8.8	4,087
Cowlitz								
2002	36,081	1,174	748	612.87	790.56	783.40	10.6	94,514
2003	35,949	1,199	739	615.64	761.24	874.55	9.9	95,146
2004	36,023	887	488	628.11	748.63	641.39	8.5	96,189
2005	36,505	1,275	703	654.03	836.55	922.43	7.2	97,325
2006	37,084	1,226	641	675.91	832.24	971.91	6.6	99,905
Douglas								
2002	8,753	D	D	438.57	D	D	7.6	33,409
2003	9,196	0	D	439.06	0	D	7.7	33,753
2004	9,820	0	D	465.27	0	D	6.3	34,427
2005	10,203	D	D	471.67	D	D	5.5	34,977
2006	10,030	D	D	493.18	D	D	5.0	35,772

(Employment and population in number of people, wages in dollars per week, unemployment in percent)

County	Average annual covered employment			Average weekly wages			Unemployment	Population
	Total	NAICS 321[a]	NAICS 113[b]	Total	NAICS 321[a]	NAICS 113[b]		
Ferry								
2002	1,743	D	D	474.03	D	D	10.7	7,268
2003	1,673	199	D	480.22	143.28	D	13.5	7,417
2004	1,711	D	69	510.24	D	544.53	10.7	7,565
2005	1,729	0	D	534.87	0	D	9.1	7,542
2006	1,684	D	D	545.33	D	D	9.5	7,560
Franklin								
2002	21,881	106	0	491.53	437.84	0	8.6	52,745
2003	22,396	123	0	505.34	475.06	0	8.7	56,126
2004	23,136	115	0	524.67	536.80	0	7.5	59,472
2005	23,750	130	0	538.19	567.94	0	6.9	63,011
2006	24,785	146	0	562.43	570.53	0	7.2	66,570
Garfield								
2002	864	0	0	522.68	0	0	6.1	2,327
2003	880	0	0	535.01	0	0	6.4	2,371
2004	894	0	0	545.81	0	0	5.2	2,311
2005	844	0	0	574.98	0	0	5.5	2,344
2006	820	0	0	598.12	0	0	5.5	2,223
Grant								
2002	30,909	19	0	464.32	263.34	0	9.4	77,983
2003	31,378	21	0	473.93	253.59	0	9.2	78,691
2004	31,958	18	0	494.30	260.21	0	8.1	79,981
2005	31,948	21	0	512.44	287.59	0	7.4	81,229
2006	33,573	D	0	539.68	D	0	6.6	82,612
Grays Harbor								
2002	23,084	1,306	672	546.82	728.03	757.72	9.4	68,470
2003	23,422	1,354	667	560.53	753.54	803.67	9.4	69,406
2004	24,222	1,428	724	571.33	782.69	756.73	8.3	70,338
2005	24,708	1,757	608	588.92	809.81	761.05	7.4	70,900
2006	24,903	1,616	576	609.04	832.68	790.34	7.1	71,587
Island								
2002	14,753	D	D	498.11	D	D	7.2	75,050
2003	14,814	D	D	511.05	D	D	7.4	76,384
2004	15,084	D	D	527.82	D	D	6.6	79,293
2005	15,150	D	D	540.12	D	D	5.8	79,252
2006	15,797	D	D	563.92	D	D	5.2	81,489
Jefferson								
2002	8,203	32	25	482.78	608.88	454.58	7.5	26,761
2003	8,520	25	24	497.60	629.54	560.15	7.1	27,716
2004	8,931	D	23	511.86	D	609.47	5.9	28,110
2005	9,016	D	31	536.35	D	591.11	5.3	28,666
2006	9,118	D	19	552.88	D	490.42	5.1	29,279
King								
2002	1,103,281	1,276	650	921.43	676.99	1,236.20	6.2	1,759,604
2003	1,088,637	1,305	398	942.30	690.84	2,092.97	6.2	1,761,411
2004	1,096,076	1,290	330	941.77	680.40	2,019.60	5.1	1,777,143
2005	1,116,434	1,534	233	964.21	760.03	2,448.47	4.8	1,793,583
2006	1,149,932	1,767	208	1,028.51	816.17	2,217.15	4.2	1,826,732
Kitsap								
2002	76,043	39	48	649.47	600.31	381.12	6.8	236,174
2003	77,501	48	45	665.58	573.21	664.71	6.8	240,719
2004	80,443	43	52	682.98	637.56	687.39	5.9	239,138
2005	82,245	29	58	701.11	715.56	817.81	5.1	240,661
2006	84,454	32	48	724.83	509.20	894.22	4.8	240,604

Table 26—Employment, wages, unemployment and population for the State of Washington, by county (continued)

(Employment and population in number of people, wages in dollars per week, unemployment in percent)

County	Average annual covered employment			Average weekly wages			Unemployment	Population
	Total	NAICS 321[a]	NAICS 113[b]	Total	NAICS 321[a]	NAICS 113[b]		
Kittitas								
2002	12,331	D	64	466.39	D	569.66	7.0	34,370
2003	12,497	D	40	475.31	D	522.74	7.4	35,206
2004	12,549	D	36	502.38	D	632.05	6.5	35,721
2005	12,621	D	36	529.44	D	639.92	5.6	36,841
2006	13,104	D	24	560.69	D	553.77	5.3	37,189
Klickitat								
2002	5,997	D	D	489.48	D	D	11.4	19,381
2003	5,861	D	D	495.57	D	D	11.9	19,547
2004	5,951	211	165	507.98	624.70	682.35	9.2	19,855
2005	5,838	D	D	535.19	D	D	7.8	19,839
2006	6,066	D	D	568.51	D	D	7.1	20,335
Lewis								
2002	24,671	1,549	650	540.13	793.30	753.90	9.2	69,710
2003	24,418	1,353	590	551.82	884.10	819.08	9.4	70,404
2004	24,637	1,439	640	574.04	920.25	814.15	8.3	71,539
2005	24,979	1,608	621	595.87	921.87	817.91	7.4	72,449
2006	25,892	1,901	632	631.00	925.22	823.11	7.0	73,585
Lincoln								
2002	2,910	D	D	468.61	D	D	6.8	10,096
2003	2,972	D	D	475.45	D	D	6.9	10,201
2004	3,027	D	D	488.74	D	D	6.4	10,412
2005	2,909	D	D	508.75	D	D	5.9	10,381
2006	2,894	D	D	531.35	D	D	5.8	10,376
Mason								
2002	12,360	890	258	524.75	725.61	764.19	8.3	51,008
2003	12,683	863	252	527.05	748.38	722.95	8.6	52,129
2004	13,208	889	239	544.76	818.30	789.21	7.4	53,637
2005	13,815	1,016	200	562.72	811.44	862.26	6.1	54,359
2006	14,510	1,213	203	571.08	778.90	1,064.18	5.9	55,951
Okanogan								
2002	15,404	69	56	403.30	476.33	603.38	10.1	39,186
2003	16,533	52	68	398.14	457.69	569.00	9.5	39,134
2004	16,921	249	119	422.14	556.69	657.59	7.8	39,444
2005	17,249	93	65	431.27	447.21	555.91	7.2	39,782
2006	17,440	87	71	446.25	461.65	656.35	6.7	40,040
Pacific								
2002	5,991	D	120	439.89	D	743.34	9.2	20,778
2003	6,138	264	122	447.50	814.23	755.03	9.2	21,103
2004	6,277	278	123	456.71	860.66	720.87	7.6	21,246
2005	6,302	280	111	481.97	865.90	766.84	6.6	21,579
2006	6,458	269	109	497.49	901.56	755.70	6.6	21,735
Pend Oreille								
2002	2,906	D	56	538.29	D	563.01	9.6	12,008
2003	2,923	D	53	550.07	D	538.83	10.3	12,254
2004	2,976	D	65	595.99	D	615.17	8.7	12,474
2005	2,973	D	65	624.63	D	610.20	7.9	12,673
2006	3,046	D	57	662.65	D	644.81	7.4	12,951
Pierce								
2002	238,158	2,589	398	625.89	671.07	735.94	8.1	732,282
2003	243,411	2,450	403	646.59	721.14	779.19	8.2	740,957
2004	249,998	2,730	232	691.01	739.63	727.52	7.1	745,411
2005	257,732	2,863	211	697.09	765.70	634.16	5.9	753,787
2006	265,719	2,648	220	724.75	764.94	755.40	5.2	766,878

Table 26—Employment, wages, unemployment and population for the State of Washington, by county (continued)

(Employment and population in number of people, wages in dollars per week, unemployment in percent)

County	Average annual covered employment			Average weekly wages			Unemployment	Population
	Total	NAICS 321[a]	NAICS 113[b]	Total	NAICS 321[a]	NAICS 113[b]		
San Juan								
2002	4,954	D	D	465.80	D	D	5.7	14,565
2003	5,100	18	D	477.26	234.67	D	5.5	14,761
2004	5,343	55	D	488.10	616.93	D	4.5	15,190
2005	5,314	50	D	502.46	649.20	D	4.1	15,274
2006	5,394	47	0	530.06	623.43	0.00	3.9	15,298
Skagit								
2002	43,642	456	340	550.89	660.41	685.92	8.2	106,906
2003	44,507	406	343	565.60	729.44	689.50	8.0	109,234
2004	45,499	261	355	575.22	916.35	734.05	6.8	111,064
2005	46,708	321	189	603.63	926.76	670.46	5.8	113,171
2006	47,877	314	151	631.24	933.68	718.56	5.2	115,700
Skamania								
2002	1,887	111	21	483.56	683.05	732.40	10.0	10,049
2003	1,963	112	21	496.83	753.45	761.10	10.1	10,292
2004	2,025	140	27	515.72	787.48	680.09	8.6	10,549
2005	2,059	D	28	527.56	D	713.03	7.5	10,664
2006	2,127	D	D	530.15	D	D	7.1	10,833
Snohomish								
2002	205,511	1,801	288	725.80	663.80	618.38	7.0	633,947
2003	207,114	2,045	256	743.65	694.83	608.95	7.0	639,409
2004	211,198	2,195	271	752.01	734.74	679.87	5.6	644,274
2005	221,081	2,160	261	788.68	747.53	689.09	5.1	655,944
2006	233,383	2,226	232	825.12	743.23	694.68	4.6	669,887
Spokane								
2002	187,611	452	D	577.61	455.67	D	7.6	427,506
2003	190,292	494	D	587.54	422.78	D	7.5	431,027
2004	192,971	571	29	604.26	430.14	571.36	6.5	435,644
2005	197,469	629	D	626.46	453.81	D	5.6	440,706
2006	204,266	676	D	653.93	471.77	D	5.0	446,706
Stevens								
2002	9,879	887	275	494.30	730.53	610.55	10.0	40,556
2003	10,041	838	255	506.58	746.78	606.51	9.6	40,776
2004	10,207	851	257	524.24	796.68	647.09	8.3	41,310
2005	10,022	803	255	539.29	784.49	584.15	7.7	42,013
2006	10,264	781	228	556.73	789.96	604.17	7.1	42,632
Thurston								
2002	86,283	282	394	650.21	598.70	753.93	6.4	217,641
2003	89,129	309	386	659.95	613.16	810.39	6.4	221,950
2004	91,286	317	447	672.15	685.96	831.67	5.7	224,673
2005	93,813	303	470	695.12	769.98	821.12	5.0	228,867
2006	96,678	204	472	726.28	755.02	877.76	4.6	234,670
Wahkiakum								
2002	776	D	D	492.45	D	D	9.6	3,793
2003	795	D	135	494.41	D	347.53	9.4	3,748
2004	818	D	145	499.61	D	666.81	7.5	3,755
2005	825	D	D	507.58	D	D	7.0	3,849
2006	846	D	D	518.53	D	D	6.5	4,026
Walla Walla								
2002	24,687	D	D	526.98	D	D	6.8	56,149
2003	25,121	26	D	542.41	523.08	D	6.9	56,751
2004	25,278	27	27	558.41	546.54	672.28	6.1	57,354
2005	24,879	27	20	574.55	558.61	476.90	5.7	57,558
2006	25,078	31	0	609.57	536.26	0.00	5.5	57,721

Table 26—Employment, wages, unemployment and population for the State of Washington, by county (continued)

(Employment and population in number of people, wages in dollars per week, unemployment in percent)

County	Average annual covered employment			Average weekly wages			Unemployment	Population
	Total	NAICS 321[a]	NAICS 113[b]	Total	NAICS 321[a]	NAICS 113[b]		
Whatcom								
2002	70,286	1,058	268	544.08	600.10	662.09	6.8	174,362
2003	72,461	1,187	310	559.98	611.98	619.44	6.6	176,571
2004	75,282	1,271	309	577.45	631.45	649.89	5.7	180,167
2005	78,477	1,365	258	598.53	646.41	673.12	4.9	183,471
2006	80,181	1,378	247	627.15	676.35	693.85	4.6	185,953
Whitman								
2002	14,985	D	D	571.17	D	D	4.6	40,631
2003	15,189	D	0	588.69	D	0	4.9	40,702
2004	15,611	D	0	605.22	D	0	4.4	40,146
2005	15,789	D	0	607.01	D	0	4.2	40,170
2006	16,005	D	0	635.86	D	0	4.1	39,838
Yakima								
2002	92,100	1,259	D	480.21	615.14	D	9.7	224,823
2003	93,474	1,139	160	496.76	637.40	675.81	9.7	226,727
2004	94,331	1,416	161	508.16	631.35	757.33	8.6	229,094
2005	95,246	1,075	155	525.59	619.63	734.92	7.6	231,586
2006	98,309	898	123	545.82	588.84	850.30	6.9	233,105
Washington								
2002	2,643,952	17,691	6,495	735.68	673.78	761.47	7.3	6,068,996
2003	2,656,604	17,573	6,087	750.68	700.01	823.76	7.4	6,131,445
2004	2,701,878	18,505	5,930	760.99	724.38	795.36	6.2	6,203,788
2005	2,766,867	19,716	5,614	782.78	756.84	825.12	5.5	6,287,759
2006	2,850,986	19,934	5,312	824.64	764.63	849.02	5.0	6,395,798

Note: D = data is not shown to avoid disclosure of data for individual employers.

[a] NAICS 321 = North America Industry Classification System for lumber and wood products.

[b] NAICS 113 = North America Industry Classification System for forestry services and logging.

Source: 2001 Employment and payrolls in Washington State by county and industry for covered employment and wage. Washington Employment Security Department for employment rates 2002 2005 is from Web site www.workforceexplorer.com

Unemployment rates are from U.S. Department of Agriculture, Economic Research Service. Web site http//:www.ers.usda.gov/Data/Unemployment. Data updated to reflect June 13 2006 numbers.

U.S. Department of Commerce, Bureau of the Census, population 2000 2005 are from Web site http//:www.ers.usda.gov/Data/Population.

Table 27—Volume of softwood log exports from Seattle and Columbia-Snake Customs Districts by species and destination, 1995-2006

(In million board feet, Scribner scale)

Year and quarter	From both customs districts				From Seattle Customs District				From Columbia-Snake Customs District				
	Total	Douglas-fir	Western hemlock	Other softwoods	Total	Douglas-fir	Western hemlock	Other softwoods	Total	Douglas-fir	Western hemlock	Port-Orford-cedar	Other softwoods
To All Countries													
1995	1,604.8	1,114.3	403.9	86.7	999.1	573.8	353.9	71.4	605.7	540.4	50.0	2.0	13.2
1996	1,502.9	1,190.4	258.8	53.6	916.7	643.8	233.1	39.9	586.1	546.6	25.7	1.3	12.5
1997	1,042.2	789.5	212.4	40.2	599.1	376.7	191.8	30.7	443.1	412.9	20.6	1.8	8.0
1998	867.1	718.8	100.0	48.3	476.6	346.6	90.5	39.5	390.5	372.2	9.5	.4	8.4
1999	793.7	668.7	91.4	33.6	434.9	322.2	85.1	27.6	358.8	346.5	6.4	.8	5.1
2000	759.2	668.8	56.2	34.2	360.2	280.1	51.3	28.7	399.0	388.7	4.9	.8	4.7
2001	642.1	553.7	46.3	42.1	289.7	207.5	41.4	40.9	352.3	346.3	4.9	.3	.9
2002	599.4	533.4	41.7	24.4	239.2	176.6	39.6	23.0	360.1	356.8	2.0	.5	.8
2003	561.6	487.4	37.6	36.7	176.7	120.7	36.1	20.1	385.0	366.7	1.6	.4	16.3
2004	621.9	540.9	40.4	40.6	225.9	153.5	38.2	34.2	396.0	387.4	2.2	a	6.3
2005:													
1st qtr.	143.8	126.6	8.6	8.6	55.8	39.3	8.5	8.0	88.1	87.4	.1	.1	.5
2d qtr.	130.4	116.6	5.3	8.5	41.8	28.5	5.2	8.1	88.6	88.1	.1	.1	.4
3d qtr.	124.6	111.6	4.4	8.6	39.2	26.5	4.3	8.4	85.4	85.1	.1	a	.1
4th qtr.	136.4	119.3	6.5	10.6	57.9	41.0	6.5	10.4	78.5	78.4	0	a	.1
2005 total	535.2	474.2	24.8	36.2	194.7	135.3	24.5	34.9	340.6	338.9	.3	.2	1.1
2006:													
1st qtr.	127.5	109.2	3.9	14.4	54.0	38.7	3.9	11.4	73.5	70.5	0	a	3.0
2d qtr.	121.4	107.1	3.0	11.3	41.4	27.4	3.0	11.0	80.0	79.7	a	a	.3
3d qtr.	137.6	122.1	2.0	13.5	46.9	32.5	2.0	12.4	90.7	89.6	0	a	1.1
4th qtr.	147.8	118.9	9.6	19.3	61.9	36.0	7.4	18.5	85.9	82.9	2.2	0	.8
2006 total	534.3	457.3	18.5	58.5	204.2	134.7	16.3	53.3	330.1	322.7	2.2	a	5.2
To Japan													
1995	1,328.5	1,088.5	202.9	37.1	742.0	549.7	169.7	22.6	586.5	538.8	33.2	1.9	12.6
1996	1,373.8	1,160.8	175.6	37.4	791.8	614.7	153.1	24.0	582.0	546.1	22.5	1.2	12.2
1997	953.9	757.4	168.7	27.7	515.7	348.4	148.2	19.2	438.1	409.0	20.5	1.5	7.0
1998	811.0	704.2	85.0	21.8	422.5	333.1	75.5	13.8	388.5	371.1	9.5	.2	7.7
1999	751.2	660.7	69.2	21.3	393.2	314.4	62.9	15.8	358.0	346.2	6.3	.8	4.7
2000	706.1	658.7	39.0	8.4	310.9	270.4	34.2	6.3	395.3	388.3	4.9	.7	1.3
2001	571.0	539.0	24.0	8.0	222.6	195.1	20.4	7.0	348.4	344.1	3.5	.3	.6
2002	535.7	514.8	14.6	6.3	176.8	159.2	12.6	5.0	358.9	355.6	2.0	.5	.8
2003	506.1	479.3	8.1	18.7	122.9	111.7	6.5	4.7	383.2	367.6	1.6	.4	13.5
2004	547.6	530.1	6.0	11.5	152.4	143.1	3.9	5.4	395.1	387.0	2.0	a	5.8
2005:													
1st qtr.	126.0	124.1	.2	1.7	38.4	37.2	.1	1.1	87.6	86.9	.1	.1	.5
2d qtr.	115.8	115.0	.1	.7	27.3	27.0	0	.3	88.5	88.0	.1	0	.4
3d qtr.	110.1	109.6	.2	.2	24.9	24.6	.2	.1	85.2	85.0	.1	0	.1
4th qtr.	119.2	117.8	.1	1.4	40.9	39.6	.1	1.2	78.3	78.2	0	.1	.1
2005 total	471.1	466.5	.7	4.0	131.5	128.3	.3	2.8	339.6	338.1	.3	.1	1.1
2006:													
1st qtr.	111.4	107.2	0	4.2	38.2	36.9	0	1.3	73.2	70.3	0	0	2.9
2d qtr.	106.1	105.2	a	.9	26.8	26.1	0	.7	79.3	79.1	a	0	.2
3d qtr.	119.9	119.7	.1	.2	30.7	30.5	.1	.1	89.2	89.2	0	a	0
4th qtr.	117.2	116.7	0	.5	34.3	33.9	0	.4	82.9	82.8	0	0	.1
2006 total	454.6	448.8	.1	5.7	130.0	127.5	.1	2.5	324.6	321.5	a	a	3.2
To Canada													
1995	133.9	6.7	93.5	33.7	133.9	6.7	93.5	33.7	0	0	0	0	0
1996	40.0	15.5	22.6	1.9	40	15.5	22.6	1.9	0	0	0	0	0
1997	11.1	5.3	1.7	4.1	11.1	5.3	1.7	4.1	0	0	0	0	0
1998	28.3	.9	2.2	25.2	28.3	.9	2.2	25.2	0	0	0	0	0
1999	8.4	.6	.6	7.3	8.4	.6	.6	7.3	0	0	0	0	0
2000	18.0	1.5	.3	16.2	18.0	1.5	.3	16.2	0	0	0	0	0
2001	28.9	1.4	1.0	26.5	28.9	1.4	1.0	26.5	0	0	0	0	0
2002	6.6	.5	.7	5.4	6.6	.5	.7	5.4	0	0	0	0	0
2003	8.8	.7	0	8.1	8.8	.7	0	8.1	0	0	0	0	0
2004	3.4	.2	0	3.1	3.4	.2	0	3.1					
2005:													
1st qtr.	.1	0	a	a	.1	0	a	a	0	0	0	0	0
2d qtr.	.1	0	0	.1	.1	0	0	.1	0	0	0	0	0
3d qtr.	.2	a	0	.2	.2	a	0	.2	0	0	0	0	0
4th qtr.	.2	0	0	.2	.2	0	0	.2	0	0	0	0	0
2005 total	.6	a	a	.5	.6	a	a	.5	0	0	0	0	0
2006:													
1st qtr.	2.0	0	0	.20	2.0	0	0	2.0	0	0	0	0	0
2d qtr.	.5	0	0	.5	.5	0	0	.5	0	0	0	0	0
3d qtr.	2.7	0	0	2.7	2.7	0	0	2.7	0	0	0	0	0
4th qtr.	.1	a	0	.1	.1	a	0	.1	0	0	0	0	0
2006 total	5.3	a	0	5.3	5.3	a	0	5.3	0	0	0	0	0

Table 27--Volume of softwood log exports from Seattle and Columbia-Snake Customs Districts by species and destination, 1995-2006 (continued)

(In million board feet, Scribner scale)

Year and quarter	From both customs districts				From Seattle Customs District				From Columbia-Snake Customs District				
	Total	Douglas-fir	Western hemlock	Other softwoods	Total	Douglas-fir	Western hemlock	Other softwoods	Total	Douglas-fir	Western hemlock	Port-Orford-cedar	Other softwoods
To South Korea													
1995	125.8	8.2	105.5	12.1	107.6	7.0	88.8	11.9	18.2	1.2	16.7	.1	.3
1996	74.2	10.6	52.5	11.1	70.8	10.4	49.3	11.0	3.4	.1	3.2	.1	.1
1997	59.9	12.9	41.4	5.6	59.4	12.7	41.4	5.3	.5	.2	0	.1	.2
1998	11.3	3.5	7.3	.7	11.3	3.5	7.3	.7	0	0	0	0	0
1999	30.3	7.1	19.9	3.3	29.8	7.0	19.8	3.0	.5	.1	.1	0	.3
2000	25.3	6.1	15.6	3.5	24.8	6.1	15.6	3.1	.5	.1	0	0	.4
2001	29.5	7.2	18.6	3.7	27.7	6.8	17.3	3.6	1.8	.4	1.3	0	.1
2002	42.0	13.1	24.2	4.8	41.7	12.7	24.2	4.8	.3	.3	0	0	0
2003	42.2	8.2	29.6	4.4	42.2	8.2	29.6	4.4	a	a	0	a	0
2004	66.0	10.0	34.2	21.8	65.7	10.0	34.2	21.5	.3	0	.1	0	.2
2005:													
1st qtr.	15.6	1.8	8.4	5.4	15.6	1.8	8.4	5.4	0	0	0	0	0
2d qtr.	11.7	.8	4.6	6.4	11.7	.8	4.6	6.4	0	0	0	0	0
3d qtr.	12.1	1.6	3.9	6.7	12.1	1.6	3.9	6.7	0	0	0	0	0
4th qtr.	16.2	1.3	6.5	8.4	16.2	1.3	6.5	8.4	0	0	0	0	0
2005 total	55.7	5.5	23.3	26.9	55.7	5.5	23.3	26.9	0	0	0	0	0
2006:													
1st qtr.	12.9	1.7	3.9	7.3	12.9	1.7	3.9	7.3	a	0	0	0	a
2d qtr.	10.5	1.2	3.0	6.3	10.3	1.2	3.0	6.1	.2	0	0	0	.2
3d qtr.	12.0	1.9	1.3	8.8	11.0	1.9	1.3	7.8	1.0	0	0	0	1.0
4th qtr.	25.2	2.1	9.2	13.9	22.4	2.1	7.0	13.3	2.8	0	2.2	0	.6
2006 total	60.6	6.9	17.4	36.3	56.6	6.9	15.2	34.5	4.0	0	2.2	0	1.8
To People's Republic of China													
1995	13.9	9.8	1.5	2.7	13.9	9.8	1.5	2.6	.1	0	0	.1	0
1996	11.9	3.0	7.7	1.2	11.9	3.0	7.7	1.2	0	0	0	0	0
1997	14.2	12.3	.4	1.5	11.8	9.8	.4	1.5	2.5	2.5	0	0	0
1998	12.4	6.4	4.2	1.8	12.4	6.4	4.2	1.8	0	0	0	0	0
1999	1.3	0	1.3	a	1.3	0	1.3	a	0	0	0	0	0
2000	5.9	2.1	.9	2.9	5.3	2.1	.9	2.2	.6	0	0	0	.6
2001	8.2	3.4	2.7	2.0	8.2	3.4	2.7	2.0	0	0	0	0	0
2002	9.7	3.5	2.1	4.1	9.4	3.5	2.1	3.8	.3	0	0	.3	0
2003	.2	a	0	.2	.1	a	0	a	.2	0	0	0	.2
2004	1.2	a	a	1.1	1.1	a	a	1.1	.1	0	0	0	.1
2005:													
1st qtr.	.5	0	0	.5	.5	0	0	.5	a	0	0	a	0
2d qtr.	.6	0	0	.6	.6	0	0	.6	a	0	0	0	a
3d qtr.	.3	0	0	.3	.3	0	0	.3	0	0	0	0	0
4th qtr.	.3	a	0	.3	.3	a	0	.3	a	0	0	a	a
2005 total	1.7	a	0	1.6	1.7	a	0	1.6	a	0	0	a	a
2006:													
1st qtr.	.3	0	0	.3	.3	0	0	.3	a	0	0	0	a
2d qtr.	2.7	0	a	2.7	2.7	0	a	2.7	a	0	0	0	a
3d qtr.	.2	0	0	.1	.1	0	0	.1	.1	0	0	0	a
4th qtr.	.4	0	a	.4	.4	0	a	.4	a	0	0	0	a
2006 total	3.7	0	a	3.7	3.5	0	a	3.5	.2	0	0	0	.2

a Less than 1,000 board feet.

Source: U.S. Department of Commerce. Columbia-Snake Customs District includes all Oregon ports and Longview and Vancouver, Washington. Seattle Customs District includes all coastal and inland ports in the State of Washington, except Longview and Vancouver. Data are compiled from Department of Commerce records at the end of each quarter.

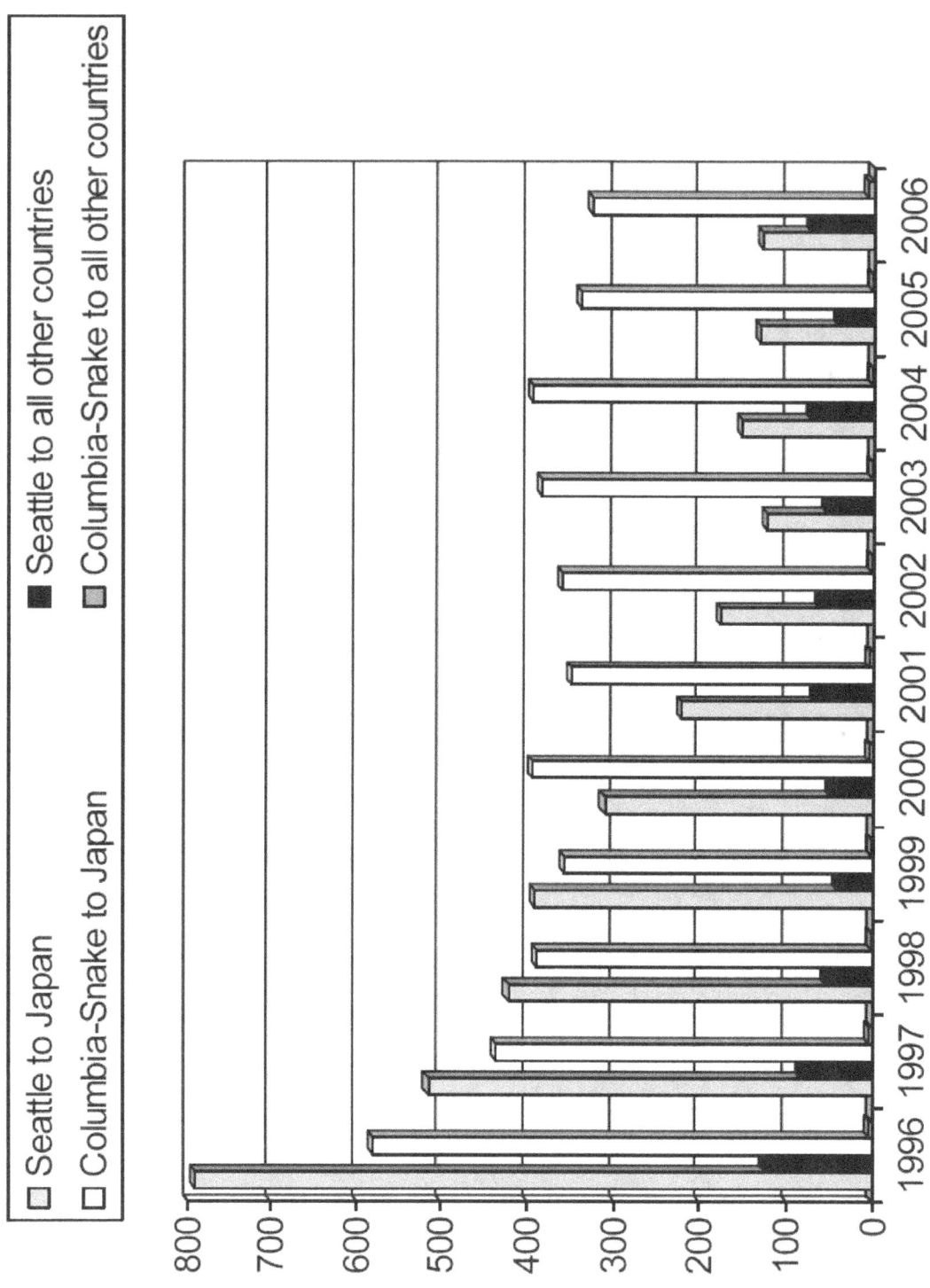

Figure 3—Log exports from Seattle and Columbia-Snake Customs Districts, 1996-2006, in million board feet

Table 28—Value of softwood log exports from Seattle and Columbia-Snake Customs Districts by species and destination, 1995-2006

(In thousand dollars)

Year and quarter	From both customs districts				From Seattle Customs District				From Columbia-Snake Customs District				
	Total	Douglas-fir	Western hemlock	Other softwoods	Total	Douglas-fir	Western hemlock	Other softwoods	Total	Douglas-fir	Western hemlock	Port-Orford-cedar	Other softwoods
To All Countries													
1995	1,509,920	1,190,580	255,683	63,657	855,512	593,612	219,301	42,599	654,408	596,968	36,382	8,911	12,147
1996	1,392,521	1,189,498	156,743	46,280	777,395	608,735	138,673	29,988	615,127	580,764	18,069	4,252	12,040
1997	888,150	718,678	134,057	35,415	483,974	339,617	120,281	24,076	404,176	379,061	13,776	5,337	6,002
1998	617,495	540,795	52,697	24,003	327,121	264,230	47,215	15,676	290,374	276,565	5,482	1,386	6,941
1999	585,715	515,483	47,623	22,608	300,985	241,244	43,889	15,853	284,729	274,240	3,734	2,869	3,887
2000	614,613	563,575	30,828	20,210	275,684	234,219	27,962	13,503	338,929	329,356	2,866	2,525	4,182
2001	446,953	410,181	20,417	16,355	183,295	150,749	18,063	14,482	263,658	259,432	2,354	1,115	756
2002	395,261	360,137	18,898	16,254	145,617	113,760	17,658	14,198	249,644	246,377	1,239	1,341	716
2003	369,591	336,272	14,812	18,507	103,785	81,742	14,058	7,985	265,806	254,531	755	1,117	9,403
2004	487,238	443,561	18,603	25,064	166,414	128,396	17,612	20,406	320,824	315,165	991	433	4,236
2005:													
1st qtr.	117,363	105,863	4,763	6,737	44,219	33,463	4,706	6,050	73,145	72,400	57	310	378
2d qtr.	104,933	98,788	2,720	3,425	32,777	27,152	2,624	3,001	72,156	71,636	96	120	304
3d qtr.	103,396	95,963	2,428	5,005	30,321	23,148	2,370	4,803	73,075	72,815	58	108	94
4th qtr.	112,689	103,108	3,887	5,694	45,847	36,522	3,887	5,438	66,841	66,586	--	115	140
2005 total	438,381	403,722	13,798	20,861	153,164	120,285	13,587	19,292	285,217	283,437	211	653	916
2006:													
1st qtr.	108,564	98,140	1,969	8,455	44,039	35,450	1,969	6,620	64,525	62,690	0	29	1,806
2d qtr.	104,843	96,410	1,736	6,697	33,502	25,334	1,729	6,439	71,341	71,076	7	48	209
3d qtr.	116,310	109,890	1,017	5,403	35,415	29,697	1,017	4,701	80,895	80,192	0	108	595
4th qtr.	118,162	104,514	4,664	8,984	44,872	33,151	3,685	8,036	73,290	71,363	979	0	948
2006 total	447,879	408,953	9,386	29,539	157,828	123,632	8,400	25,796	290,051	285,322	986	185	3,558
To Japan													
1995	1,363,250	1,173,467	151,450	38,333	721,805	578,156	124,873	18,776	641,445	595,311	26,577	7,817	11,740
1996	1,320,534	1,173,404	111,437	35,693	708,513	593,058	95,435	20,020	612,021	580,345	16,022	3,968	11,705
1997	829,133	695,639	107,942	25,552	429,246	319,600	94,201	15,445	399,887	376,039	13,741	4,886	5,221
1998	595,825	533,370	46,355	16,100	306,793	257,739	40,873	8,181	289,032	275,631	5,482	1,216	6,703
1999	564,446	510,115	37,490	16,841	280,510	236,202	33,852	10,456	283,936	273,913	3,639	2,709	3,676
2000	588,650	557,063	23,182	8,405	253,304	228,336	20,316	4,652	335,346	328,728	2,866	2,456	1,296
2001	417,217	400,017	11,718	5,482	157,441	143,720	9,874	3,846	259,776	256,297	1,844	1,115	521
2002	361,606	348,488	7,928	5,191	113,846	103,874	6,716	3,256	247,761	244,614	1,212	1,289	646
2003	346,662	330,248	3,570	12,844	82,682	77,027	2,815	2,840	263,980	253,221	755	999	9,005
2004	446,811	435,566	2,981	8,263	127,652	121,348	2,047	4,257	319,159	314,217	934	247	3,761
2005:													
1st qtr.	105,594	104,073	115	1,406	32,860	32,023	58	779	72,734	72,050	57	249	378
2d qtr.	95,430	94,756	96	578	23,644	23,324	--	320	71,786	71,432	96	--	258
3d qtr.	94,348	93,852	148	348	21,767	21,400	90	277	72,581	72,452	58	--	71
4th qtr.	102,235	101,722	25	488	35,798	35,499	25	274	66,437	66,223	--	82	132
2005 total	397,607	394,402	384	2,820	114,069	112,245	173	1,650	283,538	282,157	211	330	839
2006:													
1st qtr.	99,272	96,454	0	2,818	35,401	34,260	0	1,141	63,871	62,194	0	0	1,677
2d qtr.	96,029	94,913	7	1,109	25,414	24,397	0	1,017	70,615	70,516	7	0	92
3d qtr.	108,478	108,109	51	318	28,502	28,241	51	210	79,976	79,868	0	108	0
4th qtr.	103,515	102,902	0	613	32,179	31,644	0	535	71,336	71,258	0	0	78
2006 total	407,294	402,378	58	4,858	121,496	118,543	51	2,903	285,798	283,836	7	108	1,847
To Canada													
1995	51,693	2,376	37,180	12,137	51,693	2,376	37,180	12,137	--	--	--	--	--
1996	16,716	5,555	10,535	625	16,716	5,555	10,535	625	--	--	--	--	--
1997	3,651	1,626	554	1,471	3,651	1,626	554	1,471	--	--	--	--	--
1998	5,997	291	374	5,332	5,997	291	374	5,332	--	--	--	--	--
1999	2,035	246	88	1,702	2,035	246	88	1,702	--	--	--	--	--
2000	5,402	710	78	4,615	5,402	710	78	4,615	--	--	--	--	--
2001	6,830	592	681	5,556	6,830	592	681	5,556	--	--	--	--	--
2002	2,245	186	514	1,545	2,245	186	514	1,545	--	--	--	--	--
2003	1,881	301	--	1,580	1,881	301	--	1,580	--	--	--	--	--
2004	884	14	--	739	884	145	--	739	--	--	--	--	--
2005:													
1st qtr.	22	--	5	17	22	--	5	17	--	--	--	--	--
2d qtr.	36	--	--	36	36	--	--	36	--	--	--	--	--
3d qtr.	86	27	--	59	86	27	--	59	--	--	--	--	--
4th qtr.	70	--	--	70	70	--	--	70	--	--	--	--	--
2005 total	213	27	5	182	213	27	5	182	--	--	--	--	--
2006:													
1st qtr.	673	--	--	673	673	--	--	673	--	--	--	--	--
2d qtr.	197	--	--	197	197	--	--	197	--	--	--	--	--
3d qtr.	867	--	--	867	867	--	--	867	--	--	--	--	--
4th qtr.	45	8	--	37	45	8	--	37	--	--	--	--	--
2006 total	1,782	8	--	1,774	1,782	8	--	1,774	--	--	--	--	--

Table 28—Value of softwood log exports from Seattle and Columbia-Snake Customs Districts by species and destination, 1995-2006 (continued)

(In thousand dollars)

Year and quarter	From both customs districts				From Seattle Customs District				From Columbia-Snake Customs District				
	Total	Douglas-fir	Western hemlock	Other softwoods	Total	Douglas-fir	Western hemlock	Other softwoods	Total	Douglas-fir	Western hemlock	Port-Orford-cedar	Other softwoods
To South Korea													
1995	81,733	6,197	66,067	9,469	70,663	5,103	56,262	9,298	11,070	1,094	9,805	14	157
1996	46,061	7,878	29,834	8,350	43,729	7,786	27,765	8,179	2,332	92	2,069	117	54
1997	42,496	11,374	25,290	5,832	42,016	11,140	25,290	5,586	480	234	--	14	232
1998	6,296	2,405	3,367	524	6,296	2,405	3,367	524	--	--	--	--	--
1999	16,447	4,822	9,288	2,337	16,094	4,699	9,192	2,203	353	123	95	--	135
2000	13,636	4,088	7,122	2,426	13,247	4,056	7,122	2,069	389	32	--	--	357
2001	13,257	4,405	7,052	1,800	12,370	4,099	6,582	1,689	887	306	470	--	111
2002	19,732	7,379	9,708	2,645	19,717	7,364	9,708	2,645	15	15	--	--	--
2003	17,597	4,279	11,243	2,075	17,568	4,277	11,243	2,048	29	2	--	27	--
2004	35,630	6,777	15,529	13,323	35,418	6,777	15,507	13,134	212	--	22	--	189
2005:													
1st qtr.	10,221	1,171	4,641	4,409	10,221	1,171	4,641	4,409	--	--	--	--	--
2d qtr.	6,706	557	2,261	3,888	6,706	557	2,261	3,888	--	--	--	--	--
3d qtr.	7,183	1,411	2,164	3,608	7,183	1,411	2,164	3,608	--	--	--	--	--
4th qtr.	8,960	969	3,862	4,129	8,960	969	3,862	4,129	--	--	--	--	--
2005 total	33,069	4,107	12,928	16,034	33,069	4,107	12,928	16,034	--	--	--	--	--
2006:													
1st qtr.	7,020	1,140	1,955	3,925	6,994	1,140	1,955	3,899	26	--	--	--	26
2d qtr.	6,272	926	1,723	3,623	6,208	926	1,723	3,559	64	--	--	--	64
3d qtr.	5,332	1,393	713	3,226	4,893	1,393	713	2,787	439	--	--	--	439
4th qtr.	12,362	1,498	4,468	6,396	10,679	1,498	3,489	5,692	1,683	--	979	--	704
2006 total	30,986	4,958	8,859	17,170	28,775	4,958	7,880	15,937	2,211	--	979	--	1,232
To People's Republic of China													
1995	9,772	7,218	813	1,741	9,734	7,218	813	1,703	38	--	--	38	--
1996	7,564	2,193	4,792	579	7,564	2,193	4,792	579	--	--	--	--	--
1997	9,623	8,808	234	581	7,781	6,966	234	581	1,842	1,842	--	--	--
1998	6,429	3,644	1,962	823	6,429	3,644	1,962	823	--	--	--	--	--
1999	1,011	--	582	430	1,011	--	582	430	--	--	--	--	--
2000	2,878	1,091	325	1,462	2,525	1,091	325	1,109	353	--	--	--	353
2001	4,508	1,544	926	2,038	4,508	1,544	926	2,038	--	--	--	--	--
2002	6,651	1,599	720	4,332	6,614	1,599	720	4,295	37	--	--	37	--
2003	303	9	--	294	150	9	--	141	152	--	--	--	152
2004	630	21	25	584	528	21	25	482	102	--	--	--	102
2005:													
1st qtr.	485	--	--	485	445	--	--	445	40	--	--	40	--
2d qtr.	691	--	--	691	667	--	--	667	24	--	--	--	24
3d qtr.	211	--	--	211	211	--	--	211	--	--	--	--	--
4th qtr.	178	24	--	154	146	24	--	122	32	--	--	24	8
2005 total	1,564	24	--	1,540	1,468	24	--	1,444	96	--	--	64	32
2006:													
1st qtr.	282	--	--	282	222	--	--	222	60	--	--	--	60
2d qtr.	859	--	6	853	806	--	6	800	53	--	--	--	53
3d qtr.	284	--	--	284	128	--	--	128	156	--	--	--	156
4th qtr.	609	--	5	604	486	--	5	481	123	--	--	--	123
2006 total	2,034	--	11	2,023	1,643	--	11	1,632	391	--	--	--	391

Note: Individual columns may not add to totals because of rounding.

Source: U.S. Department of Commerce. The valuation definition used in the export statistics is the value at the seaport or border port of exportation. It is based on the selling price (or cost if not sold) and includes inland freight, insurance, and other charges to the port of exportation. Data are compiled from Department of Commerce records at the end of each quarter.

Table 29—Average value of softwood logs exported from Seattle and Columbia-Snake Customs Districts by species and destination, 1995-2006

(In dollars per thousand board feet, Scribner scale)

Year and quarter	From both customs districts				From Seattle Customs District				From Columbia-Snake Customs District				
	Total	Douglas-fir	Western hemlock	Other softwoods	Total	Douglas-fir	Western hemlock	Other softwoods	Total	Douglas fir	Western hemlock	Port-Orford-cedar	Other softwoods
To All Countries													
1995	940.89	1,068.49	633.11	734.55	856.28	1,034.48	619.71	596.66	1,080.47	1,104.61	728.06	4,355.33	918.90
1996	926.59	999.21	605.75	862.64	848.00	945.52	595.03	752.06	1,049.50	1,062.44	702.94	3,306.63	964.06
1997	852.19	910.30	631.15	880.97	807.84	901.56	627.12	784.23	912.16	918.05	668.74	2,965.00	750.30
1998	712.13	752.40	526.97	496.47	686.36	762.40	521.67	396.70	743.58	743.09	577.54	3,135.75	827.39
1999	737.98	770.89	520.92	673.45	692.07	748.75	515.93	573.47	793.62	792.89	587.74	3,388.06	764.96
2000	809.54	842.62	548.39	591.66	765.44	836.08	544.73	470.60	849.34	847.33	586.81	3,196.20	894.55
2001	696.08	740.80	440.97	388.48	632.60	726.31	436.18	354.08	748.44	749.21	483.92	3,915.17	889.41
2002	659.48	675.17	453.19	666.15	608.71	644.00	445.39	617.30	693.21	690.48	611.30	2,737.06	904.13
2003	658.05	689.93	393.94	504.28	587.23	667.34	389.33	397.26	690.55	690.33	458.51	2,944.31	576.87
2004	783.51	820.07	460.98	616.98	736.74	836.64	460.64	590.67	810.20	813.50	453.27	3,486.38	676.50
2005:													
1st qtr.	816.04	835.98	552.68	786.21	793.12	851.93	552.79	759.86	830.55	828.79	539.40	2,838.75	759.04
2d qtr.	804.46	847.30	512.14	401.15	784.00	881.43	506.82	370.68	814.11	813.53	716.12	4,181.54	734.30
3d qtr.	830.02	859.60	555.61	584.42	773.37	873.44	554.95	569.55	856.02	855.28	578.83	4,484.33	870.37
4th qtr.	826.13	864.04	596.22	539.51	791.75	891.17	596.22	522.68	851.49	849.86	--	4,274.61	1,147.54
2005 avg.	819.04	851.39	555.90	575.87	786.77	874.25	555.01	552.86	837.49	836.35	620.80	3,456.86	802.10
2006:													
1st qtr.	851.48	898.72	504.87	587.15	815.88	915.06	500.79	580.66	877.86	888.91	--	6,160.80	602.18
2d qtr.	863.62	900.19	578.67	592.65	808.42	924.56	575.45	585.41	891.99	892.36	610.31	3,905.35	695.29
3d qtr.	845.28	900.00	508.50	400.22	754.93	913.93	511.32	379.10	891.68	894.78	--	6,701.92	540.25
4th qtr.	799.47	879.00	485.83	465.49	724.73	920.22	501.00	434.36	853.10	860.37	453.00	--	1,185.90
2006 avg.	838.25	894.28	507.35	504.94	772.73	918.10	515.95	483.97	878.60	884.06	453.88	5,582.11	684.25
To Japan													
1995	1,026.17	1,078.09	746.27	1,034.13	972.76	1,051.76	735.85	830.39	1,093.74	1,104.95	799.43	4,193.67	932.26
1996	961.19	1,010.84	634.44	954.79	894.77	964.76	623.32	833.87	1,051.57	1,062.70	709.97	3,314.68	961.22
1997	869.20	918.46	639.85	922.44	832.36	917.34	635.63	804.43	912.77	919.41	670.29	3,257.33	745.79
1998	734.70	757.42	545.43	738.67	726.21	770.73	541.39	590.73	743.93	742.78	577.54	5,502.26	867.59
1999	751.41	772.13	541.79	789.49	713.49	751.25	537.88	661.55	793.04	791.09	581.06	3,433.62	776.30
2000	833.63	845.66	593.82	1,005.27	814.83	844.84	594.62	740.66	848.41	846.58	586.81	3,314.44	967.89
2001	730.68	742.15	488.25	685.25	707.37	736.77	483.83	549.43	745.63	744.91	534.17	3,915.17	930.36
2002	675.02	676.94	543.01	823.97	643.98	652.35	531.96	651.20	690.39	687.81	602.68	2,893.62	837.02
2003	684.97	689.02	440.74	686.84	672.46	689.67	431.20	604.26	688.71	688.77	458.51	2,947.33	667.04
2004	815.98	821.67	497.91	719.02	837.43	848.14	519.14	786.15	807.70	811.89	456.69	3,277.99	645.74
2005:													
1st qtr.	838.04	838.83	483.19	829.99	855.42	861.44	438.81	703.07	830.42	829.16	539.40	2,814.26	759.04
2d qtr.	824.12	824.09	716.12	850.00	865.98	864.57	--	981.60	811.21	811.69	716.12	--	730.88
3d qtr.	856.88	856.04	594.38	1,560.54	874.49	869.39	598.55	2,198.41	851.73	852.18	578.83	--	731.96
4th qtr.	857.75	863.62	597.84	358.30	876.28	897.06	597.84	221.50	848.09	846.71	--	7,714.12	1,157.89
2005 avg.	844.01	845.50	578.31	712.66	867.71	874.60	533.22	589.92	834.84	834.46	620.80	3,339.25	790.76
2006:													
1st qtr.	891.13	899.76	--	670.95	927.14	927.52	--	877.69	873.04	884.08	--	--	578.33
2d qtr.	905.08	902.21	576.55	1,232.22	946.68	933.48	--	1,452.86	890.95	891.03	610.31	--	458.32
3d qtr.	904.74	903.17	609.27	1,590.00	927.21	924.63	609.27	2,100.00	896.12	895.07	--	6,701.92	--
4th qtr.	883.23	881.77	--	1,263.92	938.66	933.37	--	1,103.09	860.47	860.41	--	--	777.95
2006 avg.	895.94	896.56	606.79	838.60	934.23	929.61	609.27	1,161.20	880.55	882.74	610.31	6,701.92	577.06
To Canada													
1995	386.07	355.80	397.70	359.84	386.07	355.80	397.70	359.84	--	--	--	--	--
1996	417.89	357.79	466.19	333.01	417.89	357.79	466.19	333.01	--	--	--	--	--
1997	328.92	306.79	325.88	358.78	328.92	306.79	325.88	358.78	--	--	--	--	--
1998	212.24	329.56	169.38	211.88	212.24	329.56	169.38	211.88	--	--	--	--	--
1999	241.35	431.15	155.27	233.19	241.35	431.15	155.27	233.19	--	--	--	--	--
2000	300.18	469.71	269.18	284.92	300.18	469.71	269.18	284.92	--	--	--	--	--
2001	236.68	412.49	705.03	209.67	236.68	412.49	705.03	209.67	--	--	--	--	--
2002	339.81	412.44	769.96	286.11	339.81	412.44	769.96	286.11	--	--	--	--	--
2003	213.12	436.75	--	195.06	213.12	436.75	--	195.06	--	--	--	--	--
2004	261.52	583.94	--	235.95	261.52	583.94	--	235.95	--	--	--	--	--
2005:													
1st qtr.	409.23	--	473.54	389.02	409.23	--	473.54	389.02	--	--	--	--	--
2d qtr.	334.38	--	--	338.35	334.38	--	--	338.35	--	--	--	--	--
3d qtr.	433.47	627.91	--	382.25	433.47	627.91	--	382.25	--	--	--	--	--
4th qtr.	324.20	--	--	323.91	324.20	--	--	323.91	--	--	--	--	--
2005 avg.	371.63	627.91	473.54	349.62	371.63	627.91	473.54	349.62	--	--	--	--	--
2006:													
1st qtr.	341.86	--	--	341.86	341.86	--	--	341.86	--	--	--	--	--
2d qtr.	433.89	--	--	433.89	433.89	--	--	433.89	--	--	--	--	--
3d qtr.	316.64	--	--	316.64	316.64	--	--	316.64	--	--	--	--	--
4th qtr.	480.51	707.92	--	370.00	480.51	707.92	--	370.00	--	--	--	--	--
2006 avg.	339.12	707.92	--	334.72	339.12	707.92	--	334.72	--	--	--	--	--

(In dollars per thousand board feet, Scribner scale)

Year and quarter	From both customs districts				From Seattle Customs District				From Columbia-Snake Customs District				
	Total	Douglas-fir	Western hemlock	Other softwoods	Total	Douglas-fir	Western hemlock	Other softwoods	Total	Douglas-fir	Western hemlock	Port-Orford-cedar	Other softwoods
						To South Korea							
1995	649.51	754.26	626.35	779.86	656.46	726.41	633.92	783.65	608.44	918.56	586.21	2,800.00	579.34
1996	621.12	745.61	568.27	752.79	617.52	745.63	562.80	740.99	697.37	744.34	653.51	3,758.43	2,317.60
1997	709.45	881.71	610.87	1,041.43	707.34	877.17	610.87	1,053.96	1,200.00	1,088.37	--	1,713.59	1,160.00
1998	559.25	680.92	462.18	791.54	559.25	680.92	462.18	791.54	--	--	--	--	--
1999	543.10	677.31	466.82	715.09	539.58	670.44	464.14	731.05	773.00	1,111.04	1,053.13	--	526.86
2000	539.40	667.70	455.96	685.69	534.06	667.61	455.96	665.38	817.99	672.14	--	--	834.18
2001	449.39	611.81	379.14	486.49	445.93	601.58	380.41	470.47	493.53	799.79	359.97	--	1,018.35
2002	469.81	563.28	400.97	551.04	472.83	578.51	400.97	551.04	457.80	457.80	--	--	--
2003	416.99	521.83	379.83	471.59	416.30	521.59	379.83	465.45	5,797.22	972.44	--	11,060.61	--
2004	539.60	676.23	453.78	611.79	538.79	676.23	453.78	609.69	717.86	--	375.22	--	804.26
2005:													
1st qtr.	654.20	648.49	554.81	808.55	654.20	648.49	554.81	808.55	--	--	--	--	--
2d qtr.	570.90	735.67	495.19	605.23	570.90	735.67	495.19	605.23	--	--	--	--	--
3d qtr.	592.14	908.49	551.04	542.56	592.14	908.49	551.04	542.56	--	--	--	--	--
4th qtr.	552.55	718.91	596.21	492.19	552.55	718.91	596.21	492.19	--	--	--	--	--
2005 avg.	593.54	751.86	554.01	595.71	593.54	751.86	554.01	595.71	--	--	--	--	--
2006:													
1st qtr.	544.19	670.59	501.28	537.67	542.84	671.27	498.81	534.10	467.03	--	--	--	467.03
2d qtr.	597.33	771.67	574.33	575.08	605.42	739.76	575.15	583.39	382.66	--	--	--	382.66
3d qtr.	444.33	733.16	548.46	366.59	443.40	744.52	529.35	357.24	426.55	--	--	--	426.55
4th qtr.	490.56	713.33	485.65	460.14	475.72	710.06	497.85	428.01	597.53	--	453.00	--	1,173.54
2006 avg.	511.32	718.55	509.14	473.00	508.18	715.23	516.05	461.93	543.72	--	453.00	--	648.56
						To People's Republic of China							
1995	703.07	739.02	548.58	656.98	701.45	739.02	548.58	648.02	1,739.13	--	--	1,739.13	--
1996	636.58	738.56	619.32	492.56	636.58	738.56	619.32	492.56	--	--	--	--	--
1997	677.68	716.10	553.19	387.33	659.41	710.82	553.19	387.33	736.80	736.80	--	--	--
1998	520.00	569.20	467.70	466.02	520.00	569.20	467.70	466.02	--	--	--	--	--
1999	527.18	--	527.18	--	527.18	--	527.18	--	--	--	--	--	--
2000	486.67	524.13	343.15	506.22	478.82	524.66	342.98	493.38	551.24	--	--	--	551.24
2001	547.52	450.33	338.56	999.02	547.52	450.33	338.56	999.02	--	--	--	--	--
2002	685.67	456.86	342.86	1,056.59	705.30	451.29	336.10	1,130.26	1,195.15	--	--	1,195.15	--
2003	1,515.00	1,229.96	--	1,470.00	2,225.92	1,229.96	--	2,346.31	810.07	--	--	--	810.07
2004	525.00	1,833.37	514.97	507.83	468.46	1,833.37	514.97	454.72	1,085.10	--	--	--	1,085.10
2005:													
1st qtr.	893.58	--	--	893.58	849.29	--	--	849.29	2,132.20	--	--	2,132.20	--
2d qtr.	1,139.93	--	--	1,139.93	1,143.52	--	--	1,143.52	1,035.38	--	--	--	1,035.38
3d qtr.	771.51	--	--	771.51	771.51	--	--	771.51	--	--	--	--	--
4th qtr.	565.08	551.85	--	488.89	493.34	542.68	--	482.21	1,685.99	--	--	2,173.91	1,006.29
2005 avg.	900.40	551.85	--	886.59	876.10	542.68	--	884.26	1,575.84	--	--	2,147.65	1,027.95
2006:													
1st qtr.	940.00	--	--	940.00	640.86	--	--	640.86	760.56	--	--	--	760.56
2d qtr.	318.15	--	685.62	315.93	300.55	--	685.62	296.51	1,669.24	--	--	--	1,669.24
3d qtr.	1,755.14	--	--	1,755.14	1,195.55	--	--	1,195.55	2,843.42	--	--	--	2,843.42
4th qtr.	1,522.50	--	453.18	1,483.80	1,299.39	--	453.18	1,203.45	2,791.94	--	--	--	2,791.94
2006 avg.	549.73	--	550.91	546.82	468.02	--	550.91	466.29	1,871.06	--	--	--	1,871.06

Source: U.S. Department of Commerce. The valuation definition used in the export statistics is the value at the seaport or border port of exportation. It is based on the selling price (or cost if not sold) and includes inland freight, insurance, and other charges to the port of exportation. Data are compiled from Department of Commerce records at the end of each quarter.

Table 30--Volume and average value of softwood log exports from the San Francisco Customs District by species and destination, 1995-2006

(In thousand board feet, Scribner scale)

Year and quarter	Total		Douglas-fir		Port-Orford-cedar		Other softwoods	
	Volume	Average value	Volume	Average value	Volume	Average value	Volume	Average value
To All Countries								
1995	21,602	808.44	7,661	1,049.47	225	5,626.67	13,716	594.78
1996	23,006	875.41	18,173	917.91	124	2,003.54	4,709	681.63
1997	15,600	823.51	13,255	788.50	377	2,296.58	1,967	776.87
1998	15,828	775.38	12,145	780.60	44	1,545.45	3,639	748.63
1999	4,266	627.12	925	699.15	0	--	3,341	607.18
2000	6,659	585.66	1,507	814.14	0	--	5,151	518.81
2001	5,766	503.37	31	2,042.33	0	--	5,735	495.12
2002	1,436	856.20	600	646.87	94	4,972.54	741	504.67
2003	76	2,033.86	10	1,996.06	0	--	66	2,039.72
2004	307	762.90	187	952.66	0	--	120	465.28
2005	140	1,240.42	74	1,262.36	0	--	66	1,220.08
2006:								
1st quarter	10	2,480.79	0	--	0	--	10	2,480.79
2d quarter	30	2,642.82	0	--	0	--	30	2,642.82
3d quarter	24	754.31	16	796.61	0	--	8	669.71
4th quarter	12	1,136.71	0	--	0	--	12	1,136.71
2006 total and average value	75	1,781.99	16	796.61	0	--	59	2,049.21
To Japan								
1995	14,514	955.56	7,603	1,044.72	225	5,626.67	6,686	696.98
1996	21,155	890.73	18,026	920.84	42	2,503.58	3,087	693.00
1997	15,470	823.33	13,249	787.96	377	2,296.58	1,843	776.07
1998	13,686	811.34	11,492	797.96	44	1,545.45	2,150	867.80
1999	1,454	885.41	576	815.57	0	--	877	931.27
2000	2,007	779.69	1,325	830.50	0	--	682	681.06
2001	784	456.58	0	--	0	--	784	456.58
2002	535	646.13	530	613.35	0	--	5	4,172.40
2003	9	1,875.19	0	--	0	--	9	1,875.19
2004	26	463.15	0	--	0	--	26	463.15
2005	15	296.46	0	--	0	--	15	296.46
2006:								
1st quarter	0	--	0	--	0	--	0	--
2d quarter	3	1,839.94	0	--	0	--	3	1,839.94
3d quarter	0	--	0	--	0	--	0	--
4th quarter	5	1,857.92	0	--	0	--	5	1,857.92
2006 total and average value	8	1,851.57	0	--	0	--	8	1,851.57
To People's Republic of China								
1995	0	--	0	--	0	--	0	--
1996	0	--	0	--	0	--	0	--
1997	0	--	0	--	0	--	0	--
1998	340	494.81	0	--	0	--	340	494.81
1999	603	478.44	0	--	0	--	603	478.44
2000	908	500.70	0	--	0	--	908	500.70
2001	836	465.31	0	--	0	--	836	465.31
2002	94	5,026.42	0	--	88	5,200.98	6	2,466.21
2003	26	3,659.99	0	--	0	--	26	3,649.99
2004	0	--	0	--	0	--	0	--
2005	0	--	0	--	0	--	0	--
2006:								
1st quarter	6	1,956.96	0	--	0		6	1,956.96
2d quarter	0	--	0	--	0	--	0	--
3d quarter	0	--	0	--	0	--	0	--
4th quarter	0	--	0	--	0	--	0	--
2006 total and average value	6	1,956.96	0	--	0	--	6	1,956.96

Source: U.S. Department of Commerce. Data are compiled from Department of Commerce records at the end of each quarter.

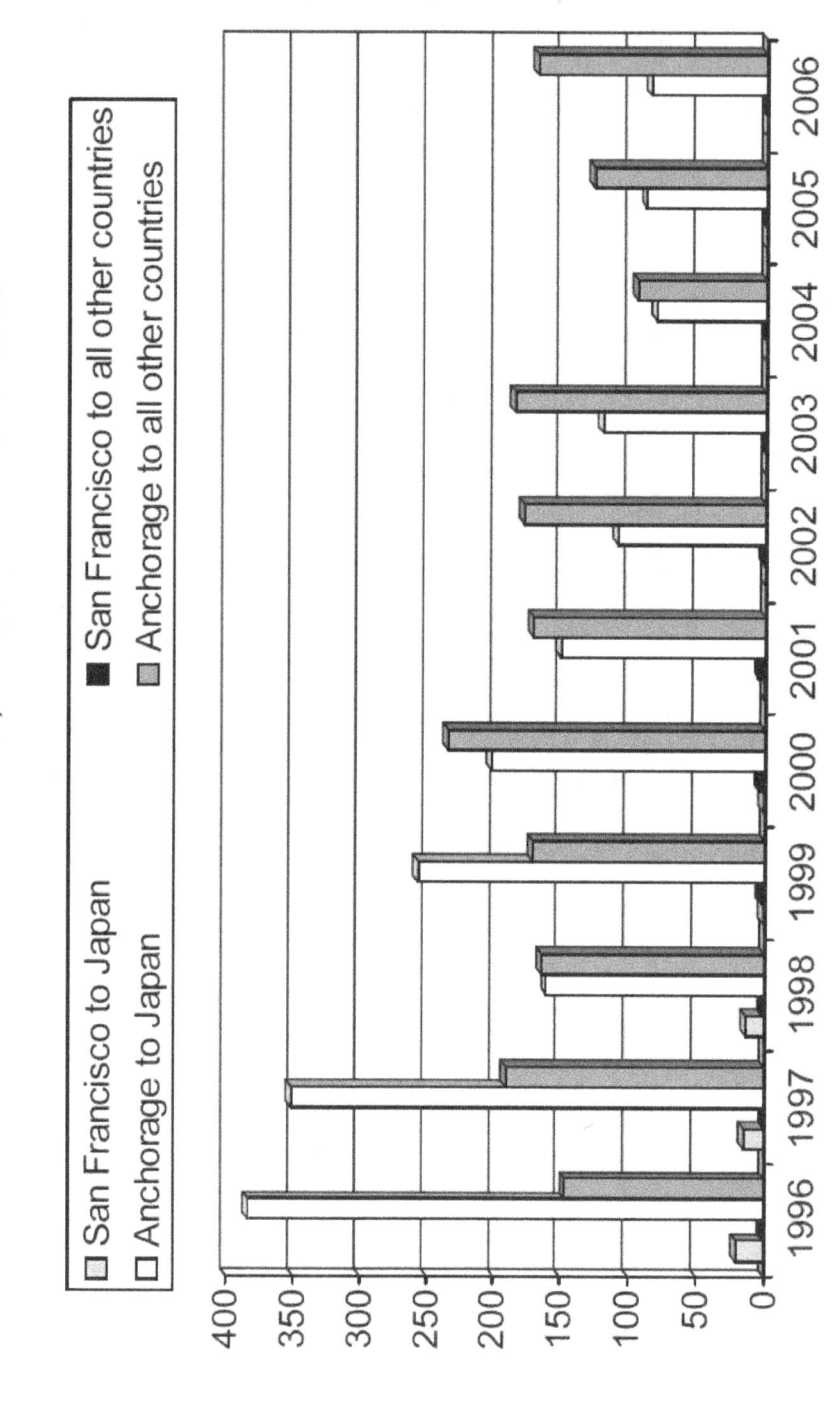

Figure 4—Log exports from San Francisco and Anchorage Customs Districts, 1996-2006, in million board feet

48

Table 31—Volume and average value of softwood log exports from Anchorage Customs District by species and destination, 1995-2006

(Volume in thousand board feet, Scribner scale; value in dollars per thousand board feet)

Year and quarter	All species Volume	All species Average value	Hemlock Volume	Hemlock Average value	Redcedar Volume	Redcedar Average value	Spruce Volume	Spruce Average value
				To All Countries				
1995	561,550	695.12	250,659	539.02	40,685	652.43	228,615	779.98
1996	530,147	705.98	223,519	537.02	22,632	678.28	257,254	817.34
1997	541,667	642.25	202,517	480.10	37,305	806.85	259,601	733.15
1998	325,386	473.55	72,186	443.51	15,232	791.62	133,334	626.71
1999	427,970	455.70	125,779	408.47	17,687	684.56	172,435	552.20
2000	436,178	426.35	127,861	403.79	22,246	766.73	148,906	541.69
2001	320,615	424.03	108,563	355.95	11,389	694.51	119,288	547.01
2002	286,976	409.70	79,406	398.67	10,820	726.22	153,548	434.34
2003	305,588	456.62	85,094	438.80	12,936	763.28	190,003	430.18
2004	175,281	552.35	50,637	490.39	7,785	804.62	104,117	576.07
2005	216,021	561.74	52,048	495.90	9,962	778.20	141,508	557.69
2006:								
1st quarter	28,486	535.76	9,834	484.73	1,500	665.96	15,278	521.10
2d quarter	64,633	422.86	16,047	479.10	1,726	703.72	45,574	382.96
3d quarter	86,598	402.26	17,237	487.21	922	662.59	66,298	363.93
4th quarter	74,335	405.08	14,848	513.18	2,151	885.26	50,277	352.82
2006 total and average value	254,053	423.30	57,967	491.19	6,299	750.70	177,427	379.20
				To Japan				
1995	356,928	798.61	116,903	633.41	18,880	679.45	189,840	815.27
1996	383,056	771.64	129,788	562.49	13,042	668.13	218,545	851.47
1997	351,497	721.67	114,246	525.60	20,198	769.29	194,755	780.93
1998	161,369	619.35	45,034	473.75	6,402	719.31	97,351	656.50
1999	257,472	565.86	78,738	435.76	8,657	767.28	124,811	594.75
2000	201,753	585.47	69,045	457.79	11,407	780.63	100,628	608.68
2001	149,923	555.73	49,441	396.11	4,359	756.08	81,800	594.93
2002	108,822	574.78	37,511	412.54	4,172	823.49	58,572	624.34
2003	120,113	624.98	37,524	446.03	7,816	820.26	65,319	662.33
2004	80,614	660.69	20,927	513.17	3,090	845.07	50,974	689.30
2005	88,581	654.02	22,778	501.97	3,263	697.43	53,424	682.86
2006:								
1st quarter	7,738	651.77	2,596	542.03	668	728.59	2,600	621.12
2d quarter	17,319	452.13	2,369	475.22	259	943.46	13,405	409.21
3d quarter	35,774	380.38	5,451	492.42	490	638.40	27,692	321.83
4th quarter	24,534	434.20	3,812	485.12	1,130	930.60	17,026	337.33
2006 total and average value	85,365	435.00	14,228	496.65	2,547	822.67	60,723	358.28
			To People's Republic of China					
1995	5,426	477.10	0	--	0	--	5,426	477.10
1996	3,062	587.89	0	--	0	--	3,062	587.89
1997	2,256	543.00	0	--	0	--	2,256	543.00
1998	2,870	652.96	1,987	604.43	0	--	883	762.17
1999	2,653	326.44	0	--	0	--	2,653	326.44
2000	6,324	408.30	507	380.71	0	--	5,817	410.73
2001	4,325	1,401.67	1,190	320.89	0	--	3,135	1,812.00
2002	5,562	658.83	129	496.36	0	--	5,433	662.69
2003	4,272	581.38	269	428.45	670	746.05	2,957	530.46
2004	3,947	644.47	944	453.07	0	--	2,928	722.73
2005	9,519	747.96	524	569.39	68	936.87	8,927	757.00
2006:								
1st quarter	2,979	707.70	0	--	383	524.74	2,595	734.71
2d quarter	2,047	382.10	401	454.25	0	--	1,646	365.54
3d quarter	0	--	0	--	0	--	0	--
4th quarter	14,417	336.97	2,081	603.51	0	--	12,218	285.90
2006 total and average value	19,443	398.51	2,481	579.41	383	524.74	16,460	364.53

Note: The three columns (hemlock, redcedar, and spruce) will not necessarily total the "all species" column because there is often "other softwood" included. The log export numbers include pulpwood volumes.

Source: U.S. Department of Commerce. Data are compiled from Department of Commerce records at the end of each quarter.

Table 32—Volume and average value of log exports by port, species, and destination, Seattle Customs District, 2006

(Volume in thousand board feet, Scribner scale; value in dollars per thousand board feet)

Port and species	All countries Volume	All countries Average value	Japan Volume	Japan Average value	People's Republic of China Volume	People's Republic of China Average value	Korea Volume	Korea Average value	Canada Volume	Canada Average value
Aberdeen:										
Douglas fir	54,935	928.45	53,811	934.07	0		1,124	659.39	0	
Hemlock	2,413	484.27	0		0		2,413	484.27	0	
Spruce	482	305.83	0		0		482	305.83	0	
All softwoods	57,829	904.73	53,811	934.07	0		4,018	511.86	0	
Everett:										
Douglas fir	993	799.92	993	799.92	0		0		0	
All softwoods	993	799.92	993	799.92	0		0		0	
Olympia:										
Douglas fir	1,679	898.12	1,679	898.12	0		0		0	
Port Orford cedar	100	1,811.84	100	1,811.84	0		0		0	
Hemlock	36	593.07	36	593.07	0		0		0	
Other softwoods	19	927.07	19	927.07	0		0		0	
All softwoods	1,833	942.16	1,833	942.16	0		0		0	
Port Angeles:										
All hardwoods	4	1,257.30	4	1,257.30	0		0		0	
Seattle:										
Douglas fir	3,528	693.91	2,592	732.33	0		738	577.73	0	
Port Orford cedar	34	991.57	11	1,623.10	0		23	685.00	0	
Redcedar	370	1,273.24	0		370	1,273.24	0		0	
Hemlock	5,262	471.76	0		19	550.91	4,335	464.45	0	
Spruce	5,313	335.45	0		0		1,051	347.69	0	
Other softwoods	22,159	512.34	1,283	1,504.47	270	872.58	20,461	433.37	0	
All softwoods	36,666	506.48	3,886	989.81	660	1,087.96	26,608	439.27	0	
All hardwoods	13,739	1,187.84	3,893	1,540.95	1,695	1,415.38	6,224	911.50	0	
Red alder	1,137	1,699.49	0		899	1,533.13	0		0	

Table 32—Volume and average value of log exports by port, species, and destination, Seattle Customs District, 2006 (continued)

(Volume in thousand board feet, Scribner scale; value in dollars per thousand board feet)

Port and species	All countries Volume	All countries Average value	Japan Volume	Japan Average value	People's Republic of China Volume	People's Republic of China Average value	Korea Volume	Korea Average value	Canada Volume	Canada Average value
Tacoma:										
Douglas fir	73,515	923.22	68,445	936.22	0		5,070	747.63	0	
Port Orford cedar	10	4,843.70	10	4,843.70	0		0		0	
Redcedar	89	572.31	0		8	866.36	0		0	
Hemlock	8,570	551.68	47	621.56	0		8,523	551.29	0	
Spruce	3,614	576.39	0		0		3,087	441.86	0	
Other softwoods	10,632	578.14	980	642.81	186	1,240.24	9,323	556.68	0	
All softwoods	96,430	839.22	69,482	932.42	194	1,224.91	26,002	578.51	0	
All hardwoods	2,419	1,989.02	214	2,908.19	1,058	1,312.79	547	2,286.09	0	
Red alder	672	1,619.21	0		639	1,577.34	0		0	
Other ports:[a]										
Douglas fir	11	707.92	0		0		0		11	707.92
Redcedar	3,288	423.51	0		0		0		3,288	423.51
Spruce	81	585.64	0		0		0		8	355.01
Other softwoods	1,970	197.73	0		0		0		1,970	197.73
All softwoods	5,351	343.43	0		0		0		5,278	339.73
All hardwoods	555	821.91	0		0		0		555	821.91
Total:										
Douglas fir	134,660	918.10	127,519	929.61	0		6,932	715.23	11	707.92
Port Orford cedar	143	1,824.01	121	2,038.88	0		23	685.00	0	
Redcedar	3,748	511.03	0		378	1,264.70	0		3,288	423.51
Hemlock	16,281	515.95	83	609.27	19	550.91	15,270	516.05	0	
Spruce	9,490	427.83	0		0		4,619	406.25	8	355.01
Other softwoods	34,780	514.86	2,282	1,129.64	456	1,022.00	29,784	471.97	1,970	197.73
All softwoods	199,102	784.41	130,005	933.94	854	1,119.05	56,628	508.36	5,278	339.73
All hardwoods	16,717	1,291.65	4,112	1,611.92	2,753	1,375.95	6,771	1,022.56	555	821.91
Red alder	1,809	1,669.68	0		1,538	1,551.50	0		0	

[a] Blaine, Metaline Falls, Oroville, and Sumas.

Source: U.S. Department of Commerce.

Table 33a—Volume and average value of log exports by port, species, and destination, Seattle Customs District, first quarter 2006

(Volume in thousand board feet, Scribner scale; value in dollars per thousand board feet)

Port and species	Destination									
	All countries		Japan		People's Republic of China		Korea		Canada	
	Volume	Average value	Volume	Average value	Volume	Average value	Volume	Average value	Volume	Average value
Aberdeen:										
Douglas fir	18,032	930.34	17,432	938.89	0		600	681.77	0	
Hemlock	1,578	488.03	0		0		1,578	488.03	0	
Spruce	327	299.51	0		0		327	299.51	0	
All softwoods	19,937	884.98	17,432	938.89	0		2,505	509.79	0	
Olympia:										
Douglas fir	1,014	956.43	1,014	956.43	0		0		0	
Other softwoods	19	927.07	19	927.07	0		0		0	
All softwoods	1,033	955.89	1,033	955.89	0		0		0	
Seattle:										
Douglas fir	2,087	687.98	1,817	720.83	0		165	461.84	0	
Port Orford cedar	6	1,796.60	6	1,796.60	0		0		0	
Redcedar	47	1,388.67	0		47	1,388.67	0		0	
Hemlock	783	443.97	0		0		770	432.98	0	
Spruce	1,278	460.17	0		0		1,051	347.69	0	
Other softwoods	2,605	963.74	533	1,364.66	192	538.32	1,853	861.45	0	
All softwoods	6,806	728.43	2,355	869.14	239	705.72	3,840	617.69	0	
All hardwoods	2,939	1,482.07	1,241	2,007.52	416	1,251.48	1,036	806.60	0	
Red alder	335	1,529.04	0		279	1,382.09	0		0	
Tacoma:										
Douglas fir	17,608	923.95	16,675	936.40	0		934	701.63	0	
Redcedar	88	535.32	0		8	866.36	0		0	
Hemlock	1,571	541.91	0		0		1,571	541.91	0	
Spruce	620	854.75	0		0		526	400.87	0	
Other softwoods	4,265	466.97	657	482.94	99	466.88	3,509	463.98	0	
All softwoods	24,152	815.21	17,331	919.21	107	496.47	6,540	511.55	0	
All hardwoods	921	2,101.58	48	2,208.22	192	1,382.90	301	1,900.26	0	
Red alder	75	1,628.40	0		75	1,628.40	0		0	

Table 33a—Volume and average value of log exports by port, species, and destination, Seattle Customs District, first quarter 2006 (continued)

(Volume in thousand board feet, Scribner scale; value in dollars per thousand board feet)

Port and species	All countries Volume	All countries Average value	Japan Volume	Japan Average value	People's Republic of China Volume	People's Republic of China Average value	Korea Volume	Korea Average value	Canada Volume	Canada Average value
Other ports:[a]										
Redcedar	1,391	414.95	0		0		0		1,391	414.95
Other softwoods	590	172.01	0		0		0		590	172.01
All softwoods	1,981	342.61	0		0		0		1,981	342.61
All hardwoods	36	4,350.56	0		0		0		36	4,350.56
Total:										
Douglas fir	38,741	915.06	36,937	927.52	0		1,698	671.27	0	
Port Orford cedar	6	1,796.60	6	1,796.60	0		0		0	
Redcedar	1,526	451.87	0		55	1,313.15	0		1,391	414.95
Hemlock	3,932	500.79	0		0		3,919	498.81	0	
Spruce	2,225	546.54	0		0		1,904	354.11	0	
Other softwoods	7,479	617.91	1,209	878.86	291	513.95	5,362	601.36	590	172.01
All softwoods	53,908	815.39	38,152	926.10	346	640.87	12,884	542.84	1,981	342.61
All hardwoods	3,895	1,654.82	1,289	2,014.98	608	1,292.92	1,337	1,052.57	36	4,350.56
Red alder	410	1,547.21	0		354	1,434.30	0		0	

[a] Blaine and Sumas.

Source: U.S. Department of Commerce.

Table 33b—Volume and average value of log exports by port, species, and destination, Seattle Customs District, second quarter 2006

(Volume in thousand board feet, Scribner scale; value in dollars per thousand board feet)

Port and species	All countries Volume	All countries Average value	Japan Volume	Japan Average value	People's Republic of China Volume	People's Republic of China Average value	Korea Volume	Korea Average value	Canada Volume	Canada Average value
Aberdeen:										
Douglas fir	8,473	938.74	8,473	938.74	0		0		0	
Olympia:										
Port Orford cedar	100	1,811.84	100	1,811.84	0		0		0	
Seattle:										
Douglas fir	924	723.25	775	759.28	0		136	510.67	0	
Port Orford cedar	23	685.00	0		0		23	685.00	0	
Hemlock	598	473.06	0		8	685.62	590	470.12	0	
Spruce	340	385.50	0		0		0		0	
Other softwoods	3,256	825.62	460	1,491.12	10	2,590.66	2,764	685.08	0	
All softwoods	5,141	736.46	1,235	1,031.79	18	1,731.07	3,512	642.25	0	
All hardwoods	5,171	1,171.68	1,896	1,372.55	382	1,504.45	1,698	1,122.13	0	
Red alder	239	1,785.06	0		188	1,453.36	0		0	
Tacoma:										
Douglas fir	18,004	928.22	16,887	938.84	0		1,117	767.57	0	
Port Orford cedar	10	4,843.70	10	4,843.70	0		0		0	
Hemlock	2,407	600.88	0		0		2,407	600.88	0	
Spruce	248	1,213.54	0		0		149	368.66	0	
Other softwoods	3,392	563.79	141	736.42	42	2,617.88	3,076	522.59	0	
All softwoods	24,060	848.61	17,037	939.40	42	2,617.88	6,748	587.66	0	
All hardwoods	632	1,631.07	4	3,199.19	432	1,078.73	112	2,825.41	0	
Red alder	198	1,555.52	0		193	1,551.32	0		0	

Table 33b—Volume and average value of log exports by port, species, and destination, Seattle Customs District, second quarter 2006 (continued)

(Volume in thousand board feet, Scribner scale; value in dollars per thousand board feet)

Port and species	Destination									
	All countries		Japan		People's Republic of China		Korea		Canada	
	Volume	Average value	Volume	Average value	Volume	Average value	Volume	Average value	Volume	Average value
Other ports:[a]										
Redcedar	454	433.89	0		0		0		454	433.89
Spruce	73	612.28	0		0		0		0	
All softwoods	526	458.51	0		0		0		454	433.89
All hardwoods	48	3,334.87	0		0		0		48	3,334.87
Total:										
Douglas fir	27,401	924.56	26,135	933.48	0		1,252	739.76	0	
Port Orford cedar	132	1,840.78	109	2,080.80	0		23	685.00	0	
Redcedar	454	433.89	0		0		0		454	433.89
Hemlock	3,005	575.45	0		8	685.62	2,996	575.15	0	
Spruce	661	720.84	0		0		149	368.66	0	
Other softwoods	6,648	692.03	600	1,314.37	51	2,612.62	5,840	599.48	0	
All softwoods	38,300	850.65	26,845	946.68	60	2,348.55	10,260	606.34	454	433.89
All hardwoods	5,852	1,239.12	1,900	1,376.37	814	1,278.42	1,810	1,227.84	48	3,334.87
Red alder	436	1,681.03	0		382	1,502.99	0		0	

[a] Blaine and Sumas.

Source: U.S. Department of Commerce.

Table 33c—Volume and average value of log exports by port, species, and destination, Seattle Customs District, third quarter 2006

(Volume in thousand board feet, Scribner scale; value in dollars per thousand board feet)

Port and species	All countries		Japan		People's Republic of China		Korea		Canada	
	Volume	Average value	Volume	Average value	Volume	Average value	Volume	Average value	Volume	Average value
Aberdeen Hoquiam:										
Douglas fir	5,527	925.59	5,527	925.59	0		0		0	
Everett:										
Douglas fir	993	799.92	993	799.92	0		0		0	
Olympia:										
Douglas fir	664	809.12	664	809.12	0		0		0	
Hemlock	36	593.07	36	593.07	0		0		0	
All softwoods	700	798.02	700	798.02	0		0		0	
Seattle:										
Douglas fir	406	706.16	0		0		327	685.19	0	
Hemlock	1,204	472.70	0		0		646	489.64	0	
Spruce	998	305.41	0		0		0		0	
Other softwoods	6,203	338.89	89	1,981.08	29	1,105.43	6,047	299.52	0	
All softwoods	8,811	370.30	89	1,981.08	29	1,105.43	7,020	334.98	0	
All hardwoods	2,411	1,117.56	30	3,435.89	536	1,401.24	1,509	898.52	0	
Red alder	357	1,809.69	0		300	1,701.97	0		0	
Tacoma:										
Douglas fir	24,903	922.08	23,358	932.99	0		1,545	757.07	0	
Hemlock	748	569.50	47	621.56	0		701	565.98	0	
Spruce	443	469.75	0		0		158	429.78	0	
Other softwoods	1,667	603.38	11	2,172.80	45	1,676.57	1,611	563.06	0	
All softwoods	27,762	886.21	23,416	932.92	45	1,676.57	4,015	632.95	0	
All hardwoods	496	1,534.06	21	1,587.84	317	1,539.04	73	945.30	0	
Red alder	312	1,639.44	0		283	1,548.97	0		0	

Table 33c—Volume and average value of log exports by port, species, and destination, Seattle Customs District, third quarter 2006 (continued)

(Volume in thousand board feet, Scribner scale; value in dollars per thousand board feet)

Port and species	Destination									
	All countries		Japan		People's Republic of China		Korea		Canada	
	Volume	Average value	Volume	Average value	Volume	Average value	Volume	Average value	Volume	Average value
Other ports:[a]										
Redcedar	1,362	427.25	0		0		0		1,362	427.25
Spruce	8	355.01	0		0		0		8	355.01
Other softwoods	1,380	208.72	0		0		0		1,380	208.72
All softwoods	2,750	317.37	0		0		0		2,750	317.37
All hardwoods	376	282.94	0		0		0		0	
Total:										
Douglas fir	32,494	913.93	30,543	924.63	0		1,872	744.52	0	
Redcedar	1,362	427.25	0		0		0		1,362	427.25
Hemlock	1,988	511.32	83	609.27	0		1,347	529.35	0	
Spruce	1,450	355.96	0		0		158	429.78	8	355.01
Other softwoods	9,250	367.13	100	2,001.44	74	1,454.27	7,658	354.97	1,380	208.72
All softwoods	46,544	756.44	30,726	927.27	74	1,454.27	11,035	443.40	2,750	317.37
All hardwoods	3,283	1,084.92	51	2,663.21	854	1,452.45	1,582	900.66	376	282.94
Red alder	669	1,730.27	0		583	1,627.61	0		0	

[a] Blaine, Oroville, and Sumas.

Source: U.S. Department of Commerce.

Table 33d—Volume and average value of log exports by port, species, and destination, Seattle Customs District, fourth quarter 2006

(Volume in thousand board feet, Scribner scale; value in dollars per thousand board feet)

Port and species	All countries Volume	All countries Average value	Japan Volume	Japan Average value	People's Republic of China Volume	People's Republic of China Average value	Korea Volume	Korea Average value	Canada Volume	Canada Average value
Aberdeen Hoquiam										
Douglas fir	22,902	923.84	22,378	930.63	0		524	633.80	0	
Hemlock	835	477.17	0		0		835	477.17	0	
Spruce	155	319.20	0		0		155	319.20	0	
All softwoods	23,892	904.32	22,378	930.63	0		1,514	515.29	0	
Port Angeles:										
All hardwoods	4	1,257.30	4	1,257.30	0		0		0	
Seattle:										
Douglas fir	111	515.87	0		0		111	515.87	0	
Port Orford cedar	6	1,449.60	6	1,449.60	0		0		0	
Redcedar	323	1,256.46	0		323	1,256.46	0		0	
Hemlock	2,678	479.17	0		11	453.18	2,329	466.44	0	
Spruce	2,697	281.14	0		0		0		0	
Other softwoods	10,094	401.39	201	1,694.83	40	1,888.58	9,797	363.99	0	
All softwoods	15,908	412.64	206	1,688.26	374	1,299.39	12,236	384.86	0	
All hardwoods	3,219	997.81	726	1,105.89	361	1,531.22	1,980	795.68	0	
Red alder	206	1,687.02	0		132	1,582.95	0		0	
Tacoma:										
Douglas fir	13,000	917.48	11,525	938.69	0		1,475	751.76	0	
Redcedar	1	3,020.00	0		0		0		0	
Hemlock	3,844	521.38	0		0		3,844	521.38	0	
Spruce	2,302	453.38	0		0		2,253	457.12	0	
Other softwoods	1,308	945.63	172	1,082.52	0		1,127	929.14	0	
All softwoods	20,456	792.76	11,697	940.81	0		8,699	596.63	0	
All hardwoods	370	2,932.48	141	3,338.13	117	1,448.59	61	4,775.66	0	
Red alder	87	1,683.55	0		87	1,683.55	0		0	

Table 33d—Volume and average value of log exports by port, species, and destination, Seattle Customs District, fourth quarter 2006 (continued)

(Volume in thousand board feet, Scribner scale; value in dollars per thousand board feet)

Port and species	Destination									
	All countries		Japan		People's Republic of China		Korea		Canada	
	Volume	Average value	Volume	Average value	Volume	Average value	Volume	Average value	Volume	Average value
Other ports:[a]										
Douglas fir	11	707.92	0		0		0		11	707.92
Redcedar	82	449.25	0		0		0		82	449.25
All softwoods	93	480.51	0		0		0		93	480.51
All hardwoods	95	353.19	0		0		0		95	353.19
Total:										
Douglas fir	36,025	920.22	33,903	933.37	0		2,110	710.06	11	707.92
Port Orford cedar	6	1,449.60	6	1,449.60	0		0		0	
Redcedar	407	1,099.62	0		323	1,256.46	0		82	449.25
Hemlock	7,356	501.00	0		11	453.18	7,007	497.85	0	
Spruce	5,154	359.22	0		0		2,408	448.26	0	
Other softwoods	11,402	463.83	373	1,412.25	40	1,888.58	10,924	422.30	0	
All softwoods	60,349	736.24	34,281	938.66	374	1,299.39	22,449	475.72	93	480.51
All hardwoods	3,687	1,175.46	872	1,467.86	478	1,510.95	2,042	915.32	95	353.19
Red alder	293	1,685.99	0		219	1,622.99	0		0	

[a] Blaine, Metaline Falls, and Sumas.

Source: U.S. Department of Commerce.

Table 34—Volume and average value of log exports by port, species, and destination, Columbia-Snake Customs District, 2006

(Volume in thousand board feet, Scribner scale; value in dollars per thousand board feet)

Port and species	All countries Volume	All countries Average value	Japan Volume	Japan Average value	People's Republic of China Volume	People's Republic of China Average value	Korea Volume	Korea Average value	Taiwan Volume	Taiwan Average value
Longview (Washington):										
Douglas fir	316,375	884.01	316,375	884.01	0		0		0	
Other softwoods	2,209	524.96	2,208	524.96	0		0		0	
All softwoods	318,584	881.52	318,584	881.52	0		0		0	
All hardwoods	1,598	905.60	1,589	906.00	0		0		0	
Portland:										
Douglas fir	6,366	886.33	5,164	805.20	0		0		0	
Port Orford cedar	33	5,582.11	16	6,701.92	0		0		17	4,520.47
Hemlock	2,173	453.88	12	610.31	0		2,161	453.00	0	
Other softwoods	2,191	795.00	16	773.88	219	1,866.50	1,906	646.60	0	
All softwoods	10,764	794.87	5,208	822.90	219	1,866.50	4,067	543.72	17	4,520.47
All hardwoods	1,812	1,507.52	0		1,120	1,616.87	45	813.09	10	1,266.53
Red alder	1,264	1,686.21	0		845	1,749.35	0		10	1,266.53
Total:										
Douglas fir	322,742	884.06	321,539	882.74	0		0		0	
Port Orford cedar	33	5,582.11	16	6,701.92	0		0		17	4,520.47
Hemlock	2,173	453.88	12	610.31	0		2,161	453.00	0	
Other softwoods	4,400	659.43	2,225	526.74	219	1,866.50	1,906	646.60	0	
All softwoods	329,348	878.69	323,792	880.58	219	1,866.50	4,067	543.72	17	4,520.47
All hardwoods	3,410	1,225.44	1,589	906.00	1,120	1,616.87	45	813.09	10	1,266.53
Red alder	1,264	1,686.21	0		845	1,749.35	0		10	1,266.53

Source: U.S. Department of Commerce.

Table 35a—Volume and average value of log exports by port, species, and destination, Columbia-Snake Customs District, first quarter 2006

(Volume in thousand board feet, Scribner scale; value in dollars per thousand board feet)

Port and species	Destination									
	All countries		Japan		People's Republic of China		Korea		Taiwan	
	Volume	Average value	Volume	Average value	Volume	Average value	Volume	Average value	Volume	Average value
Longview (Washington):										
Douglas fir	70,349	884.08	70,349	884.08	0		0		0	
Other softwoods	2,034	492.88	2,034	492.88	0		0		0	
All softwoods	72,382	873.09	72,382	873.09	0		0		0	
All hardwoods	1,589	906.00	1,589	906.00	0		0		0	
Portland:										
Douglas fir	176	2,819.45	0		0		0		0	
Port Orford cedar	5	6,160.80	0		0		0		5	6,160.80
Other softwoods	163	793.10	0		79	760.56	55	467.03	0	
All softwoods	344	1,902.75	0		79	760.56	55	467.03	5	6,160.80
All hardwoods	406	1,148.47	0		210	999.58	0		0	
Red alder	248	1,357.36	0		70	1,372.08	0		0	
Total:										
Douglas fir	70,525	888.91	70,349	884.08	0		0		0	
Port Orford cedar	5	6,160.80	0		0		0		5	6,160.80
Other softwoods	2,197	515.17	2,034	492.88	79	760.56	55	467.03	0	
All softwoods	72,726	877.96	72,382	873.09	79	760.56	55	467.03	5	6,160.80
All hardwoods	1,995	955.33	1,589	906.00	210	999.58	0		0	
Red alder	248	1,357.36	0		70	1,372.08	0		0	

Source: U.S. Department of Commerce.

Table 35b—Volume and average value of log exports by port, species, and destination, Columbia-Snake Customs District, second quarter 2006

(Volume in thousand board feet, Scribner scale; value in dollars per thousand board feet)

Port and species	All countries		Japan		People's Republic of China		Korea		Taiwan	
	Volume	Average value	Volume	Average value	Volume	Average value	Volume	Average value	Volume	Average value
Longview (Washington):										
Douglas fir	77,834	891.40	77,823	891.40	0		0		0	
Other softwoods	90	883.33	90	883.33	0		0		0	
All softwoods	77,913	891.39	77,913	891.39	0		0		0	
Portland:										
Douglas fir	1,827	933.20	1,317	869.19	0		0		0	
Port Orford cedar	12	3,905.35	0		0		0		12	3,905.35
Hemlock	12	610.31	12	610.31	0		0		0	
Other softwoods	215	602.24	16	773.88	32	1,669.24	167	382.66	0	
All softwoods	2,066	914.72	1,345	865.73	32	1,669.24	167	382.66	12	3,905.35
All hardwoods	311	1,665.45	0		188	1,638.47	0		10	1,266.53
Red alder	237	1,683.29	0		120	1,683.38	0		10	1,266.53
Total:										
Douglas fir	79,650	892.36	79,140	891.03	0		0		0	
Port Orford cedar	12	3,905.35	0		0		0		12	3,905.35
Hemlock	12	610.31	12	610.31	0		0		0	
Other softwoods	304	685.20	106	866.88	32	1,669.24	167	382.66	0	
All softwoods	79,979	891.99	79,258	890.95	32	1,669.24	167	382.66	12	3,905.35
All hardwoods	311	1,665.45	0		188	1,638.47	0		10	1,266.53
Red alder	237	1,683.29	0		120	1,683.38	0		10	1,266.53

Source: U.S. Department of Commerce.

62

Table 35c—Volume and average value of log exports by port, species, and destination, Columbia-Snake Customs District, third quarter 2006

(Volume in thousand board feet, Scribner scale; value in dollars per thousand board feet)

Port and species	Destination									
	All countries		Japan		People's Republic of China		Korea		Taiwan	
	Volume	Average value	Volume	Average value	Volume	Average value	Volume	Average value	Volume	Average value
Longview (Washington):										
Douglas fir	85,385	900.10	85,385	900.10	0		0		0	
Portland:										
Douglas fir	4,238	787.42	3,847	783.29	0		0		0	
Port Orford cedar	16	6,701.92	16	6,701.92	0		0		0	
Other softwoods	1,093	560.09	0		65	2,675.87	1,028	426.55	0	
All softwoods	5,347	758.77	3,863	807.99	65	2,675.87	1,028	426.55	0	
All hardwoods	608	1,565.28	0		388	1,774.24	0		0	
Red alder	425	1,750.34	0		351	1,784.30	0		0	
Total:										
Douglas fir	89,623	894.76	89,232	895.07	0		0		0	
Port Orford cedar	16	6,701.92	16	6,701.92	0		0		0	
Other softwoods	1,093	560.09	0		65	2,675.87	1,028	426.55	0	
All softwoods	90,732	891.77	89,248	896.12	65	2,675.87	1,028	426.55	0	
All hardwoods	608	1,565.28	0		388	1,774.24	0		0	
Red alder	425	1,750.34	0		351	1,784.30	0		0	

Source: U.S. Department of Commerce.

Table 35d—Volume and average value of log exports by port, species, and destination, Columbia-Snake Customs District, fourth quarter 2006

(Volume in thousand board feet, Scribner scale; value in dollars per thousand board feet)

Port and species	All countries Volume	All countries Average value	Japan Volume	Japan Average value	People's Republic of China Volume	People's Republic of China Average value	Korea Volume	Korea Average value	Taiwan Volume	Taiwan Average value
Longview (Washington):										
Douglas fir	82,818	860.41	82,818	860.41	0		0		0	
Other softwoods	85	912.98	85	912.98	0		0		0	
All softwoods	82,904	860.47	82,904	860.47	0		0		0	
All hardwoods	9	833.97	0		0		0		0	
Portland:										
Douglas fir	126	834.08	0		0		0		0	
Hemlock	2,161	453.00	0		0		2,161	453.00	0	
Other softwoods	720	1,209.47	0		44	2,791.94	656	1,073.96	0	
All softwoods	3,007	650.08	0		44	2,791.94	2,817	597.53	0	
All hardwoods	487	1,633.81	0		336	1,805.12	45	813.09	0	
Red alder	353	1,842.23	0		304	1,822.35	0		0	
Total:										
Douglas fir	82,944	860.37	82,818	860.41	0		0		0	
Hemlock	2,161	453.00	0		0		2,161	453.00	0	
Other softwoods	805	1,178.10	85	912.98	44	2,791.94	656	1,073.96	0	
All softwoods	85,910	853.10	82,904	860.47	44	2,791.94	2,817	597.53	0	
All hardwoods	496	1,619.58	0		336	1,805.02	45	813.09	0	
Red alder	353	1,842.23	0		304	1,822.35	0		0	

Source: U.S. Department of Commerce.

Table 36—Volume and average value of log exports by port, species, and destination, San Francisco Customs District, 2006

(Volume in thousand board feet, Scribner scale; value in dollars per thousand board feet)

Port and species	All countries Volume	All countries Average value	Japan Volume	Japan Average value	People's Republic of China Volume	People's Republic of China Average value	Korea Volume	Korea Average value	Taiwan Volume	Taiwan Average value
Oakland:										
Douglas fir	16	796.61	0		0		0		0	
Redcedar	6	1,956.96	0		6	1,956.96	0		0	
Other softwoods	128	2,531.45	83	2,766.70	0		0		0	
All softwoods	150	2,319.31	83	2,766.70	6	1,956.96	0		0	
All hardwoods	2,058	2,128.58	1,299	1,479.14	121	3,296.18	41	2,206.16	4	3,908.32
Total:										
Douglas fir	16	796.61	0		0		0		0	
Redcedar	6	1,956.96	0		6	1,956.96	0		0	
Other softwoods	128	2,531.45	83	2,766.70	0		0		0	
All softwoods	150	2,319.31	83	2,766.70	6	1,956.96	0		0	
All hardwoods	2,058	2,128.58	1,299	1,479.14	121	3,296.18	41	2,206.16	4	3,908.32

Source: U.S. Department of Commerce.

Table 37a—Volume and average value of log exports by port, species, and destination, San Francisco Customs District, first quarter 2006

(Volume in thousand board feet, Scribner scale; value in dollars per thousand board feet)

Port and species	All countries Volume	All countries Average value	Japan Volume	Japan Average value	People's Republic of China Volume	People's Republic of China Average value	Korea Volume	Korea Average value	Taiwan Volume	Taiwan Average value
Oakland:										
Redcedar	6	1,956.96	0		6	1,956.96	0		0	
Other softwoods	4	3,397.50	0		0		0		0	
All softwoods	10	2,480.79	0		6	1,956.96	0		0	
All hardwoods	509	3,259.89	190	1,907.83	28	4,231.60	4	4,119.78	0	
Total:										
Redcedar	6	1,956.96	0		6	1,956.96	0		0	
Other softwoods	4	3,397.50	0		0		0		0	
All softwoods	10	2,480.79	0		6	1,956.96	0		0	
All hardwoods	509	3,259.89	190	1,907.83	28	4,231.60	4	4,119.78	0	

Source: U.S. Department of Commerce.

Table 37b—Volume and average value of log exports by port, species, and destination, San Francisco Customs District, second quarter 2006

(Volume in thousand board feet, Scribner scale; value in dollars per thousand board feet)

Port and species	All countries Volume	All countries Average value	Japan Volume	Japan Average value	People's Republic of China Volume	People's Republic of China Average value	Korea Volume	Korea Average value	Taiwan Volume	Taiwan Average value
Oakland:										
Other softwoods	30	2,642.82	3	1,839.94	0		0		0	
All softwoods	30	2,642.82	3	1,839.94	0		0		0	
All hardwoods	378	2,143.54	247	1,693.39	23	2,939.11	12	2,471.32	0	
Total:										
Other softwoods	30	2,642.82	3	1,839.94	0		0		0	
All softwoods	30	2,642.82	3	1,839.94	0		0		0	
All hardwoods	378	2,143.54	247	1,693.39	23	2,939.11	12	2,471.32	0	

Source: U.S. Department of Commerce.

Table 37c—Volume and average value of log exports by port, species, and destination, San Francisco Customs District, third quarter 2006

(Volume in thousand board feet, Scribner scale; value in dollars per thousand board feet)

| Port and species | \multicolumn{10}{c}{Destination} | | | | | | | | | |
| | All countries | | Japan | | People's Republic of China | | Korea | | Taiwan | |
	Volume	Average value	Volume	Average value	Volume	Average value	Volume	Average value	Volume	Average value
Oakland:										
Douglas fir	16	796.61	0		0		0		0	
Other softwoods	82	2,663.69	75	2,858.22	0		0		0	
All softwoods	99	2,354.60	75	2,858.22	0		0		0	
All hardwoods	306	1,536.71	244	1,275.45	0		8	1,627.49	4	3,908.32
Total:										
Douglas fir	16	796.61	0		0		0		0	
Other softwoods	82	2,663.69	75	2,858.22	0		0		0	
All softwoods	99	2,354.60	75	2,858.22	0		0		0	
All hardwoods	306	1,536.71	244	1,375.45	0		8	1,627.49	4	3,908.32

Source: U.S. Department of Commerce.

Table 37d—Volume and average value of log exports by port, species, and destination, San Francisco Customs District, fourth quarter 2006

(Volume in thousand board feet, Scribner scale; value in dollars per thousand board feet)

| Port and species | \multicolumn{10}{c}{Destination} | | | | | | | | | |
| | All countries | | Japan | | People's Republic of China | | Korea | | Taiwan | |
	Volume	Average value	Volume	Average value	Volume	Average value	Volume	Average value	Volume	Average value
Oakland:										
Other softwoods	12	1,136.71	5	1,857.92	0		0		0	
All softwoods	12	1,136.71	5	1,857.92	0		0		0	
All hardwoods	864	1,665.07	618	1,302.81	70	3,041.04	17	1,847.48	0	
Total:										
Other softwoods	12	1,136.71	5	1,857.92	0		0		0	
All softwoods	12	1,136.71	5	1,857.92	0		0		0	
All hardwoods	864	1,665.07	618	1,302.81	70	3,041.04	17	1,847.48	0	

Source: U.S. Department of Commerce.

Table 38—Volume and average value of log exports by port, species, and destination, Anchorage Customs District, 2006

(Volume in thousand board feet, Scribner scale; value in dollars per thousand board feet)

Port and species	All countries Volume	All countries Average value	Japan Volume	Japan Average value	People's Republic of China Volume	People's Republic of China Average value	Korea Volume	Korea Average value	Canada Volume	Canada Average value
Anchorage:										
Spruce	44,845	382.04	1,572	373.68	0		43,272	382.34	0	
All softwoods	44,845	382.04	1,572	373.68	0		43,272	382.34	0	
Dalton Cache:										
Hemlock	4,061	453.48	1,598	453.90	0		2,463	453.20	0	
Spruce	36,161	331.92	16,486	299.87	0		18,282	345.97	78	432.74
All softwoods	40,222	344.19	18,084	313.48	0		20,745	358.70	78	432.74
Juneau:										
Redcedar	449	693.32	0		0		449	693.32	0	
Hemlock	3,584	467.52	0		0		3,584	467.52	0	
Spruce	1,680	652.62	0		0		1,680	652.62	0	
All softwoods	5,713	539.68	0		0		5,713	539.68	0	
Ketchikan:										
Redcedar	5,850	755.10	2,547	822.67	383	524.74	1,581	773.76	187	423.05
Hemlock	50,322	495.92	12,630	502.06	2,481	579.41	32,418	487.93	0	
Spruce	94,742	391.06	42,665	380.28	16,560	364.53	31,528	421.03	0	
Other softwoods	8,012	790.94	7,867	790.19	119	922.18	26	424.12	0	
All softwoods	158,925	457.82	65,709	469.91	19,443	398.51	65,553	462.62	187	423.05
Total:										
Redcedar	6,299	750.70	2,547	822.67	383	524.74	2,029	755.98	187	423.05
Hemlock	57,967	491.19	14,228	496.65	2,481	579.41	38,465	483.80	0	
Spruce	177,427	379.20	60,723	358.28	16,460	364.53	94,763	392.99	78	432.74
Other softwoods	8,012	790.94	7,867	790.19	119	922.18	26	424.12	0	
All softwoods	249,705	427.78	85,365	435.00	19,443	398.51	135,283	424.26	265	425.91

Source: U.S. Department of Commerce.

Table 39a—Volume and average value of log exports by port, species, and destination, Anchorage Customs District, first quarter 2006

(Volume in thousand board feet, Scribner scale; value in dollars per thousand board feet)

Port and species	Destination										
	All countries		Japan		People's Republic of China		Korea		Canada	
	Volume	Average value	Volume	Average value	Volume	Average value	Volume	Average value	Volume	Average value
Anchorage:										
Spruce	7,282	361.87	1,572	373.68	0		5,710	358.62	0	
All softwoods	7,282	361.87	1,572	373.68	0		5,710	358.62	0	
Dalton Cache:										
Spruce	10	453.40	0		0		0		10	453.40
All softwoods	10	453.40	0		0		0		10	453.40
Juneau:										
Redcedar	449	693.32	0		0		449	693.32	0	
Hemlock	3,584	467.52	0		0		3,584	467.52	0	
Spruce	1,680	652.62	0		0		1,680	652.62	0	
All softwoods	5,713	539.68	0		0		5,713	539.68	0	
Ketchikan:										
Redcedar	1,051	654.29	668	728.59	383	524.74	0		0	
Hemlock	6,250	494.60	2,596	542.03	0		3,654	460.90	0	
Spruce	6,306	670.03	1,028	999.54	2,595	734.71	2,683	481.21	0	
Other softwoods	1,873	818.98	1,873	818.98	0		0		0	
All softwoods	15,481	616.16	6,166	722.68	2,979	707.70	5,337	469.50	0	
Total:										
Redcedar	1,500	665.96	668	728.59	383	524.74	449	693.32	0	
Hemlock	9,834	484.73	2,596	542.03	0		7,238	464.18	0	
Spruce	15,278	521.10	2,600	621.12	2,595	734.71	10,073	440.31	10	453.40
Other softwoods	1,873	818.98	1,873	818.98	0		0		0	
All softwoods	28,486	535.76	7,738	651.77	2,979	707.70	17,760	456.43	10	453.40

Source: U.S. Department of Commerce.

Table 39b—Volume and average value of log exports by port, species, and destination, Anchorage Customs District, second quarter 2006

(Volume in thousand board feet, Scribner scale; value in dollars per thousand board feet)

Port and species	All countries		Japan		People's Republic of China		Korea		Canada	
	Volume	Average value	Volume	Average value	Volume	Average value	Volume	Average value	Volume	Average value
Anchorage:										
Spruce	11,963	377.22	0		0		11,963	377.22	0	
All hardwoods	11,963	377.22	0		0		11,963	377.22	0	
Dalton Cache:										
Hemlock	277	453.36	115	453.00	0		161	453.62	0	
Spruce	12,395	353.95	6,920	298.19	0		5,446	424.19	29	470.25
All softwoods	12,672	356.12	7,036	300.74	0		5,607	425.04	29	470.25
Ketchikan:										
Redcedar	1,726	703.72	259	943.46	0		448	603.67	0	
Hemlock	15,770	479.55	2,253	476.36	401	454.25	12,301	479.98	0	
Spruce	21,216	403.15	6,484	527.69	1,646	364.54	11,947	352.50	0	
Other softwoods	1,286	757.98	1,286	757.98	0		0		0	
All softwoods	39,999	457.66	10,283	555.72	2,047	382.10	24,697	420.56	0	
Total:										
Redcedar	1,726	703.72	259	943.46	0		448	603.67	0	
Hemlock	16,047	479.10	2,369	475.22	401	454.25	12,462	479.64	0	
Spruce	45,574	382.96	13,405	409.21	1,646	364.54	20,356	375.87	29	470.25
Other softwoods	1,286	757.98	1,286	757.98	0		0		0	
All softwoods	64,633	22.86	17,319	452.13	2,047	382.10	42,267	408.88	29	470.25

Source: U.S. Department of Commerce.

Table 39c—Volume and average value of log exports by port, species, and destination, Anchorage Customs District, third quarter 2006

(Volume in thousand board feet, Scribner scale; value in dollars per thousand board feet)

Port and species	All countries Volume	All countries Average value	Japan Volume	Japan Average value	People's Republic of China Volume	People's Republic of China Average value	Korea Volume	Korea Average value	Canada Volume	Canada Average value
Anchorage:										
Spruce	19,551	388.06	0		0		19,551	388.06	0	
All softwoods	19,551	388.06	0		0		19,551	388.06	0	
Dalton Cache:										
Hemlock	1,744	453.06	616	454.62	0		1,128	452.20	0	
Spruce	13,636	347.05	5,732	3098.77	0		6,559	343.05	30	414.95
All softwoods	15,380	359.07	6,348	322.92	0		7,687	359.07	30	414.95
Ketchikan:										
Redcedar	922	662.59	490	638.40	0		432	690.06	0	
Hemlock	15,494	491.05	4,835	497.24	0		9,354	497.01	0	
Spruce	33,111	356.63	21,960	325.24	0		9,235	422.99	0	
Other softwoods	2,141	793.30	2,141	793.30	0		0		0	
All softwoods	51,668	420.49	29,426	392.77	0		19,020	465.45	0	
Total:										
Redcedar	922	662.59	490	638.40	0		432	690.06	0	
Hemlock	17,237	487.21	5,451	492.42	0		10,481	492.19	0	
Spruce	66,298	363.93	27,692	321.83	0		35,345	388.84	30	414.95
Other softwoods	2,141	793.30	2,141	793.30	0		0		0	
All softwoods	86,598	402.26	35,774	380.38	0		46,258	415.07	30	414.95

Source: U.S. Department of Commerce.

Table 39d—Volume and average value of log exports by port, species, and destination, Anchorage Customs District, fourth quarter 2006

(Volume in thousand board feet, Scribner scale; value in dollars per thousand board feet)

Port and species	Destination									
	All countries		Japan		People's Republic of China		Korea		Canada	
	Volume	Average value	Volume	Average value	Volume	Average value	Volume	Average value	Volume	Average value
Anchorage:										
Spruce	6,049	396.37	0		0		6,049	396.37	0	
All softwoods	6,049	396.37	0		0		6,049	396.37	0	
Dalton Cache:										
Hemlock	2,041	453.86	867	453.51	0		1,174	454.11	0	
Spruce	10,121	284.43	3,833	289.58	0		6,277	281.16	10	357.06
All softwoods	12,161	312.86	4,700	319.82	0		7,451	308.41	10	357.06
Ketchikan:										
Redcedar	2,151	885.26	1,130	930.60	0		701	933.99	187	423.05
Hemlock	12,808	522.63	2,945	494.42	2,081	603.51	7,109	503.62	0	
Spruce	34,108	365.38	13,193	351.21	12,218	285.90	7,663	504.42	0	
Other softwoods	2,711	785.33	2,566	782.73	119	922.18	26	424.12	0	
All softwoods	51,778	447.86	19,834	461.31	14,417	336.97	15,499	523.35	187	423.05
Total:										
Redcedar	2,151	885.26	1,130	930.60	0		701	933.99	187	423.05
Hemlock	14,848	513.18	3,812	485.12	2,081	603.51	8,282	496.60	0	
Spruce	50,277	352.82	17,026	337.33	12,218	285.90	19,989	401.61	10	357.06
Other softwoods	2,711	785.33	2,566	782.73	119	922.18	26	424.12	0	
All softwoods	69,987	419.95	24,534	434.20	14,417	336.97	28,999	441.63	196	419.71

Source: U.S. Department of Commerce.

Table 40—Volume and average value of hardwood log exports from Seattle, Columbia-Snake, Anchorage, and San Francisco Customs Districts, 1995-2006

(Volume in thousand board feet, Scribner scale; value in dollars per thousand board feet)

Year and quarter	Seattle Customs District		Columbia-Snake Customs District		Anchorage Customs District		San Francisco Customs District	
	Volume	Average value	Volume	Average value	Volume	Average value	Volume	Average value
To All Countries								
1995	27,396	1,661.52	2,923	1,468.01	21	1,409.05	3,151	2,464.61
1996	25,571	1,525.33	3,485	1,806.60	0	--	2,293	1,964.93
1997	26,675	1,613.51	2,071	1,865.35	0	--	3,461	2,498.45
1998	13,531	1,559.69	2,755	1,689.58	0	--	5,823	1,844.06
1999	30,514	840.25	2,130	1,470.45	40	904.94	3,701	2,054.19
2000	15,594	1,457.01	17,247	311.74	500	116.61	2,463	2,488.06
2001	22,143	1,407.34	2,236	1,476.56	0	--	1,264	2,791.64
2002	23,125	1,223.79	2,903	1,582.81	0	--	19,156	131.72
2003	21,257	1,363.02	3,617	1,455.39	25	647.43	928	2,614.84
2004	23,285	1,271.01	1,527	1,459.38	2	17,938.80	1,403	2,481.90
2005:								
1st quarter	5,498	1,485.10	317	1,477.93	0	--	451	2,665.94
2d quarter	5,308	1,729.05	339	1,675.71	0	--	260	3,063.90
3d quarter	3,504	1,386.00	202	1,337.00	0	--	474	1,449.16
4th quarter	6,663	1,010.16	1,675	948.15	0	--	436	4,242.33
2005 total	20,973	1,379.41	2,533	1,142.85	0	--	1,622	2,798.14
2006:								
1st quarter	5,018	1,332.87	1,995	955.33	0	--	509	3,259.89
2d quarter	7,010	1,065.81	503	1,029.39	0	--	366	2,180.46
3d quarter	4,558	833.38	608	1,565.28	0	--	302	1,531.58
4th quarter	3,723	1,182.69	496	1,619.58	0	--	864	1,665.07
2006 total	20,309	1,101.06	3,602	1,160.11	0	--	2,042	2,135.70
To Japan								
1995	14,560	1,828.91	2,103	1,405.14	0	--	1,425	2,289.12
1996	14,738	1,738.16	1,343	1,905.80	0	--	898	2,564.42
1997	15,677	1,720.14	946	1,859.67	0	--	1,586	1,654.05
1998	8,342	1,726.32	2,300	1,674.89	0	--	647	2,601.62
1999	11,360	1,530.46	1,552	1,475.78	0	--	657	2,555.53
2000	8,221	1,571.70	158	1,156.83	0	--	234	2,927.00
2001	7,733	1,568.97	593	1,262.15	0	--	507	2,165.43
2002	6,854	1,174.10	1,075	1,302.69	0	--	443	2,434.98
2003	6,607	1,384.09	2,046	1,337.21	0	--	469	2,297.22
2004	10,808	975.92	624	955.91	2	17,938.80	375	3,462.49
2005:								
1st quarter	2,442	1,361.55	0	--	0	--	97	4,283.03
2d quarter	1,534	1,483.18	0	--	0	--	8	6,152.96
3d quarter	531	1,120.16	0	--	0	--	296	905.84
4th quarter	895	2,137.83	1,471	906.00	0	--	65	3,712.15
2005 total	5,402	1,501.02	1,471	906.00	0	--	466	2,093.60
2006:								
1st quarter	1,289	2,014.98	1,589	906.00	0	--	190	1,907.83
2d quarter	1,923	1,372.01	0	--	0	--	236	1,727.96
3d quarter	51	2,663.21	0	--	0	--	240	1,365.87
4th quarter	872	1,467.86	0	--	0	--	618	1,302.81
2006 total	4,134	1,608.61	1,589	906.00	0	--	1,283	1,482.09
To People's Republic of China								
1995	432	1,983.80	15	2,266.67	0	--	16	3,187.50
1996	311	1,979.05	14	1,223.02	0	--	8	2,080.78
1997	164	1,697.01	0	--	0	--	4	3,187.75
1998	425	1,229.30	13	2,470.75	0	--	38	1,460.82
1999	213	1,782.79	25	2,017.35	0	--	248	1,415.69
2000	683	1,829.79	418	761.75	0	--	468	1,744.80
2001	5,240	1,358.35	735	1,723.63	0	--	310	2,198.85
2002	4,382	1,479.76	703	1,542.18	0	--	33	2,315.66
2003	3,230	1,432.28	341	1,445.53	0	--	173	2,481.19
2004	2,822	1,818.79	339	1,657.88	0	--	188	1,350.66
2005:								
1st quarter	741	1,628.65	96	1,434.00	0	--	40	2,719.04
2d quarter	1,295	1,668.41	177	1,445.14	0	--	35	2,874.90
3d quarter	1,028	1,665.52	47	1,975.25	0	--	52	2,726.43
4th quarter	830	1,216.41	115	1,385.36	0	--	27	2,123.42
2005 total	3,894	1,563.70	435	1,484.53	0	--	154	2,652.85
2006:								
1st quarter	627	1,355.12	270	769.29	0	-	28	4,231.60
2d quarter	814	1,278.42	188	1,638.47	0	--	23	2,939.11
3d quarter	854	1,452.45	388	1,774.24	0	--	0	--
4th quarter	510	1,528.62	336	1,805.02	0	--	70	3,041.04
2006 total	2,804	1,394.04	1,182	1,531.74	0	--	121	3,296.18

Source: U.S. Department of Commerce. The valuation definition used in the export statistics is the value at the seaport or border port of exportation. It is based on the selling price (or cost if not sold) including inland freight, insurance, and other charges to the port of exportation.
Data are compiled from Department of Commerce records at the end of each quarter.

Table 41—Volume and average value of alder log exports from the Seattle Customs District, 1996-2006

(Volume in thousand board feet, Scribner scale; value in dollars per thousand board feet)

Year and quarter	Destination							
	All countries		Japan		South Korea		Taiwan	
	Volume	Average value	Volume	Average value	Volume	Average value	Volume	Average value
1996	921	453.01	397	234.05	467	571.33	33	1,057.08
1997	994	669.00	190	394.74	721	697.04	82	1,066.13
1998	164	874.23	11	554.53	69	600.38	83	1,143.20
1999	206	668.05	30	716.96	158	734.26	0	
2000	1,047	1,285.97	204	1,265.13	264	797.11	0	
2001	3,259	1,469.92	93	1,808.78	54	1,468.15	49	1,328.89
2002	4,255	1,463.94	102	966.35	4	2,910.53	0	
2003	3,370	1,420.14	0		28	3,745.52	87	1,244.40
2004	2,411	1,570.85	0		0		29	1,005.56
2005:								
1st quarter	804	1,706.88	0		0		9	4,242.82
2d quarter	785	1,538.99	0		0		9	1,264.19
3d quarter	694	1,338.86	0		0		181	1,113.22
4th quarter	462	1,508.76	0		0		21	912.46
2005 total	2,745	1,532.43	0		0		221	1,235.01
2006:								
1st quarter	410	1,547.21	0		0		9	1,265.77
2d quarter	436	1,681.03	0		0		4	1,739.52
3d quarter	669	1,730.27	0		0		4	1,815.62
4th quarter	293	1,685.99	0		0		0	
2006 total	1,809	1,669.68	0		0		18	1,512.42

Source: U.S. Department of Commerce.

Table 42—Volume and average value of log exports from southern California ports by species, 1995-2006

(Volume in thousand board feet, Scribner scale; value in dollars per thousand board feet)

Year and quarter	Total		Douglas fir		Other softwoods		Hardwoods	
	Volume	Average value	Volume	Average value	Volume	Average value	Volume	Average value
1995	12,802	1,287.06	25	560.00	7,943	869.57	4,834	1,976.83
1996	11,697	1,309.65	67	1,859.91	5,013	746.79	6,617	1,730.54
1997	15,314	1,342.39	102	502.02	8,226	853.29	6,985	1,930.85
1998	15,857	1,311.09	1,131	787.40	9,068	997.31	5,658	1,918.64
1999	13,555	1,383.73	952	491.24	3,964	765.20	8,639	1,765.89
2000	15,803	1,435.40	12	2,003.03	3,928	581.23	11,863	1,716.89
2001	17,124	2,062.54	113	489.07	3,201	702.49	13,810	2,390.71
2002	24,817	1,854.65	176	659.66	3,749	806.48	20,892	2,052.80
2003	22,149	1,811.84	52	2,056.52	5,834	606.20	16,234	2,247.58
2004	23,673	1,799.68	95	769.02	10,244	695.40	13,335	2,655.17
2005:								
1st quarter	6,812	2,432.39	26	498.60	951	1,068.81	5,835	2,663.26
2d quarter	8,414	2,323.69	9	1,091.85	2,035	811.19	6,370	2,808.50
3d quarter	6,550	2,174.31	216	850.27	1,661	917.94	4,673	2,682.07
4th quarter	8,122	2,403.22	34	609.74	2,353	812.16	5,735	3,066.80
2005 total	29,898	2,337.33	285	796.04	7,001	871.72	22,613	2,810.40
2006:								
1st quarter	12,043	2,050.11	0		3,808	977.17	8,235	2,546.30
2d quarter	14,875	1,930.32	1,879	693.07	4,018	939.00	8,978	2,632.92
3d quarter	8,413	2,090.20	18	701.47	2,745	947.03	5,649	2,650.14
4th quarter	8,595	1,868.68	0		3,614	926.26	4,981	2,552.45
2006 total	43,925	1,981.72	1,896	693.15	14,185	947.56	27,843	2,596.40

Source: U.S. Department of Commerce. Data are compiled from Department of Commerce records at the end of each quarter. Revisions that may have been made after this time are not shown. Southern California consists of the San Diego and Los Angeles Customs Districts and includes all ports south of Monterey, California.

Table 43—Volume and average value of softwood log exports to Canada from the Great Falls Customs District, 1995-2006[a]

(Volume in thousand board feet, Scribner scale; value in dollars per thousand board feet)

Year and quarter	All species		Douglas fir		Other softwoods	
	Volume	Average value	Volume	Average value	Volume	Average value
1995	5,757	402.85	1,410	471.63	4,347	380.54
1996	2,876	354.99	636	393.37	2,241	344.10
1997	1,808	396.35	300	435.14	1,508	388.63
1998	2,030	456.72	642	508.98	1,387	432.53
1999	1,863	406.72	878	506.59	985	317.70
2000	1,136	391.51	1,024	400.40	112	310.70
2001	1,195	327.50	226	433.34	970	302.87
2002	1,256	302.35	98	496.27	1,159	285.95
2003	601	374.49	315	392.75	286	354.36
2004	413	449.60	276	544.18	137	258.88
2005:						
1st quarter	0		0		0	
2d quarter	33	536.61	0		33	536.61
3d quarter	144	667.98	0		144	667.98
4th quarter	303	325.94	52	296.17	251	331.27
2005 total and average value	480	443.05	52	296.17	428	460.36
2006:						
1st quarter	663	484.20	543	459.43	119	597.14
2d quarter	140	608.10	0		140	608.10
3d quarter	55	822.17	0		55	822.17
4th quarter	87	601.03	0		87	601.03
2006 total and average value	944	532.68	543	459.43	401	631.89

[a] Great Falls Customs District includes all ports in Montana and Idaho.

Source: U.S. Department of Commerce. The valuation definition used in the export statistics is the value at the seaport or border port of exportation. It is based on the selling price (or cost if not sold) and includes inland freight, insurance, and other charges to the port of exportation. Data are compiled from Department of Commerce records at the end of each quarter.

Table 44—Volume and average value of softwood log imports of all species from Canada into Washington and Oregon, 1995-2006

(Volume in thousand board feet, Scribner scale; value in dollars per thousand board feet)

Year and quarter	Volume	Average value
1995	12,999	1,469.27
1996	18,326	845.30
1997	16,683	803.22
1998	78,925	389.81
1999	199,494	322.29
2000	274,735	365.75
2001	320,858	318.95
2002	394,004	317.43
2003	353,748	303.17
2004	300,415	360.51
2005:		
1st quarter	108,228	356.69
2d quarter	138,228	362.27
3d quarter	126,325	347.05
4th quarter	143,526	361.98
2005 total and average value	516,307	357.29
2006:		
1st quarter	127,857	401.22
2d quarter	126,056	396.79
3d quarter	117,057	455.42
4th quarter	66,457	437.16
2006 total and average value	437,426	419.91

Source: U.S. Department of Commerce. Value is declared value at port of entry. Data are compiled from Department of Commerce records at the end of each quarter.

Table 45—Volume and average value of pulpwood imports from Canada into the Seattle Customs District, 1995-2006

Year and quarter	Chips		Roundwood pulpwood	
	Volume	Average value	Volume	Average value
	Short tons[a]	*Dollars*	*Cords*	*Dollars*
1995	370,585	56.74	6,878	199.73
1996	487,095	57.39	3,108	160.56
1997	512,808	63.56	66	142.48
1998	381,260	62.36	8,523	122.21
1999	249,013	59.65	0	
2000	278,442	55.69	807	120.13
2001	139,436	49.36	1,858	16.13
2002	113,365	54.68	87	73.48
2003	207,935	51.22	673	45.02
2004	64,084	52.61		
2005:				
1st quarter	32,711	47.05	0	
2d quarter	40,329	38.67	34	67.29
3d quarter	28,908	61.37	0	
4th quarter	5,049	57.58	3	628.55
2005 total and average value	106,997	48.26	37	116.82
2006:				
1st quarter	15,040	40.83	269	16.73
2d quarter	8,848	67.08	419	24.17
3d quarter	9,938	72.02	0	
4th quarter	19,612	38.30	0	
2006 total and average value	53,438	50.05	688	21.26

[a] Dry weight basis.

Source: U.S. Department of Commerce. Data are compiled from Department of Commerce records at the end of each quarter.

Table 46—Volume of pulp exports by selected grades from Seattle, Columbia-Snake, Anchorage, and San Francisco Customs Districts, 1995-2006

(Volume in thousand short tons)

Year and quarter	Seattle Customs District		Columbia-Snake Customs District		Anchorage Customs District		San Francisco Customs District	
	Dissolving grade	Paper grades	Dissolving grade	Paper grades	Dissolving grade	Paper grades	Dissolving grade	Paper grades
To All Countries								
1995	144.1	656.0	4.0	147.7	139.5	0	16.7	172.7
1996	113.5	444.2	11.8	146.2	124.5	.1	.1	199.5
1997	69.7	379.5	7.4	120.4	49.8	0	.6	194.7
1998	59.3	247.4	1.1	78.4	0	.1	1.5	152.6
1999	82.2	359.6	6.6	111.6	0	0	.9	208.6
2000	65.0	312.3	1.6	100.3	0	.1	0	163.2
2001	62.3	172.3	.3	83.3	0	6.6	1.0	177.0
2002	77.7	251.9	.1	94.3	0	a	0	195.0
2003	88.0	197.4	0	73.4	0	0	22.8	175.2
2004	117.3	194	0	81.6	.1	.1	6.1	190.6
2005:								
1st quarter	45.7	52.1	0	24.4	0	a	.2	40.0
2d quarter	40.9	40.9	0	19.3	0	0	0	0.3
3d quarter	61.6	86.9	0	48.1	0	0	.5	3.4
4th quarter	40.2	66.1	0	39.0	0	0	0	41.5
2005 total	188.4	246.0	0	130.8	0	a	.7	85.3
2006:								
1st quarter	45.0	54.1	0	25.2	0	0	0	40.6
2d quarter	33.7	28.2	0	26.1	0	0	a	26.1
3d quarter	31.1	22.0	0	37.3	0	0	.2	20.4
4th quarter	12.3	19.5	0	35.0	0	0	.6	36.0
2006 total	122.1	123.8	0	123.6	0	0	.8	123.2
To Japan								
1995	63.9	170.4	4.0	46.7	28.0	0	16.3	3.2
1996	43.6	91.2	.8	43.3	14.2	0	.1	29.4
1997	37.7	62.6	.3	45.0	10.8	0	.1	7.6
1998	31.0	53.2	.1	11.3	0	0	1.3	5.6
1999	34.3	75.3	.1	16.7	0	0	.9	7.9
2000	33.1	51.7	.2	6.2	0	0	0	3.9
2001	32.7	20.2	.3	10.1	0	6.5	0	6.0
2002	42.2	13.9	0	5.8	0	a	0	3.7
2003	48.7	8.3	0	1.9	0	0	1.1	.5
2004	59.9	6.5	0	0	.1	0	1.9	1.5
2005:								
1st quarter	16.3	1.6	0	0	0	a	.2	a
2d quarter	11.8	1.4	0	0	0	0	0	a
3d quarter	15.2	2.2	0	0	0	0	0	0
4th quarter	21.0	1.4	0	0	0	0	0	.1
2005 total	64.3	6.5	0	0	0	a	.2	.2
2006:								
1st quarter	24.0	2.4	0	0	0	0	0	.2
2d quarter	18.0	.8	0	0	0	0	0	0
3d quarter	20.1	1.4	0	0	0	0	0	.1
4th quarter	.8	1.5	0	0	0	0	0	a
2006 total	63	6.0	0	0	0	0	0	.4

Table 46—Volume of pulp exports by selected grades from Seattle, Columbia-Snake, Anchorage, and San Francisco Customs Districts, 1995-2006 (continued)

(Volume in thousand short tons)

Year and quarter	Seattle Customs District		Columbia-Snake Customs District		Anchorage Customs District		San Francisco Customs District	
	Dissolving grade	Paper grades	Dissolving grade	Paper grades	Dissolving grade	Paper grades	Dissolving grade	Paper grades
To South Korea								
1995	.5	202.9	0	3.3	0	0	0	40.3
1996	9.5	71.7	0	2.6	0	0	0	54.7
1997	0	67.6	0	7.7	0	0	0	53.9
1998	0	32	0	2.6	0	0	0	65.5
1999	0	57.3	0	18.2	0	0	0	98.9
2000	a	60.4	0	15.0	0	0	0	66.0
2001	0	34.5	0	7.3	0	0	0	81.7
2002	.1	47.5	0	10.5	0	a	0	67.4
2003	.2	32.0	0	8.0	0	0	1.6	62.0
2004	4.5	32.1	0	6.4	0	.1	.1	47.9
2005:								
1st quarter	2.5	15.6	0	1.9	0	0	0	3.3
2d quarter	1.9	11.0	0	1.2	0	0	0	0.0
3d quarter	7.5	7.0	0	5.3	0	0	0	0.0
4th quarter	2.5	9.6	0	6.5	0	0	0	0.7
2005 total	14.3	43.2	0	14.8	0	0	0	3.9
2006:								
1st quarter	1.4	14.3	0	5.4	0	0	0	1.1
2d quarter	2.1	6.4	0	2.5	0	0	0	1.4
3d quarter	2.4	4.7	0	.9	0	0	0	1.1
4th quarter	1.8	4.0	0	.1	0	0	0	1.1
2006 total	7.6	29.4	0	8.9	0	0	0	4.6
To Western Europe								
1995	29.1	9.0	0	66.1	17.8	0	0	65.7
1996	12.3	70.7	.1	57.6	14.6	0	0	.2
1997	11.4	60.3	5.2	63.2	5.0	0	0	.4
1998	24.7	10.7	1.0	53.9	0	0	0	2.5
1999	25.9	12	6.4	50.5	0	0	0	1.2
2000	24.8	6	1.4	66.5	0	0	0	20.0
2001	26.6	6.9	0	48.4	0	0	0	58.9
2002	26.3	8	0	58.8	0	0	0	1.7
2003	29.7	10.2	0	47.3	0	0	0	16.9
2004	22.9	4.4	0	35.5	0	0	0	14.0
2005:								
1st quarter	11.3	a	0	12.3	0	0	0	0
2d quarter	6.8	a	0	11.9	0	0	0	0
3d quarter	7.0	0	0	24.4	0	0	0	0
4th quarter	0	a	0	14.6	0	0	0	0
2005 total	25.1	0.1	0	63.1	0	0	0	0
2006:								
1st quarter	0	0	0	4.4	0	0	0	0
2d quarter	0	0	0	3.0	0	0	a	0
3d quarter	0	0	0	7.3	0	0	0	0
4th quarter	0	.1	0	11.4	0	0	0	0
2006 total	0	.1	0	26.1	0	0	a	0

a Volume less than 0.1 short tons.

Note: Columns may not add to totals because of rounding.

Source: U.S. Department of Commerce.

Table 47—Average value of pulp exports by selected grades from Seattle, Columbia-Snake, Anchorage, and San Francisco Customs Districts, 1995-2006

(Value in dollars per short tons)

Year and quarter	Seattle Customs District		Columbia-Snake Customs District		Anchorage Customs District		San Francisco Customs District	
	Dissolving grade	Paper grades	Dissolving grade	Paper grades	Dissolving grade	Paper grades	Dissolving grade	Paper grades
To All Countries								
1995	661.79	349.68	758.00	511.25	878.25	--	362.16	748.76
1996	775.47	316.55	297.67	392.90	658.99	545.45	304.35	394.21
1997	844.99	313.12	463.12	316.38	553.09	--	387.41	372.60
1998	793.50	329.09	795.71	334.25	--	359.68	839.89	339.84
1999	680.25	347.81	673.39	367.78	--	--	991.22	370.34
2000	751.51	407.47	818.55	537.42	--	675.22	--	493.27
2001	738.25	381.57	905.55	373.27	--	102.16	864.86	315.69
2002	728.51	334.67	330.96	374.77	--	493.00	--	297.11
2003	733.61	341.88	--	432.08	--	--	246.33	256.86
2004	652.30	375.47	--	449.33	271.68	91.89	279.57	304.37
2005:								
1st quarter	627.40	399.08	--	426.12	--	259.40	264.84	257.87
2d quarter	593.30	376.10	--	437.77	--	--	--	413.76
3d quarter	518.99	407.76	--	337.25	--	--	326.50	313.18
4th quarter	603.67	378.19	--	459.19	--	--	--	310.56
2005 average	579.48	392.72	--	405.00	--	259.40	312.14	286.35
2006:								
1st quarter	665.77	398.84	--	468.54	--	--	--	309.33
2d quarter	739.98	458.48	--	505.65	--	--	739.21	307.29
3d quarter	727.70	505.94	--	525.66	--	--	752.58	275.42
4th quarter	435.36	542.49	--	528.32	--	--	435.36	295.73
2006 average	678.74	454.11	--	510.53	--	--	531.85	299.29
To Japan								
1995	588.90	402.95	758.00	510.88	718.39	--	361.04	636.25
1996	957.53	381.05	722.01	380.34	711.24	--	455.88	429.97
1997	868.04	352.66	775.77	314.29	568.61	--	537.18	506.26
1998	869.23	365.27	868.22	330.83	--	--	883.70	508.56
1999	805.16	366.95	868.22	380.41	--	--	998.88	421.77
2000	786.42	457.01	868.94	454.66	--	--	--	489.92
2001	801.62	385.00	905.55	370.38	--	96.00	--	334.63
2002	805.88	407.35	--	435.36	--	660.45	--	241.83
2003	802.20	475.12	--	387.35	--	--	260.47	298.88
2004	736.31	668.03	--	--	271.68	--	297.40	315.58
2005:								
1st quarter	735.99	815.46	--	--	--	259.40	264.84	266.93
2d quarter	775.51	720.56	--	--	--	--	--	720.61
3d quarter	795.20	469.03	--	--	--	--	--	--
4th quarter	776.14	614.74	--	--	--	--	--	308.38
2005 average	770.35	636.34	--	--	--	259.40	264.84	329.98
2006:								
1st quarter	787.23	549.57	--	--	--	--	--	372.54
2d quarter	777.34	754.22	--	--	--	--	--	--
3d quarter	790.39	881.28	--	--	--	--	--	308.38
4th quarter	435.36	785.14	--	--	--	--	--	380.59
2006 average	780.78	710.39	--	--	--	--	--	352.34

Table 47—Average value of pulp exports by selected grades from Seattle, Columbia-Snake, Anchorage, and San Francisco Customs Districts, 1995-2006 (continued)

(Value in dollars per short tons)

Year and quarter	Seattle Customs District		Columbia-Snake Customs District		Anchorage Customs District		San Francisco Customs District	
	Dissolving grade	Paper grades	Dissolving grade	Paper grades	Dissolving grade	Paper grades	Dissolving grade	Paper grades
To South Korea								
1995	512.00	271.50	--	641.82	--	--	--	687.97
1996	454.01	306.77	--	492.39	--	--	--	402.83
1997	--	278.08	--	278.98	--	--	--	391.95
1998	--	310.44	--	367.98	--	--	--	338.92
1999	--	346.02	--	407.80	--	--	--	373.54
2000	--	343.36	--	529.48	--	--	--	483.55
2001	--	313.24	--	380.47	--	--	--	291.72
2002	821.55	325.16	--	364.34	--	409.28	--	310.70
2003	718.53	330.97	--	400.05	--	--	274.42	267.86
2004	320.30	355.76	--	449.72	--	91.89	313.48	304.78
2005:								
1st quarter	327.19	325.24	--	444.38	--	--	--	288.69
2d quarter	325.59	314.79	--	453.42	--	--	--	--
3d quarter	307.30	383.60	--	428.12	--	--	--	--
4th quarter	326.58	356.72	--	431.07	--	--	--	308.38
2005 average	316.48	339.02	--	433.47	--	--	--	291.96
2006:								
1st quarter	325.66	354.25	--	437.19	--	--	--	309.96
2d quarter	504.78	411.84	--	440.79	--	--	--	293.32
3d quarter	576.47	434.17	--	534.96	--	--	--	308.38
4th quarter	435.36	482.29	--	557.36	--	--	--	297.18
2006 average	478.67	396.97	--	450.22	--	--	--	301.67
To Western Europe								
1995	673.37	445.11	--	503.86	848.43	--	--	809.50
1996	867.85	147.54	882.35	377.14	747.94	--	--	437.50
1997	804.32	175.76	427.85	302.64	611.79	--	--	439.13
1998	738.00	321.53	789.59	336.68	--	--	--	392.51
1999	707.33	445.46	669.38	360.62	--	--	--	363.77
2000	743.38	437.94	791.64	559.30	--	--	--	563.67
2001	690.27	427.60	--	392.14	--	--	--	353.64
2002	711.57	412.05	--	378.84	--	--	--	225.20
2003	652.69	450.40	--	442.89	--	--	--	316.20
2004	672.74	434.03	--	438.39	--	--	--	374.48
2005:								
1st quarter	715.13	391.82	--	474.20	--	--	--	--
2d quarter	699.85	388.22	--	472.50	--	--	--	--
3d quarter	693.24	--	--	307.41	--	--	--	--
4th quarter	--	111.02	--	485.40	--	--	--	--
2005 average	704.68	302.31	--	412.02	--	--	--	--
2006:								
1st quarter	--	--	--	458.01	--	--	--	--
2d quarter	--	--	--	482.95	--	--	725.58	--
3d quarter	--	--	--	531.54	--	--	--	--
4th quarter	--	478.35	--	453.38	--	--	--	--
2006 average	--	478.35	--	479.43	--	--	725.58	--

Source: U.S. Department of Commerce.

Table 48—Volume and average value of all chips exported from the Seattle, Columbia-Snake, San Francisco, and Anchorage Customs Districts, 1996-2006

(In short tons, on a dry weight basis; value in dollars per short ton)

Year and quarter	Seattle Customs District		Columbia Snake Customs District		San Francisco Customs District		Anchorage Customs District	
	Volume	Average value	Volume	Average value	Volume	Average value	Volume	Average value
1996	589,989	95.97	1,230,966	108.51	314,280	109.65	199,862	83.79
1997	611,888	72.28	1,247,092	89.54	371,554	97.71	105,653	72.10
1998	835,594	62.27	1,076,786	96.78	255,546	95.16	145,837	73.80
1999	753,147	60.51	1,024,223	82.64	285,740	90.57	131,699	41.75
2000	461,874	78.54	992,062	94.01	237,781	87.11	178,461	41.03
2001	353,074	86.00	856,164	96.58	166,558	90.59	154,880	61.28
2002	262,395	71.10	893,184	84.31	109,049	75.50	98,935	68.85
2003	252,050	82.58	760,965	82.39	63,037	69.10	109,621	49.66
2004	330,760	62.28	744,356	75.89	34,122	69.25	48,848	50.43
2005:								
1st quarter	86,318	58.07	254,551	84.63	23,116	73.17	52,020	57.19
2d quarter	169,845	67.20	189,412	78.79	1,724	105.74	19,525	47.85
3d quarter	81,561	56.21	265,670	87.19	862	95.81	7,137	29.09
4th quarter	83,319	58.31	208,841	82.65	767	99.16	35,240	86.26
2005 total and average value	421,042	61.44	918,475	83.71	26,470	76.78	113,922	62.82
2006:								
1st quarter	71,798	54.84	214,587	86.04	53	334.64	0	
2d quarter	44,888	42.39	249,350	85.05	23	491.06	929	73.21
3d quarter	38,708	46.94	161,195	94.70	3,600	44.69	5,513	39.75
4th quarter	42,899	41.41	222,957	103.72	8	529.00	0	
2006 total and average value	198,292	47.57	841,646	92.67	3,684	52.72	6,442	44.58

Source: U.S. Department of Commerce. The valuation definition used in the export statistics is the value at the seaport or border port of exportation. It is based on the selling price (or cost if not sold) and includes inland freight, insurance, and other charges to the port of exportation. Seattle Customs District includes all ports in the State of Washington, except Longview and Vancouver. Columbia Snake Customs District includes all Oregon ports and Longview and Vancouver, Washington. San Francisco Customs District includes all coastal and inland ports in the State of California from Monterey north. The Anchorage Customs District is the State of Alaska.

Table 49—Volume and average value of softwood chips exported from the Seattle, Columbia-Snake, San Francisco, and Anchorage Customs Districts, 1996-2006

(In short tons, on a dry weight basis; value in dollars per short ton)

Year and quarter	Seattle Customs District		Columbia Snake Customs District		San Francisco Customs District		Anchorage Customs District	
	Volume	Average value	Volume	Average value	Volume	Average value	Volume	Average value
1996	248,359	70.85	991,793	107.03	165,931	109.83	199,862	83.79
1997	339,109	54.87	1,033,444	85.84	171,848	86.96	104,547	72.25
1998	464,453	44.17	897,097	94.08	135,644	87.89	126,181	72.91
1999	444,956	39.96	811,978	77.73	114,002	78.75	131,699	41.75
2000	241,185	63.28	791,770	78.61	113,636	68.37	178,461	41.03
2001	195,131	70.63	709,213	83.66	101,996	84.66	154,880	61.28
2002	183,409	65.50	782,520	83.33	66,730	71.54	98,935	68.85
2003	193,327	67.18	723,012	80.72	62,591	68.71	109,621	49.66
2004	259,954	57.62	733,385	75.84	29,003	69.04	24,674	37.07
2005:								
1st quarter	68,217	52.19	254,551	84.63	20,270	74.53	7,918	85.26
2d quarter	127,636	62.82	189,412	78.79	1,711	91.70	19,525	47.85
3d quarter	80,792	55.81	265,670	87.19	862	95.81	7,137	29.09
4th quarter	82,974	57.85	208,841	82.65	767	99.16	20,824	77.35
2005 total and average value	359,619	58.08	918,475	83.71	23,611	77.35	55,404	61.87
2006:								
1st quarter	71,584	54.50	214,587	86.04	53	334.64	0	
2d quarter	44,553	41.62	249,350	85.05	23	491.06	929	73.21
3d quarter	36,870	46.62	161,195	94.70	805	78.61	5,513	39.75
4th quarter	41,938	41.10	261,474	85.76	8	529.00	0	
2006 total and average value	194,622	47.26	835,163	92.54	889	108.71	6,442	44.58

Source: U.S. Department of Commerce. The valuation definition used in the export statistics is the value at the seaport or border port of exportation. It is based on the selling price (or cost if not sold) and includes inland freight, insurance, and other charges to the port of exportation. Seattle Customs District includes all ports in the State of Washington, except Longview and Vancouver. Columbia Snake Customs District includes all Oregon ports and Longview and Vancouver, Washington. San Francisco Customs District includes all coastal and inland ports in the State of California from Monterey north. The Anchorage Customs District is the State of Alaska.

Table 50—Volume of softwood lumber exports from Seattle and Columbia-Snake Customs Districts by species and destination, 1995-2006[a]

(In thousand board feet)

Year and quarter	From both customs districts				From Seattle Customs District				From Columbia-Snake Customs District			
	Total	Douglas-fir	Western hemlock	Other soft-woods	Total	Douglas-fir	Western hemlock	Other soft-woods	Total	Douglas-fir	Western hemlock	Other soft-woods
To All Countries												
1995	1,021,509	609,231	187,967	224,310	567,220	267,181	148,744	151,295	454,289	342,050	39,223	73,015
1996	1,011,083	655,756	172,776	182,551	567,842	299,178	148,418	120,246	443,241	356,578	24,358	62,305
1997	870,870	398,345	77,081	395,444	538,402	201,087	63,220	274,095	332,468	198,258	13,861	121,349
1998	468,994	221,978	32,640	214,375	282,042	98,893	25,249	157,900	186,953	123,086	7,392	56,475
1999	438,608	225,040	44,748	168,820	237,919	89,449	30,247	118,223	200,689	135,591	14,501	50,597
2000	464,164	210,018	33,586	220,560	262,813	71,743	19,803	171,268	201,351	138,275	13,783	49,292
2001	312,022	131,461	14,899	165,662	200,544	47,281	9,917	143,346	111,478	84,180	4,982	22,316
2002	249,174	89,679	14,723	144,773	180,310	48,951	6,326	125,032	68,865	40,726	8,397	19,470
2003	254,866	77,725	16,571	160,571	193,789	44,533	5,790	143,467	61,077	33,192	10,781	17,103
2004	190,962	64,313	17,107	109,542	138,533	31,346	11,772	95,415	52,429	32,966	5,333	14,130
2005:												
1st qtr.	42,662	14,093	3,417	25,152	37,132	11,353	2,116	23,663	5,530	2,740	1,301	1,489
2d qtr.	37,630	12,151	1,145	24,334	32,395	8,822	552	23,021	5,235	3,329	593	1,313
3d qtr.	37,867	11,202	3,821	22,844	29,359	8,890	1,265	19,204	8,508	2,312	2,556	3,640
4th qtr.	33,909	9,769	981	23,159	29,589	7,783	981	20,825	4,320	1,986	0	2,334
2005 total	152,068	47,215	9,364	95,489	128,475	36,848	4,914	86,713	23,592	10,367	4,450	8,776
2006:												
1st qtr.	34,029	11,258	878	21,893	30,060	9,927	767	19,366	3,969	1,331	111	2,528
2d qtr.	40,377	15,515	1,525	23,337	34,317	12,960	1,525	19,832	6,060	2,555	0	3,505
3d qtr.	47,345	22,072	1,589	23,684	38,288	17,792	1,589	18,908	9,057	4,281	0	4,776
4th qtr.	49,569	27,014	856	21,699	42,608	23,508	807	18,292	6,961	3,506	49	3,407
2006 total	171,320	75,859	4,847	90,613	145,273	64,188	4,688	76,397	26,047	11,672	159	14,216
To Japan												
1995	669,917	355,744	177,523	136,650	367,756	144,142	139,273	84,341	302,161	211,602	38,250	52,309
1996	717,669	450,562	159,400	107,707	383,731	185,296	135,647	62,788	333,938	265,266	23,753	44,919
1997	564,065	217,985	63,914	282,166	347,236	108,183	52,216	186,837	216,829	109,802	11,698	95,329
1998	271,965	120,742	18,990	132,233	160,164	51,343	12,272	96,549	111,801	69,399	6,717	35,685
1999	256,882	141,340	18,311	97,231	130,136	54,943	10,378	64,815	126,746	86,397	7,933	32,416
2000	255,664	141,656	10,858	103,149	129,322	37,609	7,653	84,059	126,342	104,047	3,205	19,090
2001	172,092	85,321	4,855	81,914	92,978	20,087	4,331	68,558	79,114	65,234	524	13,356
2002	111,896	51,663	1,256	58,975	73,365	24,613	992	47,758	38,532	27,050	264	11,218
2003	107,669	40,710	941	66,019	73,528	15,441	693	57,394	34,142	25,269	248	8,625
2004	76,586	33,916	1,137	41,533	45,406	8,552	945	35,908	31,180	25,364	192	5,625
2005:												
1st qtr.	15,162	6,317	0	8,845	13,922	5,315	0	8,607	1,240	1,002	0	238
2d qtr.	11,386	3,989	15	7,382	10,630	3,372	15	7,243	756	617	0	139
3d qtr.	8,137	2,530	24	5,583	7,566	2,216	24	5,326	571	314	0	257
4th qtr.	9,458	2,861	0	6,597	9,126	2,653	0	6,473	332	208	0	124
2005 total	44,143	15,697	39	28,407	41,244	13,556	39	27,649	2,899	2,140	0	758
2006:												
1st qtr.	8,936	3,555	58	5,322	8,498	3,396	58	5,044	437	158	0	279
2d qtr.	8,824	3,687	39	5,097	8,242	3,387	39	4,816	582	300	0	281
3d qtr.	13,439	9,486	6	3,946	10,992	7,551	6	3,435	2,447	1,936	0	511
4th qtr.	15,806	11,724	64	4,018	13,594	10,282	54	3,258	2,212	1,442	10	760
2006 total	47,004	28,453	167	18,384	41,326	24,616	158	16,552	5,678	3,836	10	1,832

Table 50—Volume of softwood lumber exports from Seattle and Columbia-Snake Customs Districts by species and destination, 1995-2006[a] (continued)

(In thousand board feet)

Year and quarter	From both customs districts				From Seattle Customs District				From Columbia-Snake Customs District			
	Total	Douglas-fir	Western hemlock	Other soft-woods	Total	Douglas-fir	Western hemlock	Other soft-woods	Total	Douglas-fir	Western hemlock	Other soft-woods
To Canada												
1995	159,723	108,911	6,956	43,856	159,723	108,911	6,956	43,856	0	0	0	0
1996	131,786	89,581	3,282	38,924	131,786	89,581	3,282	38,924	0	0	0	0
1997	131,401	78,244	4,036	49,122	131,401	78,244	4,036	49,122	0	0	0	0
1998	80,734	35,963	2,694	42,077	80,734	35,963	2,694	42,077	0	0	0	0
1999	57,673	18,499	2,936	36,238	57,673	18,499	2,936	36,238	0	0	0	0
2000	70,022	23,026	3,617	43,379	70,022	23,026	3,617	43,379	0	0	0	0
2001	70,788	19,377	4,913	46,498	70,788	19,377	4,913	46,498	0	0	0	0
2002	65,682	17,571	4,770	43,341	65,682	17,571	4,770	43,341	0	0	0	0
2003	81,488	18,987	4,394	58,107	81,488	18,987	4,394	58,107	0	0	0	0
2004	68,331	16,441	8,215	43,675	68,331	16,441	8,215	43,675	0	0	0	0
2005:												
1st qtr.	17,597	4,489	0	13,108	17,597	4,489	0	13,108	0	0	0	0
2d qtr.	12,783	3,401	0	9,328	12,783	3,401	0	9,328	0	0	0	0
3d qtr.	12,963	4,179	5	8,779	12,963	4,179	5	8,779	0	0	0	0
4th qtr.	11,951	3,472	0	8,479	11,951	3,472	0	8,479	0	0	0	0
2005 total	55,294	15,541	5	39,748	55,294	15,541	5	39,748	0	0	0	0
2006:												
1st qtr.	13,926	4,591	703	8,632	13,926	4,591	703	8,632	0	0	0	0
2d qtr.	18,104	7,252	1,395	9,457	18,104	7,252	1,395	9,457	0	0	0	0
3d qtr.	19,902	8,163	1,505	10,234	19,902	8,163	1,505	10,234	0	0	0	0
4th qtr.	18,817	8,248	719	9,850	18,817	8,248	719	9,850	0	0	0	0
2006 total	70,749	28,253	4,322	38,173	70,749	28,253	4,322	38,173	0	0	0	0
To People's Republic of China												
1995	328	39	0	289	289	0	0	289	39	39	0	0
1996	499	59	0	440	499	59	0	440	0	0	0	0
1997	659	0	0	659	606	0	0	606	53	0	0	53
1998	1,402	0	294	1,108	1,178	0	294	884	223	0	0	223
1999	1,251	15	0	1,236	1,014	15	0	999	237	0	0	237
2000	1,224	48	83	1,093	985	48	83	855	239	0	0	239
2001	3,529	0	0	3,529	2,447	0	0	2,447	1,082	0	0	1,082
2002	5,153	0	0	5,153	4,448	0	0	4,448	705	0	0	705
2003	7,782	601	20	7,161	7,536	406	20	7,109	246	195	0	52
2004	7,965	64	20	7,881	3,943	39	20	3,884	4,022	25	0	3,997
2005:												
1st qtr.	1,266	17	0	1,249	874	17	0	857	392	0	0	392
2d qtr.	2,282	0	8	2,274	1,607	0	0	1,607	675	0	8	667
3d qtr.	3,006	98	0	2,908	1,444	68	0	1,367	1,562	30	0	1,532
4th qtr.	2,366	0	0	2,366	1,052	0	0	1,052	1,314	0	0	1,314
2005 total	8,920	115	8	8,797	4,977	85	0	4,892	3,943	30	8	3,905
2006:												
1st qtr.	1,512	0	0	1,512	328	0	0	328	1,185	0	0	1,185
2d qtr.	1,973	0	17	1,956	138	0	17	121	1,835	0	0	1,835
3d qtr	1,908	0	19	1,889	56	0	19	37	1,852	0	0	1,852
4th qtr.	1,475	17	0	1,458	182	0	0	182	1,293	17	0	1,276
2006 total	6,867	17	36	6,815	703	0	36	667	6,164	17	0	6,147

[a] Includes lumber classified as railroad crossties and not specified by species.

Source: U.S. Department of Commerce. Data are compiled from Department of Commerce records at the end of each quarter.

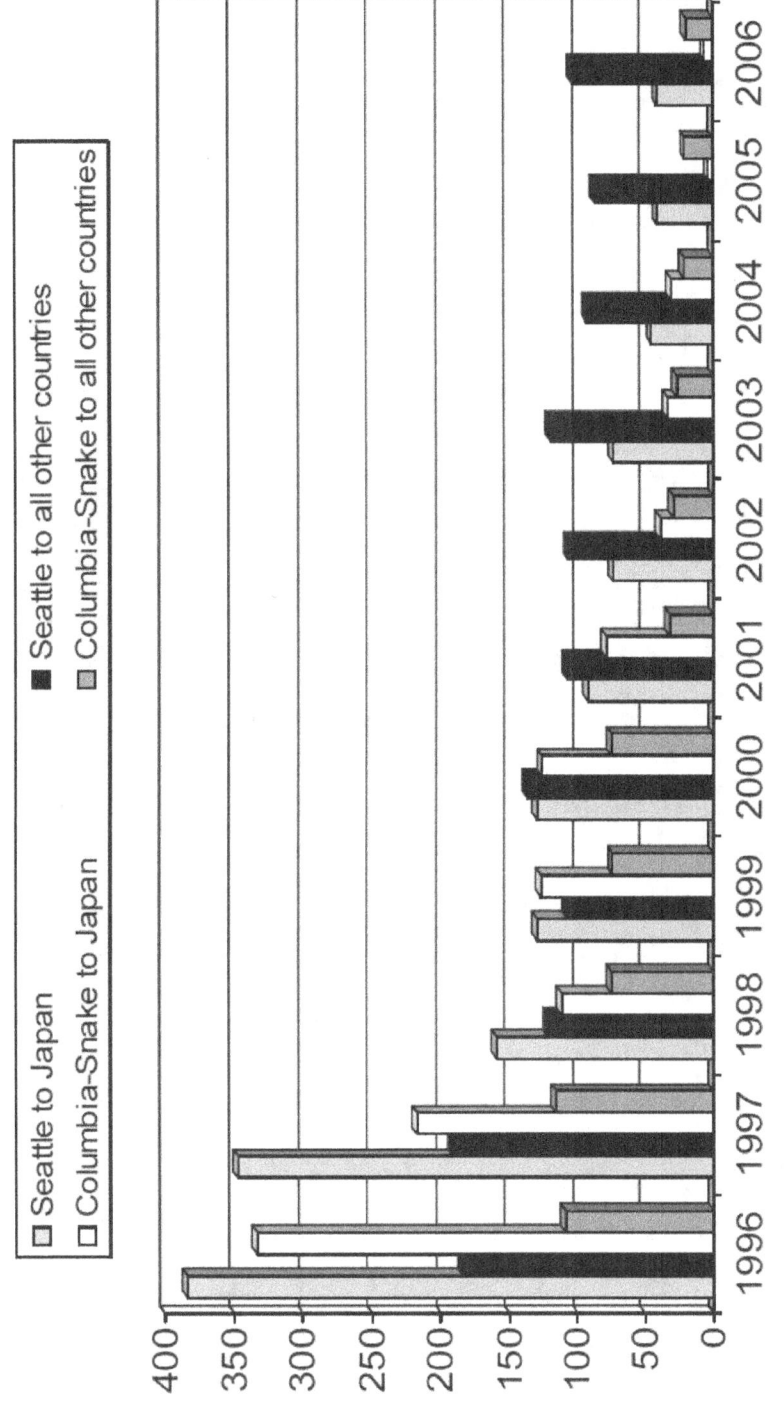

Figure 5—Lumber exports from Seattle and Columbia-Snake Customs Districts, 1996-2006, in million board feet

Seattle to Japan
Columbia-Snake to Japan
Seattle to all other countries
Columbia-Snake to all other countries

87

Table 51—Value of softwood lumber exports from Seattle and Columbia-Snake Customs Districts by species and destination, 1995-2006[a]

(In thousands of dollars)

Year and quarter	From both customs districts				From Seattle Customs District				From Columbia-Snake Customs District			
	Total	Douglas-fir	Western hemlock	Other soft-woods	Total	Douglas-fir	Western hemlock	Other soft-woods	Total	Douglas-fir	Western hemlock	Other soft-woods
To All Countries												
1995	714,815	449,115	120,102	145,599	368,109	185,081	95,378	87,650	346,706	264,033	24,724	57,949
1996	740,746	517,750	110,839	112,156	390,587	223,901	95,356	71,330	350,159	293,849	15,483	40,826
1997	609,619	322,459	52,668	234,493	355,719	153,319	45,092	157,307	253,901	169,140	7,575	77,186
1998	309,416	162,681	22,591	124,145	171,973	65,056	18,392	88,526	137,443	97,625	4,199	35,619
1999	310,806	173,412	34,987	102,407	158,856	62,266	25,780	70,810	151,951	111,146	9,207	31,598
2000	309,006	165,718	21,187	122,102	159,017	49,854	13,862	95,301	149,989	115,864	7,325	26,801
2001	206,930	96,299	6,864	103,227	121,059	30,206	4,938	85,915	85,331	66,093	1,926	17,312
2002	160,133	61,355	6,183	92,595	111,011	30,781	2,636	77,595	49,121	30,574	3,548	15,000
2003	170,218	54,782	6,887	108,549	126,146	27,464	2,896	95,786	44,072	27,318	3,991	12,763
2004	141,870	54,108	7,770	79,992	98,103	22,892	5,830	69,380	43,766	31,214	1,939	10,612
2005:												
1st qtr.	32,414	12,314	1,767	18,333	27,569	9,046	1,293	17,230	4,845	3,268	474	1,103
2d qtr.	28,900	10,901	571	17,428	24,114	7,257	358	16,499	4,786	3,644	213	929
3d qtr.	28,199	10,222	1,472	16,505	22,317	7,185	613	14,519	5,882	3,037	859	1,986
4th qtr.	25,916	8,689	628	16,599	22,344	6,332	628	15,384	3,572	2,357	0	1,215
2005 total	115,429	42,126	4,438	68,865	96,344	29,820	2,892	63,632	19,085	12,307	1,582	5,233
2006:												
1st qtr.	24,862	9,454	454	14,954	21,708	7,721	413	13,574	3,154	1,734	41	1,380
2d qtr.	30,766	13,730	862	16,174	25,775	9,411	862	15,502	4,991	4,319	0	672
3d qtr.	39,141	18,352	725	20,065	31,526	14,285	725	16,516	7,615	4,066	0	3,548
4th qtr.	41,652	23,279	580	17,792	35,570	19,802	523	15,244	6,082	3,477	57	2,548
2006 total	136,421	64,815	2,621	68,984	114,579	51,219	2,524	60,836	21,842	13,596	98	8,148
To Japan												
1995	498,991	296,212	115,673	87,106	260,286	123,597	91,565	45,124	238,705	172,615	24,108	41,982
1996	552,934	384,067	105,906	62,959	286,580	160,756	91,024	34,798	266,354	223,311	14,882	28,161
1997	404,989	196,006	46,821	162,162	243,333	99,865	40,388	103,080	161,656	96,141	6,433	59,082
1998	173,996	87,369	14,422	72,205	96,928	37,982	10,839	48,107	77,068	49,387	3,583	24,098
1999	185,884	108,648	16,380	60,850	87,933	40,197	10,148	37,588	97,951	68,452	6,232	23,267
2000	193,939	120,244	7,496	66,199	86,171	30,402	4,842	50,926	107,768	89,841	2,654	15,273
2001	119,014	66,259	2,547	50,207	57,069	15,173	2,304	39,590	61,945	51,086	243	10,617
2002	77,517	38,199	463	38,855	48,314	17,942	240	30,182	29,202	20,256	223	8,723
2003	69,980	30,141	450	39,389	43,630	11,337	338	31,955	26,350	18,804	112	7,434
2004	57,686	28,049	667	28,970	31,435	6,818	555	24,063	26,250	21,232	112	4,907
2005:												
1st qtr.	11,304	5,419	0	5,885	10,235	4,572	0	5,663	1,070	847	0	223
2d qtr.	7,848	3,550	26	4,272	7,195	3,011	26	4,158	653	539	0	114
3d qtr.	5,755	2,249	31	3,475	5,279	1,953	31	3,295	476	296	0	180
4th qtr.	6,332	2,483	0	3,849	6,013	2,276	0	3,737	319	207	0	112
2005 total	31,240	13,701	58	17,481	28,722	11,813	58	16,853	2,518	1,889	0	629
2006:												
1st qtr.	5,361	2,912	26	2,423	5,114	2,765	26	2,322	248	147	0	101
2d qtr.	5,933	3,051	17	2,865	5,538	2,817	17	2,704	395	234	0	161
3d qtr.	11,645	8,639	6	3,001	9,322	6,936	6	2,379	2,324	1,702	0	621
4th qtr.	14,462	10,933	55	3,474	12,322	9,625	45	2,653	2,140	1,308	10	821
2006 total	37,402	25,534	104	11,763	32,296	22,143	94	10,059	5,106	3,391	10	1,705

Table 51—Value of softwood lumber exports from Seattle and Columbia-Snake Customs Districts by species and destination, 1995-2006[a] (continued)

(In thousands of dollars)

Year and quarter	From both customs districts				From Seattle Customs District				From Columbia-Snake Customs District			
	Total	Douglas-fir	Western hemlock	Other soft-woods	Total	Douglas-fir	Western hemlock	Other soft-woods	Total	Douglas-fir	Western hemlock	Other soft-woods
To Canada												
1995	71,103	48,760	2,916	19,427	71,103	48,760	2,916	19,427	--	--	--	--
1996	63,617	43,920	1,407	18,290	63,617	43,920	1,407	18,290	--	--	--	--
1997	73,448	41,187	2,713	29,547	73,448	41,187	2,713	29,547	--	--	--	--
1998	47,870	16,592	1,628	29,650	47,870	16,592	1,628	29,650	--	--	--	--
1999	37,475	10,476	1,778	25,220	37,475	10,476	1,778	25,220	--	--	--	--
2000	41,236	12,443	1,964	26,829	41,236	12,443	1,964	26,829	--	--	--	--
2001	40,945	9,906	2,415	28,627	40,945	9,906	2,415	28,627	--	--	--	--
2002	40,545	8,491	2,250	29,804	40,545	8,491	2,250	29,804	--	--	--	--
2003	55,037	10,415	2,157	42,465	55,037	10,415	2,157	42,465	--	--	--	--
2004	47,488	11,639	3,308	32,541	47,488	11,639	3,308	32,541	--	--	--	--
2005:												
1st qtr.	11,837	3,268	--	8,569	11,837	3,268	--	8,569	--	--	--	--
2d qtr.	9,215	2,560	--	6,655	9,215	2,560	--	6,655	--	--	--	--
3d qtr.	9,186	2,847	4	6,335	9,186	2,847	4	6,335	--	--	--	--
4th qtr.	8,719	2,520	--	6,199	8,719	2,520	--	6,199	--	--	--	--
2005 total	38,957	11,196	4	27,758	38,957	11,196	4	27,758	--	--	--	--
2006:												
1st qtr.	9,639	3,251	366	6,023	9,639	3,251	366	6,023	--	--	--	--
2d qtr.	12,155	4,195	726	7,233	12,155	4,195	726	7,233	--	--	--	--
3d qtr.	14,218	5,116	623	8,479	14,218	5,116	623	8,479	--	--	--	--
4th qtr.	12,823	4,691	429	7,703	12,823	4,691	429	7,703	--	--	--	--
2006 total	48,835	17,253	2,144	29,438	48,835	17,253	2,144	29,438	--	--	--	--
To People's Republic of China												
1995	155	35	--	120	120	--	--	120	35	35	--	--
1996	313	54	--	259	313	54	--	259	--	--	--	--
1997	867	--	---	867	821	--	--	821	46	--	--	46
1998	901	--	374	528	794	--	374	420	108	--	--	108
1999	732	5	--	726	488	5	--	482	244	--	--	244
2000	1,271	22	39	1,210	996	22	39	935	276	--	--	276
2001	2,513	--	--	2,513	1,803	--	--	1,803	710	--	--	710
2002	2,991	--	--	2,991	2,648	--	--	2,648	344	--	--	344
2003	5,779	183	4	5,592	5,588	121	4	5,463	191	62	--	129
2004	5,656	65	41	5,550	3,406	39	41	3,326	2,250	26	--	2,224
2005:												
1st qtr.	910	27	--	883	744	27	--	717	167	--	--	167
2d qtr.	1,337	--	9	1,328	961	--	--	916	376	--	9	367
3d qtr.	1,691	98	--	1,593	910	73	--	837	782	25	--	757
4th qtr.	1,326	--	--	1,326	648	--	--	648	678	--	--	678
2005 total	5,264	125	9	5,130	3,263	100	--	3,118	2,002	25	9	1,969
2006:												
1st qtr.	868	--	--	868	157	--	--	157	710	--	--	710
2d qtr.	1,754	--	17	1,736	187	--	17	170	1,567	--	--	1,567
3d qtr.	1,250	--	27	1,223	62	--	27	35	1,188	--	--	1,188
4th qtr.	902	14	--	888	120	--	--	120	781	14	--	768
2006 total	4,773	14	44	4,715	527	--	44	483	4,246	14	--	4,233

Note: Individual columns may not add to totals because of rounding.

[a] Includes lumber classified as railroad crossties and not specified by species.

Source: U.S. Department of Commerce. Data are compiled from Department of Commerce records at the end of each quarter.

Table 52—Average value of softwood lumber exports from Seattle and Columbia-Snake Customs Districts by species and destination, 1995-2006[a]

(In dollars per thousand board feet)

Year and quarter	From both customs districts				From Seattle Customs District				From Columbia-Snake Customs District			
	Total	Douglas-fir	Western hemlock	Other soft-woods	Total	Douglas-fir	Western hemlock	Other soft-woods	Total	Douglas-fir	Western hemlock	Other soft-woods
To All Countries												
1995	699.76	737.18	638.95	649.10	648.97	692.72	641.22	579.33	763.18	771.91	630.34	793.66
1996	732.63	789.55	641.52	614.38	687.84	748.39	642.48	593.20	790.00	824.08	635.64	655.26
1997	700.01	809.50	683.28	592.99	660.69	762.45	713.26	573.92	763.69	857.46	546.54	636.06
1998	659.74	732.87	692.11	579.10	609.74	657.84	728.43	560.64	735.17	793.15	568.05	630.70
1999	708.62	770.58	781.88	606.61	667.69	696.10	852.32	598.95	757.15	819.71	634.94	624.50
2000	665.73	789.07	630.82	553.60	605.06	694.90	700.01	556.44	744.92	837.92	531.41	543.71
2001	661.46	732.53	460.70	623.12	603.65	638.86	497.93	599.35	765.45	785.14	386.60	775.77
2002	642.65	684.16	419.96	639.59	615.67	628.82	416.62	620.60	713.31	750.72	422.54	759.88
2003	667.87	704.82	415.61	676.02	650.94	616.71	500.13	667.65	721.59	823.03	370.22	746.24
2004	742.92	841.32	454.20	730.24	708.16	730.31	495.28	727.15	834.77	946.86	363.63	751.05
2005:												
1st qtr.	759.78	873.77	517.12	728.89	742.46	796.77	610.89	728.14	876.01	1,192.45	364.45	740.77
2d qtr.	767.99	897.13	498.69	716.20	744.37	822.62	647.98	716.69	914.27	1,094.77	359.94	707.54
3d qtr.	744.69	912.52	385.24	722.51	760.14	808.27	484.98	756.04	691.42	1,313.55	350.09	545.60
4th qtr.	764.29	889.45	640.16	716.74	755.15	813.60	639.99	738.73	826.95	1,187.24	--	520.57
2005 average	759.06	892.22	473.94	721.18	749.90	809.29	588.46	733.82	808.96	1,187.10	355.60	596.29
2006:												
1st qtr.	730.62	839.77	517.77	683.03	722.16	777.73	539.04	700.93	794.71	1,302.51	370.27	545.89
2d qtr.	761.97	884.96	565.21	693.06	751.08	726.13	565.21	781.69	823.63	1,690.73	--	191.65
3d qtr.	826.72	831.43	456.16	847.18	823.39	802.91	456.16	873.52	840.77	949.97	--	742.91
4th qtr.	840.28	861.74	677.94	819.97	834.82	842.34	648.33	833.38	873.72	991.79	1,168.45	748.00
2006 average	796.29	854.41	540.79	761.31	788.71	797.96	538.29	796.32	838.57	1,164.87	614.39	573.18
To Japan												
1995	744.85	832.65	651.59	637.44	707.77	857.47	657.45	535.02	789.99	815.75	630.27	802.58
1996	770.46	852.42	664.40	584.54	746.83	867.56	671.04	554.21	797.62	841.84	626.53	626.93
1997	717.98	899.17	732.56	574.70	700.77	923.11	773.48	551.71	745.55	875.57	549.90	619.77
1998	639.77	723.60	759.45	546.04	605.18	739.77	883.23	498.27	689.33	711.64	533.32	675.31
1999	723.62	768.70	894.56	625.83	675.70	731.61	977.86	579.93	772.81	792.29	785.60	717.77
2000	758.57	848.84	690.37	641.78	666.33	808.38	632.70	605.84	852.98	863.47	828.07	800.04
2001	691.57	776.58	524.61	612.92	613.79	755.39	532.07	577.47	782.98	783.11	466.29	794.92
2002	692.76	739.39	328.82	658.84	658.55	728.95	241.96	631.98	757.87	748.85	844.70	777.59
2003	649.95	740.38	478.21	596.63	593.38	734.18	488.30	556.77	771.77	744.15	451.61	861.91
2004	753.22	827.03	586.19	697.52	692.32	797.21	586.78	670.14	841.90	837.08	583.70	872.30
2005:												
1st qtr.	745.58	857.84	1,781.67	665.35	735.17	860.24	1,781.67	657.95	862.78	845.46	--	936.97
2d qtr.	689.25	889.95	--	578.70	676.82	892.90	--	574.07	863.56	873.94	--	820.14
3d qtr.	707.32	888.93	1,302.43	622.43	697.81	881.62	1,302.43	618.66	833.35	943.33	--	700.39
4th qtr.	669.53	867.88	--	583.45	658.86	858.04	--	577.32	962.81	999.13	--	903.23
2005 average	707.70	872.84	1,484.75	615.38	696.40	871.43	1,484.75	609.53	868.63	882.92	--	829.82
2006:												
1st qtr.	600.00	819.21	444.64	455.31	601.74	814.26	444.64	460.46	566.19	925.27	--	362.09
2d qtr.	672.34	827.41	423.25	562.10	671.89	831.80	423.25	561.46	678.84	777.83	--	573.13
3d qtr.	866.54	910.62	1,062.00	760.39	848.08	918.58	1,062.00	692.73	949.62	879.56	--	1,214.75
4th qtr.	914.99	932.52	862.89	864.67	906.48	936.06	833.34	814.32	967.30	907.28	1,026.09	1,080.40
2006 average	795.71	897.44	620.32	639.87	781.49	899.55	595.23	607.69	899.23	883.90	1,026.09	930.66

Table 52—Average value of softwood lumber exports from Seattle and Columbia-Snake Customs Districts by species and destination, 1995-2006[a] (continued)

(In dollars per thousand board feet)

Year and quarter	From both customs districts				From Seattle Customs District				From Columbia-Snake Customs District			
	Total	Douglas-fir	Western hemlock	Other soft-woods	Total	Douglas-fir	Western hemlock	Other soft-woods	Total	Douglas-fir	Western hemlock	Other soft-woods
To Canada												
1995	445.16	447.71	419.21	442.97	445.16	447.71	419.21	442.97	--	--	--	--
1996	482.73	490.28	428.70	469.89	482.73	490.28	428.70	469.89	--	--	--	--
1997	558.96	526.40	672.38	601.50	558.96	526.40	672.38	601.50	--	--	--	--
1998	592.93	461.36	604.30	704.65	592.93	461.36	604.30	704.65	--	--	--	--
1999	649.78	566.33	605.61	695.97	649.78	566.33	605.61	695.97	--	--	--	--
2000	588.90	540.38	542.97	618.49	588.90	540.38	542.97	618.49	--	--	--	--
2001	578.43	511.21	491.49	615.66	578.43	511.21	491.49	615.66	--	--	--	--
2002	617.29	483.24	471.70	687.66	617.29	483.24	471.70	687.66	--	--	--	--
2003	675.40	548.55	490.86	730.81	675.40	548.55	490.86	730.81	--	--	--	--
2004	694.97	707.93	402.68	745.06	694.97	707.93	402.68	745.06	--	--	--	--
2005:												
1st qtr.	672.69	727.99	--	653.72	672.69	727.99	--	653.72	--	--	--	--
2d qtr.	720.85	752.90	--	709.32	720.85	752.90	--	709.32	--	--	--	--
3d qtr.	708.64	681.36	887.79	721.61	708.64	681.36	887.79	721.61	--	--	--	--
4th qtr.	729.56	725.80	--	731.10	729.56	725.80	--	731.10	--	--	--	--
2005 average	704.54	720.41	887.79	698.35	704.54	720.41	887.79	698.35	--	--	--	--
2006												
1sr qtr.	692.17	708.13	520.25	697.69	692.17	708.13	520.25	697.69	--	--	--	--
2d qtr.	671.40	578.54	520.71	764.83	671.40	578.54	520.71	764.83	--	--	--	--
3d qtr.	714.38	626.73	413.69	828.51	714.38	626.73	413.69	828.51	--	--	--	--
4th qtr.	681.50	568.80	596.76	782.05	681.50	568.80	596.76	782.05	--	--	--	--
2006 average	690.27	610.68	496.02	771.17	690.27	610.68	496.02	771.17	--	--	--	--
To People's Republic of China												
1995	472.56	897.44	--	415.22	415.22	--	--	415.22	897.44	897.44	--	--
1996	627.25	915.25	--	588.64	627.25	915.25	--	588.64	--	--	--	--
1997	1,315.63	--	--	1,315.63	1,355.34	--	--	1,355.34	858.87	--	--	858.87
1998	642.91	--	1,270.47	476.34	673.46	--	1,270.47	475.00	481.66	--	--	481.66
1999	585.04	358.93	--	587.78	480.62	358.93	--	482.62	1,029.71	--	--	1,029.71
2000	1,038.72	459.48	472.26	1,106.91	1,010.58	459.48	472.26	1,093.50	1,154.95	--	--	1,154.95
2001	712.10	--	--	712.10	736.85	--	--	736.85	656.27	--	--	656.27
2002	580.44	--	--	580.44	595.32	--	--	595.32	487.51	--	--	487.51
2003	742.61	304.49	190.00	780.90	741.53	298.74	190.00	768.47	775.36	317.95	--	2,480.77
2004	710.09	1,017.19	2,037.75	704.24	863.89	1,011.46	2,037.75	856.41	559.29	1,029.00	--	556.37
2005:												
1st qtr.	718.86	1,614.00	--	706.97	850.73	1,614.00	--	836.64	424.79	--	--	426.02
2d qtr.	585.69	--	1,053.62	583.99	597.88	--	--	570.01	556.86	--	1,053.62	550.22
3d qtr.	562.69	1,000.00	--	547.80	629.83	1,077.86	--	608.28	500.59	847.64	--	494.13
4th qtr.	560.61	--	--	560.44	616.33	--	--	615.97	516.12	--	--	515.98
2005 average	590.20	1,086.96	1,053.62	583.15	655.47	1,176.47	--	637.37	507.85	847.64	1,053.62	504.23
2006:												
1st qtr.	573.76	--	--	573.76	480.41	--	--	480.41	599.57	--	--	599.57
2d qtr.	888.92	--	1,024.00	887.75	1,359.06	--	1,024.00	1,406.09	853.65	--	--	853.65
3d qtr.	655.21	--	1,430.80	647.56	1,107.56	--	1,430.80	945.93	641.55	--	--	641.55
4th qtr.	611.44	796.50	--	609.29	662.35	--	--	662.35	604.28	796.50	--	601.73
2006 average	695.02	796.50	1,237.09	691.94	749.48	--	1,237.09	723.48	688.81	796.50	--	688.51

[a] Includes lumber classified as railroad crossties and not specified by species.

Source: U.S. Department of Commerce. Data are compiled from Department of Commerce records at the end of each quarter.

Table 53—Volume and average value of softwood lumber exports from southern California ports by species and destination, 1995-2006[a]

(Volume in thousand board feet; value in dollars per thousand board feet)

Year and quarter	Total		Douglas-fir		Other softwoods	
	Volume	Average value	Volume	Average value	Volume	Average value
To All Countries						
1995	73,253	547.06	5,710	426.44	67,543	557.26
1996	83,953	428.82	5,128	613.45	78,825	416.81
1997	104,410	408.21	6,526	562.72	97,884	397.91
1998	102,512	406.60	10,989	249.40	91,524	425.47
1999	120,100	380.48	8,269	390.70	111,832	379.72
2000	134,728	390.62	7,558	517.96	127,169	383.05
2001	118,952	401.97	8,785	379.91	110,167	403.73
2002	125,067	397.32	12,108	367.47	112,959	400.51
2003	117,356	405.45	13,347	318.54	104,008	416.61
2004	117,298	456.80	15,211	378.79	102,087	468.42
2005:						
1st quarter	33,082	477.80	3,853	394.31	29,229	488.80
2d quarter	37,056	560.19	4,808	463.78	32,248	574.56
3d quarter	38,829	510.58	4,735	463.83	34,094	517.07
4th quarter	36,675	544.53	4,738	451.85	31,937	558.27
2005 total and average value	145,461	524.31	18,133	445.91	127,508	535.45
2006:						
1st quarter	38,031	503.37	4,606	430.51	33,425	513.41
2d quarter	31,670	680.85	2,386	645.77	29,284	683.17
3d quarter	25,128	772.24	2,558	685.67	22,570	782.04
4th quarter	25,330	769.22	3,703	723.58	21,627	777.04
2006 total and average value	120,159	662.42	13,253	600.39	106,906	670.11
To Japan						
1995	2,698	520.76	265	875.47	2,433	482.12
1996	6,227	483.24	551	1392.39	5,676	395.01
1997	11,502	508.26	775	1474.77	10,726	438.40
1998	3,228	621.81	109	953.58	3,118	610.18
1999	3,423	534.37	81	892.54	3,342	525.74
2000	2,914	573.04	219	1038.83	2,695	703.94
2001	1,860	794.75	27	974.15	1,833	792.14
2002	1,148	860.36	0	--	1,148	860.36
2003	1,307	570.02	0	--	1,307	570.02
2004	917	869.18	10	1,365.21	907	863.26
2005:						
1st quarter	112	1,363.95	24	631.28	88	1,561.67
2d quarter	141	1,286.95	17	1,051.77	124	1,320.25
3d quarter	140	1,289.62	12	1,033.09	128	1,316.23
4th quarter	72	925.49	15	1,217.56	57	856.06
2005 total and average value	466	1,250.01	67	934.23	397	1,308.59
2006:						
1st quarter	24	1,316.09	7	1,360.69	17	1,327.18
2d quarter	159	1,116.99	17	842.17	142	1,148.98
3d quarter	18	1,556.64	14	857.27	4	3,620.84
4th quarter	27	1,326.25	13	1,269.76	14	1,348.18
2006 total and average value	228	1,197.06	50	1,025.28	178	1,242.24

[a] Southern California consists of the San Diego and Los Angeles Customs Districts and includes all ports south of Monterey, California.

Source: U.S. Department of Commerce.

Table 54—Volume and average value of softwood lumber exports from northern California ports by species and destination, 1995-2006[a]

(Volume in thousand board feet; value in dollars per thousand board feet)

Year and quarter	Total Volume	Total Average value	Douglas-fir Volume	Douglas-fir Average value	Western hemlock Volume	Western hemlock Average value	Other softwoods Volume	Other softwoods Average value
			To All Countries					
1995	24,191	955.89	1,020	1,118.63	4,993	539.96	18,178	1,061.01
1996	29,954	712.19	4,732	900.43	2,619	451.38	22,603	702.99
1997	29,841	880.67	1,470	1,554.24	1,057	583.23	27,314	857.75
1998	21,524	752.66	372	1,450.88	234	823.50	20,918	739.46
1999	31,031	630.94	1,536	975.28	208	966.56	29,286	610.49
2000	34,279	842.77	2,559	818.46	26	365.99	31,694	742.46
2001	29,428	922.38	449	526.24	76	1,044.06	28,903	927.30
2002	39,019	683.46	119	583.67	20	1,867.91	38,880	683.16
2003	60,295	361.57	73	468.23	87	1,353.73	60,135	360.03
2004	30,789	777.54	530	364.92	199	426.63	30,060	787.14
2005	26,678	738.26	634	566.23	20	1,166.74	26,025	742.09
2006:								
1st quarter	6,244	706.55	154	194.95	19	1,494.67	6,071	717.04
2d quarter	5,958	852.53	23	798.11	0	--	5,935	852.95
3d quarter	6,122	886.37	0	--	19	2,262.45	6,103	882.00
4th quarter	7,140	938.23	0	--	0	--	7,140	938.23
2006 total and average value	25,464	848.97	177	274.13	38	1,878.34	25,249	851.42
			To Japan					
1995	13,782	806.99	547	795.25	4,993	539.96	8,242	969.55
1996	16,603	750.51	2,739	665.31	2,606	444.44	11,259	842.06
1997	18,757	783.18	782	1,276.00	1,057	583.23	15,919	857.31
1998	10,853	650.78	103	1,018.94	84	912.32	10,666	645.17
1999	9,658	561.23	152	797.87	208	966.56	9,297	548.29
2000	10,065	624.12	134	811.66	0	--	9,931	621.59
2001	5,784	817.74	30	1,107.89	76	1,044.06	5,678	813.24
2002	1,505	1,126.13	0	--	20	1,867.91	1,485	1,116.14
2003	675	1,701.95	16	360.21	86	1,353.73	573	1,790.57
2004	349	1,835.91	30	1,488.41	20	1,166.74	299	1,915.54
2005	182	1,113.07	0	--	20	1,166.74	162	1,105.54
2006:								
1st quarter	61	2,279.33	0	--	19	1,494.67	42	2,609.81
2d quarter	19	2,622.22	0	--	0	--	19	2,622.22
3d quarter	276	1,004.64	0	--	19	2,262.45	257	912.12
4th quarter	37	379.77	0	--	0	--	37	379.77
2006 total and average value	393	1,221.16	0	--	38	1,878.34	355	1,149.37
			To People's Republic of China					
1995	0	--	0	--	0	--	0	--
1996	33	746.94	0	--	0	--	33	746.94
1997	31	2,393.05	0	--	0	--	31	2,393.05
1998	153	287.10	0	--	0	--	153	287.10
1999	163	1,302.69	0	--	0	--	163	1,302.69
2000	42	200.43	0	--	0	--	42	200.43
2001	3,886	2,758.53	0	--	0	--	3,886	2,758.53
2002	18,211	686.73	0	--	0	--	18,211	686.73
2003	14,685	752.38	0	--	0	--	14,685	752.38
2004	16,255	850.77	0	--	0	--	16,255	850.77
2005	13,123	830.22	127	1,809.33	0	--	12,996	820.66
2006:								
1st quarter	1,925	884.93	0	--	0	--	1,925	884.93
2d quarter	2,675	988.05	0	--	0	--	2,675	988.05
3d quarter	2,558	1,018.68	0	--	0	--	2,558	1,108.68
4th quarter	2,564	1,119.81	0	--	0	--	2,564	1,119.81
2006 total and average value	9,722	1,010.45	0	--	0	--	9,722	1,010.45

[a] Northern California consists of the San Francisco Customs District and includes Monterey, California, and all ports north of Monterey.

Source: U.S. Department of Commerce.

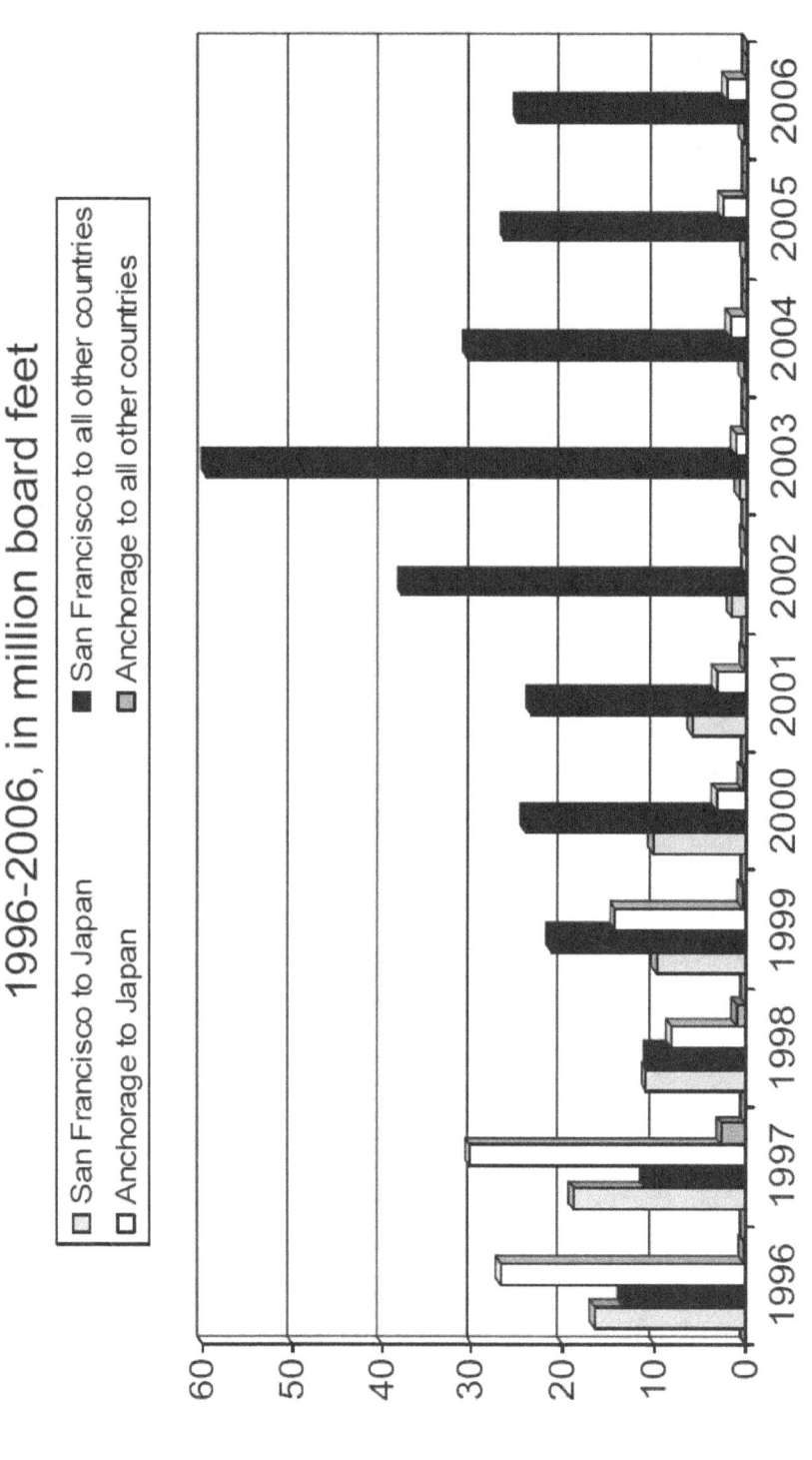

Figure 6—Lumber exports from San Francisco and Anchorage Customs Districts, 1996–2006, in million board feet

Table 55—Volume and average value of softwood lumber exports from Anchorage Customs District by species and destination, 1995-2006

(Volume in thousand board feet; value in dollars per thousand board feet)

Year and quarter	Total Volume	Total Average value	Western hemlock Volume	Western hemlock Average value	Sitka spruce Volume	Sitka spruce Average value	Cedar Volume	Cedar Average value	Other softwoods Volume	Other softwoods Average value
To All Countries										
1995	50,379	775.01	28,367	608.59	20,352	1,010.91	1,407	817.34	253	221.34
1996	26,854	715.05	14,831	557.28	11,934	914.09	20	688.30	69	204.08
1997	32,764	599.48	18,524	499.05	13,093	759.35	84	100.11	1,063	420.12
1998	9,048	460.22	4,447	386.06	3,874	540.98	261	392.86	466	534.46
1999	14,674	735.78	1,492	371.20	8,624	682.96	0	--	4,558	955.05
2000	3,609	901.62	0	--	3,254	854.45	278	1,235.94	77	1,691.68
2001	3,292	208.21	0	--	3,247	200.58	0	--	44	770.89
2002	85	49.56	0	--	0	--	0	--	85	49.56
2003	1,217	1,023.87	0	--	1,217	1,023.87	0	--	0	--
2004	1,825	1,087.76	0	--	1,825	1,087.76	0	--	0	--
2005	2,669	561.77	0	--	2,669	561.77	0	--	0	--
2006:										
1st quarter	609	1,012.60	0	--	609	1,012.60	0	--	0	--
2d quarter	243	1,061.18	0	--	243	1,061.18	0	--	0	--
3d quarter	897	952.48	0	--	897	952.48	0	--	0	--
4th quarter	417	1,075.91	0	--	417	1,075.91	0	--	0	--
2006 total and average value	2,166	1,005.35	0	--	2,166	1,005.35	0	--	0	--
To Japan										
1995	49,351	763.63	28,019	607.44	19,672	989.27	1,407	817.34	253	221.34
1996	26,784	716.24	14,761	558.77	11,934	914.09	20	688.30	69	204.08
1997	30,238	625.93	17,364	511.95	12,246	793.07	0	--	627	518.20
1998	8,105	487.32	3,856	420.46	3,791	550.00	0	--	458	531.56
1999	14,370	739.47	1,492	371.20	8,388	687.02	0	--	4,491	959.61
2000	3,161	858.77	0	--	3,161	858.77	0	--	0	--
2001	3,247	200.58	0	--	3,247	200.58	0	--	0	--
2002	0	--	0	--	0	--	0	--	0	--
2003	1,217	1,023.87	0	--	1,217	1,023.87	0	--	0	--
2004	1,825	1,087.76	0	--	1,825	1,087.76	0	--	0	--
2005	2,669	561.77	0	--	2,669	561.77	0	--	0	--
2006:										
1st quarter	609	1,012.60	0	--	609	1,012.60	0	--	0	--
2d quarter	243	1,061.18	0	--	243	1,061.18	0	--	0	--
3d quarter	897	952.48	0	--	897	952.48	0	--	0	--
4th quarter	417	1,075.91	0	--	417	1,075.91	0	--	0	--
2006 total and average value	2,166	1,005.35	0	--	2,166	1,005.35	0	--	0	--
To South Korea										
1995	1,028	1,320.04	348	701.15	680	1,636.76	0	--	0	--
1996	0	--	0	--	0	--	0	--	0	--
1997	380	289.49	0	--	0	--	0	--	380	289.49
1998	0	--	0	--	0	--	0	--	0	--
1999	223	531.13	0	--	156	480.13	0	--	67	649.85
2000	0	--	0	--	0	--	0	--	0	--
2001	0	--	0	--	0	--	0	--	0	--
2002	0	--	0	--	0	--	0	--	0	--
2003	0	--	0	--	0	--	0	--	0	--
2004	0	--	0	--	0	--	0	--	0	--
2005	0	--	0	--	0	--	0	--	0	--
2006:										
1st quarter	0	--	0	--	0	--	0	--	0	--
2d quarter	0	--	0	--	0	--	0	--	0	--
3d quarter	0	--	0	--	0	--	0	--	0	--
4th quarter	0	--	0	--	0	--	0	--	0	--
2006 total and average value	0	--	0	--	0	--	0	--	0	--

Source: U.S. Department of Commerce.

Table 56—Volume and average value of lumber exports by port, species, and destination, Seattle Customs District, 2006

(Volume in thousand board feet; value in dollars per thousand board feet)

Port and species	Destination									
	All countries		Japan		People's Republic of China		Korea		Canada	
	Volume	Average value	Volume	Average value	Volume	Average value	Volume	Average value	Volume	Average value
Port Angeles:										
Cedars	26	1,676.02	0		0		0		26	1,676.02
All softwoods	26	1,676.02	0		0		0		26	1,676.02
All hardwoods	32	1,470.65	0		32	1,470.65	0		0	
Seattle:										
Douglas fir	19,850	989.16	10,713	927.98	0		0		86	335.61
Other firs	116	810.41	116	810.41	0		0		0	
Cedars	376	1,909.29	78	1,439.57	9	2,798.29	77	1,558.68	0	
Hemlock	157	1,316.14	0		0		0		0	
Spruce	2,646	817.81	370	974.37	149	227.13	342	524.08	0	
Pines	521	667.29	131	1,028.34	264	596.95	0		0	
Redwood	63	2,072.97	50	2,319.66	0		0		0	
Other softwoods	15,977	959.42	1,216	818.98	0		0		0	
All softwoods	39,706	972.75	12,673	927.44	422	512.95	419	714.47	86	335.61
Red alder	32,369	860.03	1,051	1,705.94	24,794	803.78	246	1,400.00	0	
All hardwoods	51,329	991.03	5,988	1,652.11	32,771	846.56	990	1,650.36	5	2,195.78
Tacoma:										
Douglas fir	15,530	881.43	13,798	878.73	0		42	497.96	0	
Other firs	128	872.53	128	872.53	0		0		0	
Cedars	369	1,918.32	339	1,913.90	23	2,001.28	0		0	
Hemlock	175	636.86	158	595.23	17	1,024.00	0		0	
Spruce	441	1,306.31	268	814.60	26	2,665.81	15	809.14	0	
Pines	85	755.20	85	755.20	0		0		0	
Redwood	260	1,256.65	260	1,256.65	0		0		0	
Other softwoods	3,763	747.84	2,982	707.90	57	540.82	0		0	
All softwoods	20,750	886.77	18,017	871.32	124	1,333.30	57	576.64	0	
Red alder	7,456	820.86	36	1,967.06	5,315	833.94	0		0	
All hardwoods	15,000	983.53	1,011	1,467.97	10,099	951.74	61	2,202.65	0	

Table 56—Volume and average value of lumber exports by port, species, and destination, Seattle Customs District, 2006 (continued)

(Volume in thousand board feet; value in dollars per thousand board feet)

Port and species	All countries Volume	Average value	Japan Volume	Average value	People's Republic of China Volume	Average value	Korea Volume	Average value	Canada Volume	Average value
Other ports:[a]										
Douglas fir	26,039	626.05	86	675.45	0		0		25,866	625.26
Other firs	1,194	1,641.09	54	646.68	0		0		461	450.37
Cedars	15,720	906.09	0		0		0		15,720	906.09
Hemlock	3,367	520.72	0		0		0		3,367	520.72
Spruce	428	547.68	47	611.01	0		0		381	539.79
Pines	2,725	711.36	0		0		0		2,725	711.36
Redwood	130	1,445.12	0		0		0		52	946.82
Other softwoods	11,982	388.85	8,314	368.55	0		525	392.65	2,800	457.38
All softwoods	61,586	670.26	8,501	374.77	0		525	392.65	51,372	697.88
Red alder	23,026	1,105.78	31	2,232.43	18	631.36	0		13,534	711.18
All hardwoods	60,130	945.68	33	2,239.43	18	631.36	0		50,153	803.52
Total:										
Douglas fir	61,419	807.98	24,597	899.47	0		42	497.96	25,951	624.31
Other firs	1,437	1,505.99	297	807.42	0		0		461	450.37
Cedars	16,492	952.89	417	1,825.21	32	2,221.51	77	1,558.68	15,747	907.38
Hemlock	3,699	560.00	158	595.23	17	1,024.00	0		3,367	520.72
Spruce	3,516	846.19	685	886.75	175	593.23	357	535.93	381	539.79
Pines	3,331	705.58	216	921.22	264	596.95	0		2,725	711.36
Redwood	453	1,423.95	309	1,427.02	0		0		52	946.82
Other softwoods	31,722	718.80	12,511	493.19	57	540.82	525	392.65	2,800	457.38
All softwoods	122,068	805.67	39,191	781.76	545	699.08	1,001	537.97	51,484	697.78
Red alder	62,850	945.42	1,118	1,729.01	30,127	809.00	246	1,399.69	13,534	711.18
All hardwoods	126,492	968.70	7,032	1,628.35	42,920	817.69	1,051	1,682.64	50,158	803.69

[a] Bellingham, Blaine, Frontier, Laurier, Lynden, Metaline Falls, Oroville, Sea Tac Int'l. Airport, and Sumas.

Source: U.S. Department of Commerce.

Table 57a—Volume and average value of lumber exports by port, species, and destination, Seattle Customs District, first quarter 2006

(Volume in thousand board feet; value in dollars per thousand board feet)

Port and species	Destination									
	All countries		Japan		People's Republic of China		Korea		Canada	
	Volume	Average value	Volume	Average value	Volume	Average value	Volume	Average value	Volume	Average value
Port Angeles:										
Cedars	26	1,676.02	0		0		0		26	1,676.02
Seattle:										
Douglas fir	2,995	887.69	1,455	846.45	0		0		0	
Cedars	108	1,756.35	30	1,063.66	0		8	6,381.58	0	
Spruce	1,173	638.40	262	731.24	140	212.55	169	212.40	0	
Pines	197	682.52	43	958.02	154	606.07	0		0	
Redwood	50	2,319.66	50	2,319.66	0		0		0	
Other softwoods	4,484	965.94	796	831.02	0		0		0	
All softwoods	9,007	908.04	2,636	862.33	294	418.95	178	512.55	0	
Red alder	9,248	774.96	157	1,768.66	7,602	736.90	17	818.69	0	
All hardwoods	14,453	893.99	1,880	1,486.67	9,629	756.16	166	1,661.34	4	1,595.83
Tacoma:										
Douglas fir	2,341	772.08	1,942	790.15	0		0		0	
Other firs	36	1,038.48	36	1,038.48	0		0		0	
Cedars	6	3,177.57	6	3,177.57	0		0		0	
Spruce	91	1,097.10	79	723.44	0		0		0	
Pines	22	756.98	22	756.98	0		0		0	
Other softwoods	102	724.06	102	724.06	0		0		0	
All softwoods	2,657	783.07	2,245	785.82	0		0		0	
Red alder	1,872	743.45	0		1,348	729.88	0		0	
All hardwoods	4,010	863.56	275	1,355.61	2,700	812.69	12	2,313.78	0	

Table 57a—Volume and average value of lumber exports by port, species, and destination, Seattle Customs District, first quarter 2006 (continued)

(Volume in thousand board feet; value in dollars per thousand board feet)

Port and species	Destination									
	All countries		Japan		People's Republic of China		Korea		Canada	
	Volume	Average value	Volume	Average value	Volume	Average value	Volume	Average value	Volume	Average value
Other ports:[a]										
Douglas fir	4,254	718.79	0		0		0		4,254	718.79
Other firs	127	2,657.10	0		0		0		3	1,640.54
Cedars	3,872	840.08	0		0		0		3,872	840.08
Hemlock	678	511.12	0		0		0		678	511.12
Spruce	85	547.15	41	540.76	0		0		44	553.06
Pines	698	705.98	0		0		0		698	705.98
Redwood	61	1,458.07	0		0		0		31	928.28
Other softwoods	4,203	251.41	3,280	200.56	0		277	200.59	646	531.28
All softwoods	13,977	620.86	3,320	204.73	0		277	200.59	10,226	738.41
Red alder	6,602	1,169.38	0		0		0		3,299	657.97
All hardwoods	13,019	1,170.03	0		0		0		9,622	991.32
Total:										
Douglas fir	9,590	784.55	3,396	814.26	0		0		4,254	718.79
Other firs	163	2,295.54	36	1,038.48	0		0		3	1,640.54
Cedars	4,012	873.78	36	1,411.84	0		8	6,831.58	3,898	845.71
Hemlock	736	505.84	58	444.64	0		0		678	511.12
Spruce	1,349	663.65	382	709.33	140	212.55	169	212.40	44	553.06
Pines	918	702.19	65	888.83	154	606.07	0		698	705.98
Redwood	110	1,845.78	50	2,319.66	0		0		31	928.28
Other softwoods	8,789	621.44	4,178	333.46	0		277	200.59	646	531.28
All softwoods	25,668	739.51	8,201	575.15	294	418.95	455	322.41	10,253	740.81
Red alder	17,721	918.56	157	1,768.66	8,950	735.85	17	818.69	3,299	657.97
All hardwoods	31,482	1,004.27	2,155	1,469.94	12,329	768.54	178	1,706.39	9,627	991.58

[a] Blaine, Laurier, Lynden, Metaline Falls, Oroville, and Sumas.

Source: U.S. Department of Commerce.

Table 57b—Volume and average value of lumber exports by port, species, and destination, Seattle Customs District, second quarter 2006

(Volume in thousand board feet; value in dollars per thousand board feet)

Port and species	Destination									
	All countries		Japan		People's Republic of China		Korea		Canada	
	Volume	Average value	Volume	Average value	Volume	Average value	Volume	Average value	Volume	Average value
Seattle:										
Douglas fir	3,441	959.46	1,330	877.00	0		0		86	335.61
Other firs	31	514.15	31	514.15	0		0		0	
Cedars	103	1,643.75	0		9	2,798.29	25	968.12	0	
Hemlock	74	1,372.90	0		0		0		0	
Spruce	413	937.00	17	3,009.00	9	456.27	96	704.88	0	
Pines	142	665.08	16	2,487.89	0		0		0	
Redwood	13	1,141.94	0		0		0		0	
Other softwoods	3,950	981.42	251	850.12	0		0		0	
All softwoods	8,166	974.82	1,644	903.50	18	1,627.28	121	759.19	86	335.61
Red alder	8,256	867.38	304	1,528.27	6,727	820.96	120	1,214.73	0	
All hardwoods	13,119	982.04	1,747	1,549.63	9,063	848.32	298	1,486.54	0	
Tacoma:										
Douglas fir	2,256	826.99	1,991	807.42	0		4	802.40	0	
Other firs	60	924.22	60	924.22	0		0		0	
Cedars	92	1,094.91	69	789.08	23	2,001.28	0		0	
Hemlock	56	603.93	39	423.25	17	1,024.00	0		0	
Spruce	185	1,118.50	157	878.56	13	4,339.36	15	809.14	0	
Pines	62	754.56	62	754.56	0		0		0	
Redwood	133	1,513.40	133	1,513.40	0		0		0	
Other softwoods	1,421	637.09	1,232	659.12	54	524.83	0		0	
All softwoods	4,266	801.01	3,744	783.38	107	1,392.11	19	807.64	0	
Red alder	2,507	829.77	18	2,071.86	1,944	843.60	0		0	
All hardwoods	4,212	947.22	276	1,258.61	2,887	923.10	0		0	

Table 57b—Volume and average value of lumber exports by port, species, and destination, Seattle Customs District, second quarter 2006 (continued)

(Volume in thousand board feet; value in dollars per thousand board feet)

Port and species	All countries		Japan		People's Republic of China		Korea		Canada	
	Volume	Average value	Volume	Average value	Volume	Average value	Volume	Average value	Volume	Average value
Other ports:[a]										
Douglas fir	6,822	590.39	66	656.56	0		0		6,756	589.74
Other firs	403	1,963.49	54	646.68	0		0		54	405.51
Cedars	4,529	878.06	0		0		0		4,529	878.06
Hemlock	1,374	518.31	0		0		0		1,374	518.31
Spruce	131	572.07	7	10,323.50	0		0		124	546.92
Pines	581	937.62	0		0		0		581	937.62
Other softwoods	3,174	346.43	2,330	327.59	0		92	608.31	506	456.96
All softwoods	17,014	659.91	2,457	345.38	0		92	608.31	13,923	685.08
Red alder	6,291	1,131.58	0		0		0		3,458	679.08
All hardwoods	16,776	944.52	1	2,411.92	0		0		13,694	780.48
Total:										
Douglas fir	12,518	734.46	3,387	831.80	0		4	802.40	6,842	586.56
Other firs	494	1,748.13	144	733.71	0		0		54	405.51
Cedars	4,724	898.92	69	789.08	32	2,221.51	25	968.12	4,529	878.06
Hemlock	1,504	563.65	39	423.25	17	1,024.00	0		1,374	518.31
Spruce	729	917.57	181	1,083.90	22	2,771.19	111	718.81	124	546.92
Pines	785	873.97	78	1,103.11	0		0		581	937.62
Redwood	147	1,480.12	133	1,513.40	0		0		0	
Other softwoods	8,545	688.31	3,813	469.12	54	524.83	92	608.31	506	456.96
All softwoods	29,446	767.68	7,845	671.39	125	1,425.59	232	703.60	14,009	682.95
Red alder	17,054	959.30	322	1,558.31	8,672	826.03	120	1,214.73	3,458	679.08
All hardwoods	34,107	959.29	2,024	1,510.51	11,950	866.39	298	1,486.54	13,694	780.48

[a] Bellingham, Blaine, Laurier, Lynden, Metaline Falls, Oroville, and Sumas.

Source: U.S. Department of Commerce.

Table 57c—Volume and average value of lumber exports by port, species, and destination, Seattle Customs District, third quarter 2006

(Volume in thousand board feet; value in dollars per thousand board feet)

Port and species	All countries		Japan		People's Republic of China		Korea		Canada	
	Volume	Average value	Volume	Average value	Volume	Average value	Volume	Average value	Volume	Average value
Port Angeles:										
All hardwoods	32	1,470.65	0		32	1,470.65	0		0	
Seattle:										
Douglas fir	5,061	986.85	3,226	916.81	0		0		0	
Other firs	52	869.75	52	868.75	0		0		0	
Cedars	108	2,587.71	35	1,211.28	0		0		0	
Hemlock	49	1,143.43	0		0		0		0	
Spruce	605	899.74	73	921.67	0		17	1,846.97	0	
Pines	76	723.90	62	668.31	14	979.25	0		0	
Other softwoods	3,967	996.39	58	838.48	0		0		0	
All softwoods	9,917	1,000.64	3,506	913.46	14	979.25	17	1,846.97	0	
Red alder	8,427	907.92	448	1,711.22	6,271	840.31	72	1,431.77	0	
All hardwoods	12,504	1,023.38	1,249	1,845.00	8,123	883.41	242	1,657.73	1	5,195.54
Tacoma:										
Douglas fir	4,457	917.42	4,325	919.89	0		0		0	
Other firs	31	581.17	31	581.17	0		0		0	
Cedars	55	709.61	55	709.61	0		0		0	
Hemlock	6	1,062.00	6	1,062.00	0		0		0	
Spruce	165	1,632.91	32	724.30	13	992.27	0		0	
Redwood	70	1,275.82	70	1,275.82	0		0		0	
Other softwoods	744	758.84	718	752.75	0		0		0	
All softwoods	5,529	918.15	5,237	896.51	13	992.27	0		0	
Red alder	1,912	822.33	18	1,862.27	1,247	843.92	0		0	
All hardwoods	3,808	1,005.90	209	1,529.23	2,502	998.22	49	2,174.86	0	

Table 57c—Volume and average value of lumber exports by port, species, and destination, Seattle Customs District, third quarter 2006 (continued)

(Volume in thousand board feet; value in dollars per thousand board feet)

| Port and species | \multicolumn{10}{c}{Destination} |
| | All countries | | Japan | | People's Republic of China | | Korea | | Canada | |
	Volume	Average value	Volume	Average value	Volume	Average value	Volume	Average value	Volume	Average value
Other ports:[a]										
Douglas fir	7,715	638.44	0		0		0		7,628	636.46
Other firs	329	1,513.21	0		0		0		158	419.97
Cedars	3,206	1,079.47	0		0		0		3,206	1,079.47
Hemlock	883	484.25	0		0		0		883	484.25
Spruce	213	532.89	0		0		0		213	532.89
Pines	735	585.99	0		0		0		735	585.99
Redwood	66	1,440.34	0		0		0		17	909.13
Other softwoods	2,441	544.78	1,405	607.36	0		46	607.99	920	441.29
All softwoods	15,588	723.68	1,405	607.36	0		46	607.99	13,760	710.41
Red alder	5,877	1,141.69	31	2,232.43	0		0		3,403	753.43
All hardwoods	18,365	848.37	31	2,232.43	0		0		15,792	715.86
Total:										
Douglas fir	17,233	812.70	7,551	918.58	0		0		7,628	636.46
Other firs	412	1,361.36	83	760.17	0		0		158	419.97
Cedars	3,369	1,122.04	90	906.02	0		0		3,206	1,079.47
Hemlock	938	522.15	6	1,062.00	0		0		883	484.25
Spruce	983	943.31	105	861.98	13	992.27	17	1,846.97	213	532.89
Pines	811	598.89	62	668.31	14	979.25	0		735	585.99
Redwood	136	1,355.53	70	1,275.82	0		0		17	909.13
Other softwoods	7,152	817.54	2,180	661.34	0		46	607.99	920	441.29
All softwoods	31,034	846.83	10,147	862.34	27	985.66	63	934.48	13,760	710.41
Red alder	16,215	982.55	497	1,749.51	7,518	840.91	72	1,431.77	3,403	753.43
All hardwoods	34,708	929.27	1,490	1,808.79	10,657	909.79	292	1,744.92	15,793	716.10

[a] Blaine, Laurier, Lynden, Metaline Falls, Oroville, and Sumas.

Source: U.S. Department of Commerce.

Table 57d—Volume and average value of lumber exports by port, species, and destination, Seattle Customs District, fourth quarter 2006

(Volume in thousand board feet; value in dollars per thousand board feet)

Port and species	All countries		Japan		People's Republic of China		Korea		Canada	
	Volume	Average value	Volume	Average value	Volume	Average value	Volume	Average value	Volume	Average value
Seattle:										
Douglas fir	8,353	1,039.62	4,702	9,975.29	0		0		0	
Other firs	33	990.30	33	990.30	0		0		0	
Cedars	57	1,384.97	13	2,960.86	0		44	930.38	0	
Hemlock	34	1,438.73	0		0		0		0	
Spruce	455	1,063.08	17	2,882.37	0		60	751.30	0	
Pines	107	601.92	11	1,269.21	96	528.43	0		0	
Other softwoods	3,576	885.92	111	651.43	0		0		0	
All softwoods	12,615	995.70	4,887	980.65	96	528.43	104	827.32	0	
Red alder	6,438	910.14	142	2,000.60	4,194	842.82	36	2,221.89	0	
All hardwoods	11,253	1,090.23	1,112	1,876.14	5,956	939.77	284	1,809.57	0	
Tacoma:										
Douglas fir	6,476	915.16	5,541	903.25	0		38	464.13	0	
Cedars	217	2,540.24	209	2,563.72	0		0		0	
Hemlock	54	833.34	54	833.34	0		0		0	
Redwood	56	619.86	56	619.86	0		0		0	
Other softwoods	1,495	849.24	931	736.12	3	794.73	0		0	
All softwoods	8,297	943.16	6,791	928.64	3	794.73	38	464.13	0	
Red alder	1,165	923.63	0		775	974.62	0		0	
All hardwoods	2,971	1,168.24	251	1,769.76	2,010	1,134.32	0		0	

Table 57d—Volume and average value of lumber exports by port, species, and destination, Seattle Customs District, fourth quarter 2006 (continued)

(Volume in thousand board feet; value in dollars per thousand board feet)

Port and species	All countries		Japan		People's Republic of China		Korea		Canada	
	Volume	Average value	Volume	Average value	Volume	Average value	Volume	Average value	Volume	Average value
Other ports:[a]										
Douglas fir	7,248	592.00	20	738.13	0		0		7,228	591.60
Other firs	335	993.66	0		0		0		247	465.24
Cedars	4,114	863.97	0		0		0		4,114	863.97
Hemlock	432	617.95	0		0		0		432	617.95
Pines	710	661.23	0		0		0		710	661.23
Redwood	3	1,306.85	0		0		0		3	1,306.85
Other softwoods	2,165	542.07	1,300	607.83	0		110	606.32	728	412.40
All softwoods	15,007	672.50	1,319	609.80	0		110	606.32	13,462	667.53
Red alder	4,257	919.41	0		18	631.36	0		3,373	753.50
All hardwoods	11,970	852.58	0		18	631.36	0		11,044	793.84
Total:										
Douglas fir	22,077	856.16	10,263	935.93	0		38	464.13	7,228	591.60
Other firs	368	993.36	33	990.30	0		0		247	465.24
Cedars	4,387	953.44	222	2,586.45	0		44	930.38	4,114	863.97
Hemlock	520	694.37	54	833.34	0		0		432	617.95
Spruce	455	1,063.08	17	2,882.37	0		60	751.30	0	
Pines	817	653.48	11	1,269.21	96	528.43	0		710	661.23
Redwood	59	659.11	56	619.86	0		0		3	1,306.85
Other softwoods	7,236	775.47	2,341	660.89	3	794.73	110	606.32	728	412.40
All softwoods	35,920	848.53	12,997	915.83	100	537.50	252	675.81	13,462	667.53
Red alder	11,860	914.79	142	2,000.60	4,987	862.56	36	2,221.89	3,374	753.50
All hardwoods	26,194	990.48	1,363	1,856.53	7,984	988.06	284	1,809.57	11,044	793.84

[a] Blaine, Frontier, Laurier, Lynden, Metaline Falls, Oroville, and Sumas.

Source: U.S. Department of Commerce.

Table 58—Volume and average value of lumber exports by port, species, and destination, Columbia-Snake Customs District, 2006

(Volume in thousand board feet; value in dollars per thousand board feet)

Port and species	All countries Volume	All countries Average value	Japan Volume	Japan Average value	People's Republic of China Volume	People's Republic of China Average value	Korea Volume	Korea Average value	Taiwan Volume	Taiwan Average value
Coos Bay:										
Red alder	188	593.12	0		130	524.90	0		0	
All hardwoods	435	544.21	0		366	500.99	0		0	
Longview/Vancouver::										
Douglas fir	1,029	870.69	0		0		0		0	
Spruce	2	3,047.35	0		0		0		0	
Other softwoods	3	2,286.05	0		0		0		0	
All softwoods	1,033	877.75	0		0		0		0	
All hardwoods	204	1,540.64	0		30	1,059.31	0		0	
Portland:										
Douglas fir	10,685	1,018.89	3,836	883.90	17	796.50	0		333	812.30
Other firs	230	402.96	41	631.73	0		0		0	
Cedars	105	1,666.31	64	1,569.13	0		0		0	
Hemlock	159	614.39	10	1,026.09	0		0		0	
Spruce	132	1,279.62	0		86	1,182.33	0		0	
Pines	6,181	687.96	243	1,193.60	5,853	665.37	0		0	
Redwood	439	1,090.60	428	1,074.40	0		0		12	1,674.34
Other softwoods	1,486	808.86	1,056	785.01	153	1,311.11	0		0	
All softwoods	19,418	893.74	5,678	899.23	6,108	689.14	0		345	841.95
Red alder	16,750	906.29	267	1,573.31	13,275	866.53	140	1,448.82	523	747.64
All hardwoods	21,660	951.04	297	1,597.34	16,222	911.11	324	1,481.71	563	733.30
Total:										
Douglas fir	11,714	1,005.87	3,836	883.90	17	796.50	0		333	812.30
Other firs	230	402.96	41	631.73	0		0		0	
Cedars	105	1,666.31	64	1,569.13	0		0		0	
Hemlock	159	614.39	10	1,026.09	0		0		0	
Spruce	134	1,302.00	0		86	1,182.33	0		0	
Pines	6,181	687.96	243	1,193.60	5,853	665.37	0		0	
Redwood	439	1,090.60	428	1,074.40	0		0		12	1,674.34
Other softwoods	1,489	811.38	1,056	785.01	153	1,311.11	0		0	
All softwoods	20,451	892.93	5,678	899.23	6,108	689.14	0		345	841.98
Red alder	16,938	902.82	267	1,573.31	13,406	863.22	140	1,448.82	523	747.64
All hardwoods	22,299	98.51	297	1,597.34	16,618	902.34	324	1,481.71	563	733.30

Source: U.S. Department of Commerce.

Table 59a—Volume and average value of lumber exports by port, species, and destination, Columbia-Snake Customs District, first quarter 2006

(Volume in thousand board feet; value in dollars per thousand board feet)

Port and species	Destination									
	All countries		Japan		People's Republic of China		Korea		Taiwan	
	Volume	Average value	Volume	Average value	Volume	Average value	Volume	Average value	Volume	Average value
Coos Bay:										
Red alder	95	510.25	0		56	517.50	0		0	
All hardwoods	311	510.25	0		273	465.90	0		0	
Longview and Vancouver, Wash.:										
Douglas fir	139	988.05	0		0		0		0	
All softwoods	139	988.05	0		0		0		0	
All hardwoods	174	1,623.70	0		0		0		0	
Portland:										
Douglas fir	1,192	1,339.18	158	925.27	0		0		19	717.49
Other firs	22	438.55	22	438.51	0		0		0	
Hemlock	111	370.27	0		0		0		0	
Pines	1,173	609.72	43	1,120.35	1,093	576.59	0		0	
Other softwoods	305	402.74	214	200.74	92	874.07	0		0	
All softwoods	2,803	886.59	437	566.18	1,185	599.57	0		19	717.49
Red alder	4,883	880.86	54	1,112.16	3,940	855.33	48	793.77	219	831.35
All hardwoods	5,860	889.50	54	1,112.16	4,380	867.73	64	974.55	219	831.35
Total:										
Douglas fir	1,331	1,302.51	158	925.27	0		0		19	717.49
Other firs	22	438.55	22	438.51	0		0		0	
Hemlock	111	370.27	0		0		0		0	
Pines	1,173	609.72	43	1,120.35	1,093	576.59	0		0	
Other softwoods	305	402.74	214	200.74	92	874.07	0		0	
All softwoods	2,942	891.39	437	566.18	1,185	599.57	0		19	717.49
Red alder	4,978	876.31	54	1,112.16	3,996	850.57	48	793.77	219	831.36
All hardwoods	6,345	891.04	54	1,112.16	4,663	844.16	64	974.55	219	831.36

Source: U.S. Department of Commerce.

Table 59b—Volume and average value of lumber exports by port, species, and destination, Columbia-Snake Customs District, second quarter 2006

(Volume in thousand board feet; value in dollars per thousand board feet)

Port and species	All countries Volume	All countries Average value	Japan Volume	Japan Average value	People's Republic of China Volume	People's Republic of China Average value	Korea Volume	Korea Average value	Taiwan Volume	Taiwan Average value
Coos Bay:										
Red alder	19	591.42	0		0		0		0	
All hardwoods	19	591.42	0		0		0		0	
Longview, WA:										
Douglas fir	820	842.26	0		0		0		0	
All softwoods	820	842.26	0		0		0		0	
Portland:										
Douglas fir	1,734	1,046.65	300	777.83	0		0		14	1,317.18
Other firs	177	323.68	0		0		0		0	
Cedars	41	1,819.17	0		0		0		0	
Spruce	46	1,460.82	0		0		0		0	
Pines	1,792	819.04	17	1,193.70	1,774	815.37	0		0	
Redwood	93	1,033.73	81	940.31	0		0		12	1,674.34
Other softwoods	336	617.36	183	350.53	61	1,966.67	0		0	
All softwoods	4,219	897.18	582	678.83	1,835	853.65	0		25	1,483.85
Red alder	4,508	879.21	89	1,577.96	3,592	837.50	44	1,994.97	214	659.35
All hardwoods	5,772	940.02	119	1,636.65	4,514	893.66	89	1,696.52	234	649.53
Total:										
Douglas fir	2,555	981.01	300	777.83	0		0		14	1,317.18
Other firs	177	323.68	0		0		0		0	
Cedars	41	1,819.17	0		0		0		0	
Spruce	46	1,460.82	0		0		0		0	
Pines	1,792	819.04	17	1,193.70	1,774	815.37	0		0	
Redwood	93	1,033.73	81	940.31	0		0		12	1,674.34
Other softwoods	336	617.36	183	350.53	61	1,966.67	0		0	
All softwoods	5,039	888.24	582	678.84	1,835	853.65	0		25	1,483.85
Red alder	4,527	878.00	89	1,577.96	3,592	837.50	44	1,994.97	214	659.35
All hardwoods	5,791	938.87	119	1,636.65	4,514	893.66	89	1,696.52	234	649.53

Source: U.S. Department of Commerce.

Table 59c—Volume and average value of lumber exports by port, species, and destination, Columbia-Snake Customs District, third quarter 2006

(Volume in thousand board feet; value in dollars per thousand board feet)

Port and species	Destination									
	All countries		Japan		People's Republic of China		Korea		Taiwan	
	Volume	Average value	Volume	Average value	Volume	Average value	Volume	Average value	Volume	Average value
Coos Bay:										
Red alder	74	530.57	0		74	530.57	0		0	
All hardwoods	104	637.06	0		93	603.71	0		0	
Longview, WA:										
Douglas fir	49	863.35	0		0		0		0	
All softwoods	49	863.35	0		0		0		0	
All hardwoods	30	1,059.31	0		30	1,059.31	0		0	
Portland:										
Douglas fir	4,231	950.98	1,936	879.56	0		0		35	794.34
Other firs	4	628.47	0		0		0		0	
Cedars	7	2,761.05	7	2,761.05	0		0		0	
Spruce	86	1,182.33	0		86	1,182.33	0		0	
Pines	1,865	665.64	106	1,503.06	1,710	613.97	0		0	
Redwood	155	1,165.78	155	1,165.78	0		0		0	
Other softwoods	307	1,021.49	244	1,076.95	0		0		0	
All softwoods	6,655	883.89	2,447	949.62	1,796	641.19	0		35	794.34
Red alder	3,865	926.20	88	1,746.67	3,019	879.44	33	2,076.19	73	789.74
All hardwoods	5,194	972.77	88	1,746.67	3,790	922.74	133	1,689.37	73	789.74
Total:										
Douglas fir	4,281	949.97	1,936	879.56	0		0		35	794.34
Other firs	4	628.47	0		0		0		0	
Cedars	7	2,761.05	7	2,761.05	0		0		0	
Spruce	86	1,182.33	0		86	1,182.33	0		0	
Pines	1,865	665.64	106	1,503.06	1,710	613.97	0		0	
Redwood	155	1,165.78	155	1,165.78	0		0		0	
Other softwoods	307	1,021.49	244	1,076.95	0		0		0	
All softwoods	6,704	883.74	2,447	949.62	1,796	641.19	0		35	794.34
Red alder	3,939	918.79	88	1,746.67	3,092	871.12	33	2,076.19	73	789.74
All hardwoods	5,328	966.69	88	1,746.67	3,914	916.19	133	1,689.37	73	789.74

Source: U.S. Department of Commerce.

Table 59d—Volume and average value of lumber exports by port, species, and destination, Columbia-Snake Customs District, fourth quarter 2006

(Volume in thousand board feet; value in dollars per thousand board feet)

Port and species	Destination									
	All countries		Japan		People's Republic of China		Korea		Taiwan	
	Volume	Average value	Volume	Average value	Volume	Average value	Volume	Average value	Volume	Average value
Longview, WA:										
Douglas fir	20	1,233.49	0		0		0		0	
Spruce	2	3,047.35	0		0		0		0	
Other softwoods	3	2,286.05	0		0		0		0	
All softwoods	25	1,467.47	0		0		0		0	
Portland:										
Douglas fir	3,528	978.48	1,442	907.28	17	796.50	0		266	795.56
Other firs	27	855.32	19	855.00	0		0		0	
Cedars	57	1,427.87	57	1,427.87	0		0		0	
Hemlock	49	1,168.45	10	1,026.09	0		0		0	
Pines	1,352	612.93	76	801.40	1,276	601.73	0		0	
Redwood	192	1,057.56	192	1,057.56	0		0		0	
Other softwoods	538	1,037.78	417	1,104.31	0		0		0	
All softwoods	5,742	906.12	2,212	967.30	1,293	604.28	0		266	795.56
Red alder	3,494	954.76	36	1,829.65	2,725	906.70	16	608.62	18	608.49
All hardwoods	4,835	1,015.44	36	1,829.65	3,538	974.63	39	1,105.39	37	574.42
Total:										
Douglas fir	3,548	979.95	1,442	907.28	17	796.50	0		266	795.56
Other firs	27	855.32	19	855.00	0		0		0	
Cedars	57	1,427.87	57	1,427.87	0		0		0	
Hemlock	49	1,168.45	10	1,026.09	0		0		0	
Spruce	2	3,047.35	0		0		0		0	
Pines	1,352	612.93	76	801.40	1,276	601.73	0		0	
Redwood	192	1,057.56	192	1,057.56	0		0		0	
Other softwoods	540	1,043.66	417	1,104.31	0		0		0	
All softwoods	5,766	908.52	2,212	967.30	1,293	604.28	0		266	795.56
Red alder	3,494	954.76	36	1,829.65	2,725	906.70	16	608.62	18	608.49
All hardwoods	4,835	1,015.44	36	1,829.65	3,538	974.63	39	1,105.39	37	574.42

Source: U.S. Department of Commerce.

Table 60—Volume and average value of lumber exports by port, species, and destination, San Francisco Customs District, 2006

(Volume in thousand board feet; value in dollars per thousand board feet)

Port and species	All countries Volume	All countries Average value	Japan Volume	Japan Average value	People's Republic of China Volume	People's Republic of China Average value	Korea Volume	Korea Average value	Taiwan Volume	Taiwan Average value
Oakland:										
Douglas fir	178	274.13	0		0		0		154	194.95
Cedars	23,116	843.19	239	902.41	8,789	1,015.44	0		0	
Hemlock	38	1,878.56	38	1,878.56	0		0		0	
Pines	677	464.51	37	379.77	0		0		0	
Redwood	364	1,849.89	78	2,270.50	66	1,550.72	9	332.55	134	1,343.26
Other softwoods	70	352.22	0		0		0		0	
All softwoods	24,443	843.78	393	1,221.16	8,855	1,019.43	9	332.55	289	729.48
Red alder	42	1,888.00	0		42	1,888.00	0		0	
All hardwoods	3,209	1,374.87	1,114	1,429.26	1,134	1,081.39	10	2,807.61	24	1,376.43
San Francisco and Airport:										
Cedars	792	995.28	0		792	995.28	0		0	
All softwoods	792	995.28	0		792	995.28	0		0	
All hardwoods	21	15,522.49	10	12,317.46	0		0		0	\
Total:										
Douglas fir	178	274.13	0		0		0		154	194.95
Cedars	23,908	848.22	239	902.41	9,850	1,013.77	0		0	
Hemlock	38	1,878.56	38	1,878.56	0		0		0	
Pines	677	464.51	37	379.77	0		0		0	
Redwood	364	1,849.89	78	2,270.50	66	1,550.72	9	332.55	134	1,343.26
Other softwoods	70	352.22	0		0		0		0	
All softwoods	25,235	848.53	393	1,221.16	9,646	1,017.45	9	332.55	289	729.48
Red alder	42	1,888.00	0		42	1,888.00	0		0	
All hardwoods	3,230	1,465.81	1,124	1,523.90	1,134	1,081.39	10	2,807.61	24	1,376.43

Source: U.S. Department of Commerce.

Table 61a—Volume and average value of lumber exports by port, species, and destination, San Francisco Customs District, first quarter 2006

(Volume in thousand board feet; value in dollars per thousand board feet)

Port and species	All countries Volume	All countries Average value	Japan Volume	Japan Average value	People's Republic of China Volume	People's Republic of China Average value	Korea Volume	Korea Average value	Taiwan Volume	Taiwan Average value
Oakland:										
Douglas fir	154	194.95	0		0		0		154	194.95
Cedars	5,547	678.88	11	2,553.16	1,679	871.30	0		0	
Hemlock	19	1,494.67	19	1,494.67	0		0		0	
Redwood	175	1,542.38	31	2,670.86	17	1,430.75	9	332.55	118	1,361.92
Other softwoods	64	224.72	0		0		0		0	
All softwoods	5,958	689.42	61	2,279.31	1,696	876.89	9	332.55	272	700.27
All hardwoods	1,350	1,319.21	425	1,592.70	650	935.74	0		0	
San Francisco and Airport:										
Cedars	228	944.60	0		228	944.60	0		0	
All softwoods	228	944.60	0		228	944.60	0		0	
All hardwoods	1	12,404.16	1	12,404.16	0		0		0	
Total:										
Douglas fir	154	194.95	0		0		0		154	194.95
Cedars	5,775	689.39	11	2,553.16	1,908	880.08	0		0	
Hemlock	19	1,494.67	19	1,494.67	0		0		0	
Redwood	175	1,542.38	31	2,670.86	17	1,430.75	9	332.55	118	1,361.02
Other softwoods	64	224.72	0		0		0		0	
All softwoods	6,187	698.84	61	2,279.33	1,925	884.93	9	332.55	272	700.27
All hardwoods	1,351	1,322.69	425	1,603.48	650	935.74	0		0	

Source: U.S. Department of Commerce.

Table 61b—Volume and average value of lumber exports by port, species, and destination, San Francisco Customs District, second quarter 2006

(Volume in thousand board feet; value in dollars per thousand board feet)

Port and species	Destination									
	All countries		Japan		People's Republic of China		Korea		Taiwan	
	Volume	Average value	Volume	Average value	Volume	Average value	Volume	Average value	Volume	Average value
Oakland:										
Douglas fir	23	798.11	0		0		0		0	
Cedars	4,736	854.23	0		2,185	993.56	0		0	
Pines	601	448.42	0		0		0		0	
Redwood	116	2,494.52	19	2,622.22	16	1,569.08	0		17	1,210.26
Other softwoods	7	1,547.57	0		0		0		0	
All softwoods	5,483	844.99	19	2,622.22	2,200	997.68	0		17	1,210.26
Red alder	42	1,888.00	0		42	1,888.00	0		0	
All hardwoods	1,180	1,180.29	579	1,129.28	363	1,167.11	6	1,537.09	24	1,376.43
San Francisco:										
Cedars	475	943.48	0		475	943.48	0		0	
All softwoods	475	943.48	0		475	943.48	0		0	
All hardwoods	9	15,642.19	6	11,629.57	0		0		0	
Total:										
Douglas fir	23	798.11	0		0		0		0	
Cedars	5,211	862.36	0		2,659	984.64	0		0	
Pines	601	448.42	0		0		0		0	
Redwood	116	2,494.52	19	2,622.22	16	1,569.08	0		17	1,210.26
Other softwoods	7	1,547.57	0		0		0		0	
All softwoods	5,958	852.83	19	2,622.22	2,675	988.06	0		17	1,210.26
Red alder	42	1,888.00	0		42	1,888.00	0		0	
All hardwoods	1,189	1,288.56	585	1,235.80	363	1,167.11	6	1,537.09	24	1,376.43

Source: U.S. Department of Commerce.

Table 61c—Volume and average value of lumber exports by port, species, and destination, San Francisco Customs District, third quarter 2006

(Volume in thousand board feet; value in dollars per thousand board feet)

Port and species	All countries Volume	All countries Average value	Japan Volume	Japan Average value	People's Republic of China Volume	People's Republic of China Average value	Korea Volume	Korea Average value	Taiwan Volume	Taiwan Average value
Oakland:										
Cedars	5,990	877.21	228	822.78	2,504	1,017.74	0		0	
Hemlock	19	2,262.45	19	2,262.45	0		0		0	
Pines	21	726.79	0		0		0		0	
Redwood	44	1,598.06	29	1,613.82	16	1,569.08	0		0	
All softwoods	6,075	886.32	276	1,004.64	2,519	1,021.17	0		0	
All hardwoods	368	1,910.65	56	2,141.16	66	1,541.86	0		0	
San Francisco and Airport:										
Cedars	39	857.71	0		39	857.71	0		0	
All softwoods	39	857.71	0		39	857.71	0		0	
All hardwoods	8	14,914.08	1	16,048.00	0		0		0	
Total:										
Cedars	6,029	877.09	228	822.78	2,543	1,015.29	0		0	
Hemlock	19	2,262.45	19	2,262.45	0		0		0	
Pines	21	726.79	0		0		0		0	
Redwood	44	1,598.06	29	1,613.82	16	1,569.08	0		0	
All softwoods	6,114	886.14	276	1,004.64	2,558	1,018.68	0		0	
All hardwoods	376	2,189.19	58	2,447.93	66	1,541.86	0		0	

Source: U.S. Department of Commerce.

Table 61d—Volume and average value of lumber exports by port, species, and destination, San Francisco Customs District, fourth quarter 2006

(Volume in thousand board feet; value in dollars per thousand board feet)

Port and species	All countries Volume	All countries Average value	Japan Volume	Japan Average value	People's Republic of China Volume	People's Republic of China Average value	Korea Volume	Korea Average value	Taiwan Volume	Taiwan Average value
Oakland:										
Cedars	6,843	938.95	0		2,421	1,132.76	0		0	
Pines	55	539.74	37	379.77	0		0		0	
Redwood	30	1,523.45	0		18	1,632.61	0		0	
All softwoods	6,927	938.30	37	379.77	2,439	1,136.41	0		0	
All hardwoods	311	1,720.53	54	2,611.54	56	1,676.32	5	4,309.15	0	
San Francisco and Airport:										
Cedars	50	1,832.81	0		50	1,832.81	0		0	
All softwoods	50	1,832.81	0		50	1,832.81	0		0	
All hardwoods	3	17,043.04	2	11,987.86	0		0		0	
Total:										
Cedars	6,892	945.38	0		2,470	1,146.81	0		0	
Pines	55	539.74	37	379.77	0		0		0	
Redwood	30	1,523.45	0		18	1,632.61	0		0	
All softwoods	6,977	944.66	37	379.77	2,488	1,150.28	0		0	
All hardwoods	315	1,885.51	56	2,964.00	56	1,676.32	5	4,309.15	0	

Source: U.S. Department of Commerce.

Table 62—Volume and average value of lumber exports by port, species, and destination, Anchorage Customs District, 2006

(Volume in thousand board feet; value in dollars per thousand board feet)

Port and species	All countries		Japan		People's Republic of China		Korea		Canada	
	Volume	Average value	Volume	Average value	Volume	Average value	Volume	Average value	Volume	Average value
Anchorage:										
All hardwoods	31	9,558.10	24	11,800.67	8	2,581.18	0		0	
Ketchikan:										
Spruce	2,166	1,005.35	2,166	1,005.35	0		0		0	
Total:										
Spruce	2,166	1,005.35	2,166	1,005.35	0		0		0	
All softwoods	2,166	1,005.35	2,166	1,005.35	0		0		0	
All hardwoods	35	9,558.10	24	11,800.67	8	2,581.18	0		0	

Source: U.S. Department of Commerce.

Table 63—Volume and average value of lumber exports by port, species, and destination, Anchorage Customs District, all quarters 2006

(Volume in thousand board feet; value in dollars per thousand board feet)

Port and species	All countries Volume	All countries Average value	Japan Volume	Japan Average value	People's Republic of China Volume	People's Republic of China Average value	Korea Volume	Korea Average value	Canada Volume	Canada Average value
1ˢᵗ quarter										
Anchorage:										
All hardwoods	11	11,688.99	11	11,688.99	0		0		0	
Ketchikan:										
Spruce	609	1,012.60	609	1,021.60	0		0		0	
Total:										
Spruce	609	1,012.60	609	1,021.60	0		0		0	
All hardwoods	11	11,688.99	11	11,688.99	0		0		0	
2ⁿᵈ quarter										
Anchorage:										
All hardwoods	3	6,025.75	3	6,025.75	0		0		0	
Ketchikan:										
Spruce	243	1,061.18	243	1,061.18	0		0		0	
Total:										
Spruce	243	1,061.18	243	1,061.18	0		0		0	
All hardwoods	3	6,025.75	3	6,025.75	0		0		0	
3ʳᵈ quarter										
Anchorage:										
All hardwoods	4	13,191.69	4	13,191.69	0		0		0	
Ketchikan:										
Spruce	897	952.48	896	952.48	0		0		0	
Total:										
Spruce	897	952.48	897	952.48	0		0		0	
All hardwoods	4	13,191.69	4	13,191.69	0		0		0	
4ᵗʰ quarter										
Anchorage:										
All hardwoods	14	7,530.54	6	13,893.99	8	2,581.18	0		0	
Ketchikan:										
Spruce	417	1,075.91	417	1,075.91	0		0		0	
Total:										
Spruce	417	1,075.91	417	1,075.91	0		0		0	
All hardwoods	14	7,530.54	6	13,893.99	8	2,581.18	0		0	

Source: U.S. Department of Commerce.

Table 64—Volume and average value of softwood lumber exports to Canada from the Great Falls Customs District, 1995-2006[a]

(Volume in thousand board feet; value in dollars per thousand board feet)

Year and quarter	Total		Douglas fir		Western hemlock		Other softwoods	
	Volume	Average value	Volume	Average value	Volume	Average value	Volume	Average value
1995	13,636	551.63	5,839	653.02	772	624.35	7,025	459.36
1996	12,804	592.79	4,575	716.13	1,071	565.02	7,158	518.13
1997	17,370	574.27	7,595	643.85	854	731.12	8,921	500.01
1998	17,454	657.76	3,112	694.55	7	1,173.45	14,336	649.53
1999	10,367	702.40	2,635	762.91	14	388.76	7,718	682.32
2000	9,694	706.96	3,172	741.76	19	605.10	6,522	688.31
2001	8,303	654.85	2,964	611.50	31	400.73	5,307	680.57
2002	9,997	634.37	4,045	654.34	41	764.74	5,911	619.86
2003	7,777	619.59	2,414	693.61	69	554.97	5,293	573.55
2004	6,697	706.49	2,852	831.54	69	551.16	3,776	614.90
2005:								
1st quarter	3,108	752.96	1,895	816.86	0		1,213	652.85
2d quarter	2,177	884.74	1,300	1,066.52	0		877	615.17
3d quarter	2,081	744.10	944	911.29	36	520.16	1,101	608.16
4th quarter	2,157	702.40	1,183	825.66	0		974	552.83
2005 total	9,523	769.70	5,323	896.56	36	520.16	4,164	609.71
2006:								
1st quarter	2,028	830.47	1,041	946.21	0		987	708.63
2d quarter	2,101	716.92	1,178	760.85	0		923	660.76
3d quarter	2,266	688.55	1,258	765.49	0		1,008	592.88
4th quarter	2,399	660.00	1,139	717.57	98	326.82	1,162	631.79
2006 total	8,794	720.27	4,616	793.24	98	326.82	4,080	647.32

[a] Great Falls Customs District includes all ports in Montana and Idaho.

Source: U.S. Department of Commerce.

Table 65—Volume and average value of hardwood lumber exports from Seattle, Columbia-Snake, Anchorage, and San Francisco Customs Districts, 1995-2006

(Volume in thousand board feet; value in thousands of dollars)

Year and quarter	Seattle Customs District Volume	Seattle Customs District Average value	Columbia-Snake Customs District Volume	Columbia-Snake Customs District Average value	Anchorage Customs District Volume	Anchorage Customs District Average value	San Francisco Customs District Volume	San Francisco Customs District Average value
				To All Countries				
1995	93,216	1,174.13	27,333	1,316.39	0	--	5,715	1,326.68
1996	106,015	1,212.20	29,067	1,252.99	0	--	2,049	1,386.24
1997	107,322	1,174.36	31,172	1,269.97	0	--	2,709	1,257.86
1998	63,018	1,080.08	21,992	1,073.06	27	1,362.09	4,158	1,414.48
1999	90,968	1,082.53	26,635	1,119.37	51	1,201.04	2,791	1,424.17
2000	101,053	1,055.81	21,203	1,019.87	0	--	3,714	1,383.54
2001	86,789	968.17	26,807	1,040.45	0	--	2,112	1,524.31
2002	105,556	934.43	26,670	855.97	24	2,665.93	2,444	1,542.09
2003	105,445	954.39	28,547	851.74	181	1,688.60	5,705	1,477.02
2004	116,014	939.45	28,368	822.51	193	717.49	2,000	1,908.81
2005	131,542	992.91	25,226	888.75	176	10,493.72	3,195	1,511.17
2006:								
1st quarter	30,182	1,022.99	6,345	891.04	17	17,478.28	1,291	1,256.61
2d quarter	28,174	1,086.04	5,731	936.30	8	3,181.02	1,083	1,279.45
3d quarter	27,083	1,091.77	5,167	954.67	16	14,966.19	341	2,459.77
4th quarter	22,023	1,109.36	4,476	988.25	14	7,515.74	301	1,906.51
2006 total	107,461	1,074.55	21,719	938.15	54	12,153.48	3,017	1,465.77
				To Japan				
1995	38,123	1,456.84	8,953	1,378.98	0	--	2,239	1,360.88
1996	34,415	1,477.41	9,504	1,387.38	0	--	938	1,315.57
1997	34,630	1,387.85	8,192	1,416.19	0	--	1,319	1,399.16
1998	15,051	1,334.98	5,064	1,132.25	0	--	1,080	1,514.01
1999	16,479	1,334.22	4,355	1,323.06	25	864.12	683	1,423.07
2000	14,578	1,305,57	2,872	1,409.66	0	--	1,292	1,352.31
2001	15,445	1,204.73	4,401	1,153.21	0	--	455	1,900.21
2002	15,272	1,056.41	1,239	1,317.87	24	2,665.93	551	2,228.55
2003	9,413	1,347.55	800	1,582.53	132	2,066.84	4,250	1,328.92
2004	10,363	1,338.46	859	1,664.76	193	717.49	390	2,464.65
2005	9,372	1,432.77	133	1,768.07	158	11,536.27	637	3,027.02
2006:								
1st quarter	2,153	1,469.89	54	1,112.15	17	17,478.28	425	1,603.48
2d quarter	3,403	878.72	119	1,636.65	8	3,181.02	585	1,235.80
3d quarter	1,490	1,808.79	88	1,746.67	16	14,966.19	59	3,411.26
4th quarter	1,350	1,861.98	36	1,829.65	6	13,437.21	56	2,964.04
2006 total	8,397	1,353.49	297	1,597.34	47	13,719.86	1,125	1,575.86
				To People's Republic of China				
1995	1,138	790.86	381	687.66	0	--	0	--
1996	704	1,445.01	55	896.45	0	--	49	1,204.08
1997	2,640	1,042.77	743	1,677.76	0	--	90	1,283.48
1998	4,662	700.68	640	702.06	0	--	41	1,408.03
1999	13,305	702.49	3,339	748.23	0	--	39	1,496.78
2000	23,623	726.82	5,664	631.98	0	--	141	1,881.80
2001	23,356	722.30	7,610	717.61	0	--	131	1,498.34
2002	32,101	684.60	13,143	675.22	0	--	302	832.87
2003	35,363	692.69	14,417	679.76	0	--	206	1,142.51
2004	43,472	665.11	16,751	657.80	0	--	236	1,929.80
2005	55,354	765.36	18,571	829.06	0	--	1,905	937.08
2006:								
1st quarter	12,329	768.54	4,653	844.16	0	--	626	851.56
2d quarter	11,932	865.47	4,462	888.06	0	--	281	1,145.34
3d quarter	10,503	904.89	3,777	900.73	0	--	54	1,590.53
4th quarter	7,833	981.72	3,194	934.08	8	25,812.76	49	1,790.90
2006 total	42,597	868.51	16,086	887.48	8	25,812.76	1,011	1,014.76

Source: U.S. Department of Commerce.

Table 66—Volume of lumber exports from British Columbia ports by species and destination, 1996-2006

(In thousand board feet)

Year	Total, all species	Douglas fir	Hem fir	Cedars	Spruce	Other softwoods
To All Countries						
1996	12,256,620	801,192	1,863,155	1,141,084	106,854	8,344,335
1997	11,516,058	747,305	1,731,186	969,891	93,266	7,974,410
1998	10,699,390	848,775	1,461,984	783,467	51,253	7,553,911
1999	10,896,046	905,239	1,478,558	753,819	64,930	7,693,500
2000	10,920,898	1,025,082	1,323,279	1,011,484	53,631	7,507,422
2001	11,216,905	859,790	1,209,516	921,139	64,886	8,161,574
2002	11,995,659	846,587	1,049,543	891,409	38,636	9,169,484
2003	12,375,244	781,128	1,063,829	785,179	44,229	9,700,879
2004	13,755,601	1,044,341	1,218,119	903,130	31,177	10,558,834
2005	14,238,972	861,183	1,252,424	887,019	32,310	11,206,036
2006	14,050,773	660,410	1,167,641	976,587	21,417	11,224,718
To Japan						
1996	2,616,214	435,525	977,918	198,872	98,232	905,667
1997	2,130,206	354,049	832,481	188,103	86,169	669,404
1998	1,575,471	343,745	561,473	118,118	47,409	504,726
1999	1,795,303	373,161	617,881	101,618	60,023	642,620
2000	1,904,164	442,334	615,091	131,272	48,821	666,647
2001	1,577,689	291,417	495,500	110,964	60,167	619,641
2002	1,515,500	318,703	403,887	100,731	34,177	658,002
2003	1,446,886	275,597	363,806	104,697	35,206	667,580
2004	1,666,167	340,037	444,470	105,038	23,413	753,209
2005	1,360,769	251,079	329,831	90,783	22,803	666,273
2006	1,467,758	199,726	333,694	101,701	17,503	815,134
To United States [a]						
1996	9,148,980	261,063	704,737	844,579	6,643	7,331,958
1997	8,863,227	263,282	742,535	681,492	5,910	7,170,008
1998	8,743,274	416,637	782,098	579,870	3,237	6,961,432
1999	8,659,092	425,062	717,046	563,981	2,097	6,950,906
2000	8,508,678	454,021	548,691	772,799	3,527	6,729,640
2001	9,225,342	468,626	575,162	731,885	2,840	7,446,829
2002	9,939,938	383,029	483,165	695,993	803	8,376,948
2003	10,258,496	355,059	492,107	574,501	2,074	8,834,755
2004	11,386,786	568,916	539,938	669,446	3,474	9,605,012
2005	12,265,247	492,402	720,961	674,482	3,453	10,373,949
2006	11,860,091	347,425	627,608	725,937	579	10,158,542
To People's Republic of China						
1996	18,964	1,433	13,251	158	34	4,088
1997	8,267	130	6,936	16	48	1,137
1998	8,667	638	5,199	26	76	2,728
1999	10,017	365	3,764	136	139	5,613
2000	22,376	3,051	9,754	1,622	403	7,546
2001	38,187	4,185	20,488	3,680	850	8,984
2002	60,032	4,701	31,978	6,275	1,868	15,210
2003	85,930	11,820	33,695	13,680	2,539	24,196
2004	108,924	7,164	49,475	21,245	1,635	29,405
2005	106,596	6,417	54,965	22,471	2,687	20,056
2006	140,757	4,453	60,686	34,129	1,361	40,128

[a] Figures do not include shipments of railroad crossties.

Source: Statistics Canada, Vancouver, B.C., "Canadian Exports Cleared Through B.C. Custom Ports.

Table 67—Average value of lumber exports from British Columbia ports by species and destination, 1996-2006

(In Canadian dollars per thousand board feet)

Year	Total, all species	Douglas fir	Hem fir	Cedars	Spruce	Other softwoods
To All Countries						
1996	644.30	954.14	768.75	1,005.34	1,428.22	527.36
1997	696.87	925.00	793.90	1,274.44	1,432.79	575.58
1998	620.34	752.38	656.24	1,338.80	1,119.91	520.65
1999	686.78	822.00	713.61	1,251.29	1,049.42	607.35
2000	646.63	773.65	708.67	1,366.12	1,181.52	517.59
2001	597.67	736.90	645.55	1,329.11	970.16	490.39
2002	540.66	702.35	630.26	1,333.18	1,245.37	435.47
2003	437.23	641.67	537.92	1,144.81	1,133.74	349.28
2004	509.59	664.75	541.10	1,068.58	1,082.56	441.10
2005	449.19	618.19	470.37	957.62	1,115.72	391.67
2006	424.07	655.34	482.11	959.74	1,034.32	356.65
To Japan						
1996	937.88	1,137.11	907.80	1,501.09	1,453.21	694.99
1997	1,004.87	1,100.91	952.76	1,575.25	1,434.74	803.26
1998	856.86	927.09	776.49	1,452.38	1,138.05	732.67
1999	862.85	970.53	799.76	1,448.62	1,066.29	749.34
2000	863.17	904.12	799.43	1,587.74	1,205.24	727.08
2001	856.69	986.75	810.67	1,584.67	975.09	690.47
2002	814.95	937.03	846.93	1,545.15	1,257.22	601.44
2003	761.96	872.85	786.88	1,445.27	1,213.03	571.64
2004	758.91	918.09	720.02	1,330.00	1,203.56	616.54
2005	713.22	845.08	672.32	1,241.82	1,265.89	592.83
2006	674.91	844.08	684.70	986.91	1,067.36	582.09
To United States [a]						
1996	538.79	603.52	551.49	790.82	1,021.98	505.80
1997	597.70	608.24	563.05	1,078.14	1,204.23	554.74
1998	553.12	540.97	518.95	1,193.45	726.29	504.27
1999	630.08	631.34	607.17	1,093.96	506.44	594.77
2000	570.29	576.18	563.58	1,206.69	792.17	497.25
2001	538.17	552.91	480.88	1,223.02	1,011.62	474.18
2002	480.03	477.26	425.08	1,211.82	1,571.61	422.42
2003	368.09	386.09	318.60	955.09	466.25	331.93
2004	455.79	448.75	383.95	902.45	497.99	429.10
2005	401.34	413.95	344.44	811.78	427.45	378.00
2006	373.09	431.15	344.53	847.22	687.39	338.96
To People's Republic of China						
1996	403.13	495.46	353.56	1,335.44	1,411.76	487.28
1997	433.77	253.85	408.45	1,625.00	1,333.33	554.09
1998	455.98	280.56	432.97	1,769.23	473.68	527.86
1999	451.43	441.10	330.77	823.53	1,280.58	503.47
2000	499.78	560.14	344.17	737.98	1,590.57	567.06
2001	496.50	677.42	347.42	968.48	424.71	565.67
2002	510.33	374.39	392.55	1,185.34	836.19	481.46
2003	521.40	429.53	402.31	939.55	870.03	459.13
2004	520.32	456.17	413.60	964.46	739.42	382.42
2005	511.59	543.09	366.29	828.13	967.62	483.94
2006	464.96	663.60	367.10	775.67	1,012.49	308.06

[a] Figures do not include shipments of railroad crossties.

Source: Statistics Canada, Vancouver, B.C., "Canadian Exports Cleared Through B.C. Custom Ports."

Table 68—Volume of all species of softwood lumber imports into the Seattle Customs District, 1996-2006

(Volume in thousand board feet, Scribner scale)

Year and quarter	Countries of origin						
	All countries	Canada	Chile	China	New Zealand	Russia	Uruguay
1996	3,803,422	3,783,666	18,255	0	230	84	21
1997	3,392,218	3,366,792	18,282	17	699	163	1,326
1998	3,050,317	3,035,612	11,319	11	604	407	1,499
1999	3,246,662	3,198,835	17,066	0	2,458	2,725	3,254
2000	3,213,148	3,177,351	23,385	0	3,928	3,547	1,351
2001	3,745,653	3,730,488	6,736	0	4,589	1,593	731
2002	3,594,476	3,583,615	5,551	0	2,809	1,294	279
2003	3,930,411	3,919,095	4,657	8	2,122	2,763	809
2004	4,585,078	4,539,547	20,453	319	20,466	1,870	1,640
2005:							
1st quarter	1,186,048	1,175,171	6,965	341	2,604	544	436
2d quarter	1,386,620	1,371,967	9,178	694	3,444	944	250
3d quarter	1,360,650	1,344,089	9,164	483	5,682	744	354
4th quarter	1,261,255	1,246,359	7,375	1,119	4,498	1,035	312
2005 total	5,194,572	5,137,586	32,682	2,638	16,228	3,268	1,353
2006:							
1st quarter	1,373,161	1,356,763	10,490	1,042	3,685	497	420
2d quarter	1,352,480	1,327,424	11,315	4,832	6,438	750	421
3d quarter	1,077,117	1,055,001	8,878	3,053	8,372	852	356
4th quarter	737,772	723,436	5,061	1,211	6,418	908	335
2006 total	4,540,529	4,462,624	35,744	10,138	24,912	3,008	1,533

Source: U.S. Department of Commerce.

Table 69—Average value of all species of softwood lumber imports into the Seattle Customs District, 1996-2006

(Value in dollars per thousand board feet)

Year and quarter	All countries	Canada	Chile	China	New Zealand	Russia	Uruguay
				Countries of origin			
1996	376.33	373.77	852.49	--	1,352.17	940.48	683.98
1997	426.33	424.01	813.92	1,004.45	1,001.67	792.03	496.19
1998	352.24	350.44	738.05	1,567.49	943.97	901.68	430.37
1999	411.43	412.54	638.18	--	635.25	591.91	390.58
2000	395.23	393.90	475.61	--	836.82	462.26	361.87
2001	350.52	349.13	524.62	--	1,069.82	502.85	374.40
2002	325.48	324.31	679.19	--	944.07	479.15	480.55
2003	267.51	266.66	640.73	852.58	598.26	419.12	460.60
2004	352.61	347.68	814.09	708.65	905.67	438.72	697.50
2005:							
1st quarter	358.82	353.70	788.63	570.58	1,331.95	419.72	1,005.24
2d quarter	346.56	341.03	704.94	609.41	1,461.49	461.38	698.74
3d quarter	311.81	305.49	671.34	682.83	1,145.16	443.73	709.03
4th quarter	318.87	313.40	758.83	415.46	954.09	440.35	733.26
2005 average	333.54	327.93	725.51	535.53	1,189.30	443.76	808.27
2006:							
1st quarter	352.67	347.03	747.01	779.51	1,088.76	540.19	780.24
2d quarter	349.63	340.89	845.12	734.77	966.35	486.34	882.04
3d quarter	347.87	337.63	847.73	834.24	858.13	456.32	1,109.03
4th quarter	355.79	346.11	794.52	994.67	877.15	514.77	1,360.44
2006 average	351.13	342.83	809.81	800.38	925.11	495.33	1,011.48

Source: U.S. Department of Commerce.

Table 70—Volume of all species of softwood lumber imports into the Columbia-Snake Customs District, 1996-2006

(Volume in thousand board feet, Scribner scale)

Year and quarter	Countries of origin							
	All countries	Argentina	Brazil	Canada	Chile	China	New Zealand	Russia
1996	43,438	37	9,359	0	659	1	29,970	0
1997	64,478	198	5,503	366	12,395	51	41,445	0
1998	89,300	0	3,789	2,469	28,907	16	52,475	0
1999	130,253	22	15,925	1,662	41,354	0	70,085	0
2000	112,464	405	7,448	2,180	48,569	15	51,398	53
2001	125,108	0	3,067	17	46,550	0	73,897	128
2002	163,874	418	4,412	0	73,136	22	83,824	685
2003	166,063	319	1,891	0	71,951	0	89,750	1,642
2004	124,527	70	1,348	0	47,180	36	73,358	2,164
2005:								
1st quarter	19,838	0	285	0	896	0	18,440	174
2d quarter	26,555	0	198	5,764	654	0	19,167	772
3d quarter	16,101	0	833	0	1,051	59	12,726	1,339
4th quarter	18,335	0	253	0	1,266	1,093	14,828	546
2005 total	80,828	0	1,570	5,764	3,867	1,153	65,160	2,830
2006								
1st quarter	15,225	0	61	0	1,048	275	13,043	498
2d quarter	19,453	0	179	21	4,158	362	14,228	486
3d quarter	23,488	0	759	0	4,461	1,528	15,907	729
4th quarter	20,906	0	238	0	6,119	1,317	12,767	321
2006 total	79,071	0	1,236	21	15,786	3,482	55,944	2,033

Source: U.S. Department of Commerce.

Table 71—Average value of all species of softwood lumber imports into the Columbia-Snake Customs District, 1996-2006

(Value in dollars per thousand board feet)

Year and quarter	Countries of origin							
	All countries	Argentina	Brazil	Canada	Chile	China	New Zealand	Russia
1996	742.56	1,024.65	839.52	--	1,641.08	1,428.59	709.58	--
1997	826.50	740.36	906.97	400.71	943.35	1,040.00	789.19	--
1998	708.72	--	796.88	307.35	758.92	1,038.90	691.26	--
1999	647.57	763.13	660.15	333.47	725.65	--	603.02	--
2000	565.05	519.36	478.02	128.37	621.84	1,378.63	534.83	353.12
2001	567.50	--	491.24	1,506.51	565.30	--	567.87	482.30
2002	652.45	593.36	459.91	--	602.81	871.86	705.06	790.00
2003	586.64	396.80	438.77	--	543.77	--	618.08	901.68
2004	822.90	223.80	572.05	--	738.14	947.18	876.55	1,086.58
2005:								
1st quarter	790.05	--	427.77	--	805.25	--	791.20	1,112.50
2d quarter	646.53	--	678.55	300.52	755.67	--	726.15	1,152.93
3d quarter	758.08	--	598.91	--	690.13	834.04	724.67	1,252.24
4th quarter	664.61	--	572.92	--	741.21	305.46	670.05	1,288.91
2005 average	708.08	--	573.69	300.52	744.61	332.66	731.50	1,223.66
2006:								
1st quarter	710.12	--	623.11	--	734.97	724.52	705.66	982.22
2d quarter	684.10	--	680.31	434.43	650.33	677.00	683.45	1,014.10
3d quarter	749.14	--	788.06	--	917.62	710.90	697.51	906.11
4th quarter	676.49	--	693.58	--	724.78	671.50	648.55	915.61
2006 average	706.42	--	746.17	434.43	760.34	693.55	684.66	952.05

Source: U.S. Department of Commerce.

Table 72—Volume and average value of plywood exports from Seattle and Columbia-Snake Customs Districts by destination, 1995-2006

(Volume in thousand square feet; value in dollars per thousand square feet)

Year and quarter	From both customs districts Softwood 3/8-inch basis Volume	Average value	Hardwood 3/8-inch basis Volume	Average value	From Seattle Customs District Softwood 3/8-inch basis Volume	Average value	Hardwood 3/8-inch basis Volume	Average value	From Columbia-Snake Customs District Softwood 3/8-inch basis Volume	Average value	Hardwood 3/8-inch basis Volume	Average value
					To All Countries							
1995	107,205	275.89	51,540	314.59	57,437	246.41	49,754	316.05	49,768	309.92	1,786	273.80
1996	114,058	240.04	50,407	286.43	76,352	221.54	47,189	288.48	37,706	277.49	3,219	256.29
1997	102,496	251.05	48,400	320.29	62,832	245.33	43,373	320.44	39,663	260.13	5,117	313.39
1998	43,805	279.43	29,367	358.35	24,661	283.53	28,793	358.18	19,144	274.14	574	367.06
1999	39,698	301.39	23,570	432.00	27,159	308.25	23,235	431.93	12,539	286.53	335	436.90
2000	39,587	325.48	25,455	453.49	28,402	337.76	25,324	451.16	11,185	289.20	131	904.71
2001	31,101	342.72	22,593	435.37	22,881	329.88	22,227	438.43	8,219	378.47	366	249.24
2002	30,637	298.52	5,282	454.34	24,922	290.87	5,282	454.35	5,715	331.87	0	--
2003	29,415	314.22	466	418.34	23,610	312.73	486	418.34	5,806	320.04	0	--
2004	36,565	332.34	445	262.14	33,436	322.79	446	262.14	3,129	434.44	0	--
2005	35,459	322.73	1,459	410.06	31,059	315.74	1,425	405.99	4,400	372.06	34	584.13
2006:												
1st quarter	8,684	353.79	73	883.37	7,225	356.60	73	883.37	1,459	340.00	0	--
2d quarter	7,211	366.98	0	--	7,211	366.98	0	--	0	--	0	--
3d quarter	8,711	367.96	5	816.41	8,444	364.76	5	816.41	267	469.58	0	--
4th quarter	5,830	382.44	96	740.88	5,272	376.38	96	740.88	558	439.38	0	--
2006 total	30,436	366.46	174	802.98	28,153	365.41	174	802.98	2,284	379.42	0	--
					To Japan							
1995	9,194	295.74	3,077	547.61	3,621	265.95	2,331	631.06	5,573	315.09	746	286.86
1996	22,484	249.60	1,590	522.64	16,218	251.59	571	968.48	6,266	244.50	1,019	272.82
1997	14,712	292.81	4,045	426.51	12,608	289.14	1,887	468.16	2,104	314.77	2,159	390.01
1998	1,905	337.85	1,746	486.39	1,078	318.35	1,356	512.18	827	363.27	390	396.69
1999	7,462	236.58	489	417.97	5,098	235.76	338	406.42	2,364	238.33	151	443.81
2000	5,924	419.00	376	510.05	2,751	540.52	258	326.70	3,173	313.57	118	910.92
2001	4,141	502.65	544	329.94	1,650	473.47	221	436.93	2,492	521.82	323	255.97
2002	1,407	436.18	44	102.34	501	380.01	44	102.34	906	467.31	0	--
2003	1,169	530.39	0	--	130	848.88	0	--	1,038	490.86	0	--
2004	359	489.97	0	--	112	570.20	0	--	247	453.06	0	--
2005	146	829.73	496	216.38	95	1,046.06	496	216.38	51	425.92	0	--
2006:												
1st quarter	69	360.28	0	--	69	360.28	0	--	0	--	0	--
2d quarter	19	381.90	0	--	19	381.90	0	--	0	--	0	--
3d quarter	42	605.40	0	--	17	365.09	0	--	25	773.93	0	--
4th quarter	250	429.43	0	--	82	577.25	0	--	168	354.84	0	--
2006 total	380	434.09	0	--	188	458.34	0	--	193	408.76	0	--
					To Western Europe							
1995	40,772	319.14	236	394.07	4,618	414.03	203	413.79	36,154	307.02	33	272.73
1996	33,358	270.16	877	256.56	9,477	256.09	0	--	23,881	275.74	877	256.56
1997	28,369	269.88	1,856	310.53	3,751	388.33	596	243.08	24,617	251.83	1,261	342.25
1998	12,475	293.05	219	245.38	3,299	380.61	171	227.36	9	261.57	49	308.71
1999	6,477	296.13	15	1,133.62	1,520	466.51	15	1,133.62	4,957	243.91	0	--
2000	5,874	270.45	0	--	1,345	380.99	0	--	4,529	237.66	0	--
2001	1,878	428.06	102	598.77	371	996.30	102	598.77	1,507	288.35	0	--
2002	2,898	353.73	102	598.77	524	914.47	102	598.77	2,373	229.96	0	--
2003	694	460.21	0	--	228	911.65	0	--	466	239.08	0	--
2004	694	483.83	0	--	270	751.09	0	--	424	236.56	0	--
2005	2,227	319.11	362	672.74	95	1,161.26	362	672.74	2,132	297.28	0	--
2006:												
1st quarter	45	935.47	73	883.37	45	935.27	73	883.37	0	--	0	--
2d quarter	0	--	0	--	0	--	0	--	0	--	0	--
3d quarter	51	549.64	0	--	51	549.64	0	--	0	--	0	--
4th quarter	0	--	96	740.88	0	--	96	740.88	0	--	0	--
2006 total	96	731.11	169	802.62	96	731.11	169	802.62	0	--	0	--

Source: U.S. Department of Commerce. Columbia-Snake Customs District includes all Oregon ports plus Longview and Vancouver, Washington.
Seattle Customs District includes all coastal and inland ports in the State of Washington, except Longview and Vancouver.

Table 73—Volume and average value of plywood exports from California, 1995-2006[a]

(Volume in thousand square feet; value in dollars per thousand square feet)

Year and quarter	All California — All Plywood		Northern California — Softwood 3/8-inch basis		Northern California — Hardwood surface measure		Southern California — Softwood 3/8-inch basis		Southern California — Hardwood surface measure	
	Volume	Average value	Volume	Average value	Volume	Average value	Volume	Average value	Volume	Average value
1995	49,444	288.57	581	294.32	781	304.74	30,902	277.52	17,180	307.51
1996	82,880	217.46	1,626	249.69	1,041	208.45	53,155	196.18	27,058	257.67
1997	90,535	211.92	888	370.39	201	231.10	64,639	181.88	24,807	284.37
1998	82,031	247.48	1,444	278.24	283	810.35	54,539	197.56	25,765	345.25
1999	110,579	264.22	4,994	253.83	350	286.53	63,980	228.97	41,254	319.94
2000	134,302	296.36	5,716	247.25	181	333.44	92,053	294.20	36,351	309.36
2001	130,286	240.10	920	310.58	107	165.73	97,660	222.76	31,599	291.91
2002	83,963	242.28	331	481.75	0	--	76,207	234.95	7,425	306.77
2003	89,166	207.36	458	558.18	47	251.57	85,016	202.82	3,645	268.69
2004	70,260	278.45	629	669.62	0	--	63,989	275.48	5,641	268.55
2005:										
1st quarter	15,498	277.56	124	749.65	0	--	14,575	270.12	799	272.04
2d quarter	15,958	279.36	6	833.49	0	--	14,573	273.04	1,379	344.02
3d quarter	17,703	277.23	15	3,284.71	130	219.91	15,947	265.09	1,611	374.60
4th quarter	15,342	280.85	16	2,079.50	98	156.66	13,922	268.71	1,306	397.65
2005 total	64,501	278.69	160	1,115.80	228	192.67	59,017	269.15	5,095	356.16
2006:										
1st quarter	16,649	242.21	81	500.95	0	--	14,379	240.20	2,189	245.79
2d quarter	12,001	316.38	11	1,080.76	0	--	10,771	302.06	1,219	435.82
3d quarter	10,242	332.81	49	249.47	0	--	9,034	315.71	1,159	469.67
4th quarter	13,836	321.39	86	1,032.83	0	--	12,392	303.73	1,358	437.63
2006 total	52,728	297.47	227	677.10	0	--	46,575	286.06	5,925	372.66

[a] Northern California is the San Francisco Customs District and includes all coastal and inland ports from Monterey north.
Southern California consists of the San Diego and Los Angeles Customs Districts and includes all ports south of Monterey.

Source: U.S. Department of Commerce.

Table 74—Volume and average value of veneer exports from Seattle and Columbia-Snake Customs Districts by destination, 1995-2006

(Volume in thousand square feet; value in dollars per thousand square feet)

Year and quarter	From both customs districts Softwood surface measure Volume	Average value	Hardwood surface measure Volume	Average value	From Seattle Customs District Softwood surface measure Volume	Average value	Hardwood surface measure Volume	Average value	From Columbia-Snake Customs District Softwood surface measure Volume	Average value	Hardwood surface measure Volume	Average value
To All Countries												
1995	108,048	153.07	160,438	109.38	77,668	124.71	150,514	107.39	30,380	225.54	9,924	139.56
1996	111,737	151.32	149,396	129.87	83,803	126.69	129,311	132.15	27,934	225.17	20,085	115.21
1997	154,909	89.94	163,193	143.96	151,374	86.67	147,043	145.53	3,536	229.89	16,150	129.67
1998	139,313	70.35	95,541	137.95	136,135	67.34	85,665	138.10	3,178	199.08	9,876	136.65
1999	137,092	86.69	98,520	140.70	135,484	83.23	81,065	141.07	1,608	378.05	17,455	138.99
2000	134,179	99.22	121,051	125.37	131,038	96.35	116,295	126.06	3,141	218.69	4,756	108.42
2001	91,920	123.04	130,900	128.93	82,031	116.83	128,382	127.21	9,878	174.76	2,517	216.52
2002	63,427	163.92	235,368	115.22	59,461	157.42	233,939	114.83	3,965	261.38	1,429	180.10
2003	80,738	158.24	145,927	118.21	78,888	158.68	134,763	119.29	1,850	139.49	11,164	105.22
2004	160,833	95.25	233,097	154.27	160,222	94.96	232,899	154.40	611	170.78	198	135.00
2005	154,617	78.00	143,093	127.39	152,143	75.79	142,913	127.35	2,474	214.25	180	159.82
2006:												
1st quarter	37,941	78.52	26,042	133.63	37,941	78.52	26,042	133.63	0	--	0	--
2d quarter	37,146	83.08	33,746	140.13	37,146	83.08	33,685	139.54	0	--	61	460.38
3d quarter	23,504	89.42	22,395	150.34	23,504	89.42	22,057	149.39	0	--	338	211.93
4th quarter	23,443	90.52	26,165	134.85	22,100	90.70	25,398	132.61	1,343	87.57	767	209.28
2006 total	122,034	84.32	108,348	139.40	120,691	84.28	107,181	138.49	1,343	87.57	1,166	223.28
To Japan												
1995	91,833	141.66	59,448	91.31	62,025	101.83	56,664	88.05	29,808	224.54	2,784	157.33
1996	94,020	131.85	13,380	125.19	66,476	93.31	5,733	123.32	27,544	224.84	7,647	126.59
1997	60,271	93.48	22,327	161.07	57,325	86.12	16,600	162.85	2,946	236.73	5,727	155.91
1998	17,736	78.08	13,726	149.14	16,595	67.25	8,891	169.88	1,141	235.77	4,835	111.00
1999	16,448	101.99	29,529	141.42	16,032	97.63	15,766	171.42	415	269.98	13,763	107.06
2000	14,605	87.92	28,435	105.48	12,313	75.79	26,588	104.56	2,293	153.07	1,847	118.77
2001	3,668	110.15	8,759	130.00	1,334	77.51	8,759	130.00	2,333	128.82	0	--
2002	1,187	171.02	11,576	89.43	323	278.69	10,935	88.46	864	130.77	640	106.18
2003	1,398	92.10	13,648	121.03	0	--	7,771	128.26	1,398	92.10	5,877	111.48
2004	0	--	20,193	105.97	0	--	20,193	105.97	0	--	0	--
2005	9	684.54	24,214	148.52	9	684.54	24,214	148.52	0	--	0	--
2006:												
1st quarter	12	373.83	1,037	214.65	12	373.83	1,037	214.65	0	--	0	--
2d quarter	0	--	1,275	162.36	0	--	1,275	162.36	0	--	0	--
3d quarter	0	--	696	158.07	0	--	696	158.07	0	--	0	--
4th quarter	293	126.86	2,097	143.34	293	126.86	2,097	143.34	0	--	0	--
2006 total	305	136.67	5,104	164.58	305	136.67	5,104	164.58	0	--	0	--
To Western Europe												
1995	235	255.32	3,197	151.70	235	255.32	1,250	180.80	0	--	1,947	133.03
1996	2,088	238.51	3,280	137.80	1,971	236.94	2,635	143.83	117	264.96	645	114.73
1997	1,531	169.97	13,544	131.71	1,162	162.26	12,914	131.38	370	193.61	630	138.62
1998	400	224.50	2,828	111.82	400	224.50	2,828	111.82	0	--	0	--
1999	304	222.51	5,119	140.19	0	--	5,119	140.19	304	222.51	0	--
2000	1,725	184.71	477	282.36	1,725	184.71	477	22.36	0	--	0	--
2001	1,340	215.85	1,125	225.86	1,340	215.85	1,125	225.86	0	--	0	--
2002	0	--	564	121.84	0	--	564	121.81	0	--	0	--
2003	1,409	250.59	291	111.48	1,409	250.59	0	--	0	--	291	111.48
2004	4,691	198.20	0	--	4,086	203.57	0	--	605	161.86	0	--
2005	3,473	229.13	504	210.82	1,070	266.91	504	210.82	2,403	212.35	0	--
2006:												
1st quarter	0	--	0	--	0	--	0	--	0	--	0	--
2d quarter	0	--	0	--	0	--	0	--	0	--	0	--
3d quarter	0	--	0	--	0	--	0	--	0	--	0	--
4th quarter	1,343	87.57	0	--	0	--	0	--	1,343	87.57	0	--
2006 total	1,343	87.57	0	--	0	--	0	--	1,343	87.57	0	--

Source: U.S. Department of Commerce. Columbia-Snake Customs District includes all Oregon ports plus Longview and Vancouver, Washington. Seattle Customs District includes all coastal and inland ports in the State of Washington, except Longview and Vancouver.

128

Table 75—Volume of timber sold on publicly owned or managed lands, Montana and Idaho, 2001-2006

(In thousand board feet, Scribner scale)

Agency	2001	2002	2003	2004	2005		2006				
					Tota	4th qtr.	1st qtr.	2d qtr.	3d qtr.	4th qtr.	Tota
Montana:											
USDA Forest Service[a]	176,159	132,434	57,699	126,450	198,892	32,791	3,262	16,536	51,917	11,915	83,631
U.S. Bur. of Land Manage.[b]	7,644	2,078	5,103	10,454	NA	NA	NA	NA	NA	NA	73
State of Montana	34,011	36,140	39,785	48,346	54,673	7,781	2,119	24,040	12,755	11,435	50,349
Tota	217,814	170,652	102,587	185,250	NA	NA	NA	NA	NA	NA	134,052
Idaho:											
USDA Forest Service[a]	170,477	102,118	118,627	83,482	24,765	6,139	39,898	6,595	36,635	5,091	88,219
U.S. Bur. of Land Manage.[b]	6,245	8,078	5,331	10,692	NA	NA	NA	NA	NA	NA	19
State of Idaho	307,315	293,823	392,663	321,984	414,702	136,336	55,184	142,986	117,831	104,687	420,688
Tota	484,037	404,019	516,621	416,158	NA	NA	NA	NA	NA	NA	508,926
All public lands:											
USDA Forest Service[a]	346,636	234,552	176,326	209,932	223,657	38,930	43,160	23,131	88,552	17,007	171,850
U.S. Bur. of Land Manage.[b]	13,899	10,156	10,434	21,146	NA	NA	NA	NA	NA	NA	92
State of Montana	34,011	36,140	39,785	48,346	54,673	7,781	2,119	24,040	12,755	11,435	50,349
State of Idaho	307,315	293,823	392,663	321,984	414,702	136,336	55,184	142,986	117,831	104,687	420,688
Tota	701,851	574,671	619,208	601,408	NA	NA	NA	NA	NA	NA	642,979

Note: The U.S. Bureau of Indian Affairs land is now privately owned and no longer managed by the BIA. That category has been dropped.

NA = not available.

[a] Convertible products only.

[b] Does not include culog sales.

Source: Respective agencies listed.

Table 76—Average stumpage prices of timber sold on publicly owned or managed lands, Montana and Idaho, 2001-2006

(in dollars per thousand board feet)

| Agency | 2001 | 2002 | 2003 | 2004 | 2005 | | 2006 | | | | |
					Average	4th qtr	1st qtr	2d qtr	3d qtr	4th qtr	Average
Montana											
USDA Forest Service[a]	101 26	56 22	58 96	124 78	106 96	129 65	83 16	77 84	148 83	70 28	121 04
U S Bureau of Land Manage[b]	74 91	88 97	43 89	181 16	NA	NA	NA	NA	NA	NA	30 37
State of Montana	170 03	198 78	174 23	281 62	270 79	295 29	284 91	303 03	228 73	18 52	256 53
Average	111 07	86 81	102 91	168 90	NA	NA	NA	NA	NA	NA	171 88
Idaho											
USDA Forest Service[a]	103 00	76 97	118 19	130 42	107 54	100 91	55 96	77 21	126 16	18 56	84 54
U S Bureau of Land Manage[b]	76 79	67 28	36 79	212 68	NA	NA	NA	NA	NA	NA	365 12
State of Idaho	116 93	140 18	78 52	170 28	178 54	110 83	309 74	154 62	208 36	48 63	163 64
Average	111 50	122 75	87 20	163 37	NA	NA	NA	NA	NA	NA	149 94
All public lands											
USDA Forest Service[a]	102 12	62 25	98 81	127 02	107 03	125 12	58 02	77 66	139 45	54 80	102 30
U S Bureau of Land Manage[b]	75 75	71 72	40 26	197 10	NA	NA	NA	NA	NA	NA	99 94
State of Montana	170 03	198 78	174 23	281 62	270 79	295 29	28 91	303 03	228 73	184 52	256 53
State of Idaho	116 93	140 18	78 52	170 28	178 54	110 83	309 74	154 62	208 36	48 63	163 64
Average	111 37	112 08	89 80	165 07	NA	NA	NA	NA	NA	NA	154 51

Note: The U.S. Bureau of Indian Affairs land is now privately owned and no longer managed by the BIA. That category has been dropped.

NA = not available

[a] Prices received for individual sales may vary significantly from the averages shown in this table because of differences in species mix, quality, road costs, logging and processing costs, size and length of sale, number of bidders, and other related price determinants. Prices for stumpage on National Forest lands are high bid value. Road costs and an allowance for sale-area betterment are included in the bid.

[b] Does not include cull log prices

Source: Respective agencies listed

Table 77—Volume of sawtimber sold on National Forests by selected species, Northern Region, 1996-2006

(n thousand board feet Scr bner sca e)

Year and quarter	Doug as-fr	Ponderosa p ne	Western wh te p ne	Lodgepo e p ne	Enge man spruce	Western hem ock	Cedars	Larch	True f rs	A spec es
1996	77 900	10 289	10 422	87 680	18 565	5 129	9 966	13 070	67 062	317 211
1997	62 564	12 902	8 627	68 777	7 592	4 435	6 987	6 122	35 381	233 690
1998	56 276	7 460	1 659	45 070	4 482	1 366	4 227	8 158	23 879	172 575
1999	50 383	1 060	1 061	28 755	1 727	210	3 910	2 326	15 452	147 584
2000	22 599	5 735	471	3 860	7 086	43	2 073	1 824	15 916	99 547
2001	88 366	885	1 277	47 807	11 458	1 737	4 710	12 650	27 209	207 217
2002	66 832	7 099	303	27 830	10 210	103	382	2 308	9 078	160 994
2003	20 870	10 742	802	11 160	3 225	162	4 127	1 487	21 315	109 661
2004	58 845	1 987	2 723	28 845	5 264	309	2 773	13 548	39 044	163 714
2005										
1st quarter	33 003	0	1 058	4 169	19 389	23	23	11 426	5 258	76 561
2d quarter	10 790	59	27	1 810	5 072	10	52	2 882	638	25 567
3d quarter	19 038	7 614	1	7 568	654	0	510	1 158	1 449	43 580
4th quarter	16 603	173	0	3 912	614	115	111	1 717	1 741	26 373
2005 tota	79 433	7 846	1 086	17 458	25 729	148	696	17 183	9 086	172 082
2006										
1st quarter	4 000	536	117	17 070	88	49	574	180	1 849	39 922
2d quarter	2 271	4 931	5	3 054	20	0	16	329	336	11 723
3d quarter	14 777	1 486	3	27 252	5 073	19	280	179	10 640	71 957
4th quarter	4 983	0	5	798	236	0	122	1 501	924	8 763
2006 tota	26 031	6 953	130	48 175	5 417	68	992	2 189	13 748	132 366

Source Forest Serv ce U S Department of Agr cu ture Northern Reg on nc udes Montana northeastern Wash ngton northern daho North Dakota and northwestern South Dakota

Table 78—Average stumpage prices for sawtimber sold on National Forests by selected species, Northern Region, 1996-2006 [a]

(in dollars per thousand board feet)

Year and quarter	Douglas-fir	Ponderosa pine	Western white pine	Lodgepole pine	Engelmann spruce	Western hemlock	Cedars	Larch	True firs	All species
1996	166.95	172.15	228.96	226.32	118.08	161.75	262.69	196.82	169.59	185.83
1997	207.11	188.76	320.36	184.07	296.60	188.26	370.45	216.28	225.78	207.96
1998	168.68	115.50	246.92	201.42	255.02	146.04	290.10	115.48	176.38	176.51
1999	203.18	173.90	321.71	234.61	194.59	234.20	337.40	246.43	277.45	212.88
2000	321.05	145.85	298.10	199.29	354.72	259.65	309.03	250.07	171.02	203.85
2001	117.90	176.30	257.92	127.51	134.42	145.48	406.94	115.21	132.00	131.34
2002	63.08	34.96	84.33	70.88	88.81	148.84	140.66	72.14	59.26	75.21
2003	134.18	36.36	185.01	127.21	68.68	175.36	281.90	168.99	172.81	137.31
2004	172.09	126.71	129.60	163.91	204.05	113.45	169.78	146.44	121.25	155.00
2005										
1st quarter	137.32	—	81.11	194.99	61.86	69.22	61.38	80.67	66.01	105.37
2d quarter	174.40	124.58	74.88	210.52	174.05	121.20	533.11	123.09	103.68	182.73
3d quarter	121.28	169.67	239.57	153.79	128.75	—	118.81	83.46	73.51	136.63
4th quarter	185.93	274.89	—	160.50	238.37	304.84	298.04	156.77	203.50	176.78
2005 total	148.67	171.64	81.05	171.01	89.89	256.26	176.56	95.58	96.20	135.73
2006										
1st quarter	59.90	137.29	42.02	18.33	59.35	266.80	104.20	226.04	110.76	57.82
2d quarter	204.56	36.02	271.40	167.51	166.97	—	305.56	214.39	190.76	119.61
3d quarter	206.15	133.56	335.02	159.28	158.18	197.03	221.15	260.87	51.44	167.44
4th quarter	77.76	—	218.70	48.91	14.65	—	25.64	85.94	32.53	70.84
2006 total	158.97	64.67	65.33	108.03	150.36	247.34	130.90	131.07	61.55	123.75

[a] Prices received for individual sales may vary significantly from the averages shown in this table because of differences in species mix, quality, road costs, logging and processing costs, size and length of sale, number of bidders, and other related price determinants. Prices for stumpage on National Forest and are high bid value. Road costs and an allowance for sale-area betterment are not included in the bid.

Source: Forest Service, U.S. Department of Agriculture, Northern Region, includes Montana, northeastern Washington, northern Idaho, North Dakota, and northwestern South Dakota.

132

Table 79—Volume and average value of timber harvested on the National Forests of the Northern Region, 2006

(Volume in million board feet; value in dollars per thousand board feet)

Quarter	Beaverhead/Deerlodge Volume	Beaverhead/Deerlodge Average value	Bitterroot Volume	Bitterroot Average value	Clearwater Volume	Clearwater Average value	Custer Volume	Custer Average value	Flathead Volume	Flathead Average value
1st qtr.	1.6	112.19	1.1	33.71	2.9	131.23	.4	109.41	16.5	125.62
2d qtr.	.4	10.21	.9	41.28	2.0	154.55	.4	85.24	1.1	24.31
3d qtr.	1.9	36.60	.9	29.53	6.8	147.24	.7	75.81	4.4	75.81
4th qtr.	2.1	27.66	2.7	41.32	4.0	145.87	.8	22.36	6.9	64.51
Total	6.1	32.36	5.6	37.93	15.7	144.90	2.2	49.90	28.9	99.65

Quarter	Gallatin Volume	Gallatin Average value	Helena Volume	Helena Average value	Kootenai Volume	Kootenai Average value	Lewis and Clark Volume	Lewis and Clark Average value	Lolo Volume	Lolo Average value
1st qtr.	.6	118.46	2.3	105.79	3.5	164.64	.2	8.47	7.9	122.43
2d qtr.	.1	15.00	.8	23.27	4.4	152.39	.1	10.00	5.5	125.90
3d qtr.	3.2	214.73	.7	112.36	10.2	127.77	.7	18.95	4.5	94.57
4th qtr.	1.6	146.26	.8	37.24	8.0	106.14	1.0	16.93	3.0	100.45
Total	5.5	179.72	4.6	80.46	26.2	130.32	2.0	16.31	20.9	85.51

Quarter	Nezperce Volume	Nezperce Average value	Panhandle Volume	Panhandle Average value	Northern Idaho Volume	Northern Idaho Average value	Montana Volume	Montana Average value	All Forests Volume	All Forests Average value
1st qtr.	.1	9.86	4.3	101.17	7.3	111.47	34.2	122.93	41.5	120.87
2d qtr.	.1	10.13	1.2	73.90	3.3	120.98	13.7	108.55	17.0	110.92
3d qtr.	2.7	55.77	9.4	218.09	18.9	169.22	27.2	108.84	46.2	133.64
4th qtr.	7.4	46.31	9.7	32.55	21.0	28.81	27.0	49.94	48.0	40.68
Total	10.3	47.99	24.6	92.02	50.6	99.38	102.1	97.94	152.7	98.40

Source: Forest Service, U.S. Department of Agriculture. Northern Region includes northern Idaho and Montana and a small portion of northeastern Washington.

Table 80—Volume of sawtimber sold on National Forests by selected species, Intermountain Region, 1996-2006

(Volume in thousand board feet, Scribner scale)

Year and quarter	Douglas fir	Lodgepole pine	Ponderosa pine	Engelmann spruce	Larch	True firs	All species
1996	69,863	16,164	40,297	18,667	0	49,195	245,329
1997	40,960	11,716	19,425	6,636	20	27,569	119,645
1998	19,854	18,416	13,191	16,625	0	20,425	97,342
1999	4,953	13,235	5,407	6,617	0	434	37,901
2000	1,419	7,777	1,143	7,329	0	2,041	22,691
2001	24,548	5,437	9,330	9,154	0	12,353	67,256
2002	8,545	2,445	7,519	5,014	0	3,515	31,773
2003	6,968	2,930	3,298	2,125	0	8,178	27,452
2004	27,256	2,622	13,368	4,804	0	30,562	84,583
2005:							
1st quarter	3,245	1,514	1,379	758	0	4,049	10,945
2d quarter	2,628	29	699	4	0	26	4,974
3d quarter	1,442	1,967	738	3,668	0	1,435	13,287
4th quarter	1,033	2,869	1,865	3,308	0	940	11,535
2005 total	8,348	6,377	4,681	7,738	0	6,450	40,741
2006:							
1st quarter	5,200	0	1,993	25	0	750	8,102
2d quarter	2,067	3,001	785	568	0	3,112	11,546
3d quarter	7,008	8,023	5,809	594	0	1,730	30,339
4th quarter	9,280	24	6,281	982	0	3,761	21,528
2006 total	23,555	11,048	14,868	2,169	0	9,353	71,515

Source: Forest Service, U.S. Department of Agriculture. Intermountain Region includes eastern California, Nevada, Utah, and Wyoming.

Table 81—Average stumpage prices for sawtimber sold on National Forests by selected species, Intermountain Region, 1996-2006

(In dollars per thousand board feet)

Year and quarter	Douglas fir	Lodgepole pine	Ponderosa pine	Engelmann spruce	Larch	True firs	All species
1996	64.69	134.84	129.40	120.81		64.67	82.23
1997	174.56	150.89	305.58	182.01	325.73	172.52	178.37
1998	148.34	131.23	244.84	207.45		148.47	157.56
1999	173.54	133.19	115.02	191.09		145.65	129.43
2000	188.93	177.34	116.18	284.71		96.06	185.36
2001	84.21	172.86	193.07	173.76		62.05	118.23
2002	130.93	207.27	79.65	203.87		41.96	124.51
2003	63.29	63.97	60.14	192.64		42.98	69.80
2004	95.08	123.69	101.92	133.32		79.50	92.71
2005:							
1st quarter	192.93	152.81	17.87	119.02		69.59	114.57
2d quarter	53.92	112.92	127.62	136.81		79.90	70.18
3d quarter	70.64	105.69	121.46	166.51		102.86	112.99
4th quarter	68.27	102.43	118.38	174.12		74.35	119.21
2005 average	112.62	115.44	90.63	165.10		77.72	109.95
2006:							
1st quarter	79.83		112.95	142.84		103.93	89.31
2d quarter	158.54	102.54	233.58	130.40		79.02	113.75
3d quarter	58.00	112.91	70.92	260.25		34.50	89.92
4th quarter	55.19	62.08	51.57	69.08		58.02	56.14
2006 average	70.54	109.99	67.09	138.37		64.35	83.53

[a] Prices received for individual sales may vary significantly from the averages shown in this table because of differences in species mix, quality, road costs, logging and processing costs, size and length of sale, number of bidders, and other related price determinants. Prices for stumpage on National Forest lands are high bid value. Road costs and an allowance for sale area betterment are included in the bid.

Source: Forest Service, U.S. Department of Agriculture. Intermountain Region includes eastern California, Nevada, Utah, and Wyoming.

Table 82—Volume and average value of timber harvested on the National Forests of the Intermountain Region, 2006

(Volume in million board feet; value in dollars per thousand board feet)

Quarter	Ashley Volume	Ashley Average value	Boise Volume	Boise Average value	Bridger/Teton Volume	Bridger/Teton Average value	Caribou/Targhee Volume	Caribou/Targhee Average value	Dixie Volume	Dixie Average value
1st qtr.	.2	11.14	1.2	24.37	.3	32.93	.5	27.57	3.1	107.80
2d qtr.	.1	147.54	.1	3.97	.1	75.82	.1	138.11	1.7	110.37
3d qtr.	1.4	59.14	4.4	53.70	2.7	20.75	1.0	38.88	2.9	74.34
4th qtr.	1.9	21.86	3.3	30.75	2.6	12.12	3.5	53.73	2.4	52.89
Total	3.7	38.68	9.0	40.98	5.7	18.00	4.9	50.90	10.1	85.45

Quarter	Fishlake Volume	Fishlake Average value	Humboldt/Toiyabe Volume	Humboldt/Toiyabe Average value	Manti Lasal Volume	Manti Lasal Average value	Payette Volume	Payette Average value	Salmon Challis Volume	Salmon Challis Average value
1st qtr.	.3	10.39	.8	25.97	.2	40.23	1.1	18.05	.3	38.49
2d qtr.	.1	11.73	.6	22.82	.4	72.23	.3	72.29	.2	23.65
3d qtr.	1.4	104.40	.8	23.10	.7	155.95	6.6	92.45	1.9	31.22
4th qtr.	2.2	84.42	1.7	24.85	1.4	18.70	6.1	36.58	2.3	19.95
Total	4.0	85.00	3.9	24.42	2.8	31.44	14.2	61.92	4.8	25.90

Quarter	Sawtooth Volume	Sawtooth Average value	Wasatch Volume	Wasatch Average value	Southern Idaho Volume	Southern Idaho Average value	Nevada Volume	Nevada Average value	Utah Volume	Utah Average value
1st qtr.	.1	41.27	.3	92.48	3.3	31.65	.2	22.09	4.2	88.76
2d qtr.	.7	83.41	.2	76.77	1.2	59.47	.5	23.45	2.3	99.09
3d qtr.	2.5	52.61	1.1	59.69	16.6	65.37	.5	20.16	9.0	83.33
4th qtr.	2.3	30.26	1.9	78.27	17.5	35.88	.6	20.33	12.2	66.83
Total	5.7	47.20	3.5	73.32	38.6	48.99	1.8	21.36	27.7	78.17

Quarter	Wyoming Volume	Wyoming Average value	All Forests Volume	All Forests Average value
1st qtr.	.3	32.93	8.6	59.00
2d qtr.	.2	76.55	4.4	76.02
3d qtr.	2.7	20.95	29.1	65.63
4th qtr.	2.6	12.12	34.1	44.56
Total	5.9	19.96	74.1	56.90

[a] Less than 0.1 million board feet.

Source: Forest Service, U.S. Department of Agriculture. Intermountain Region includes Idaho, Nevada, Utah, and Wyoming.

Table 83—Volume of timber sold on publicly owned or managed lands in California, 2001-2006

(In thousand board feet Scribner scale)

| Agency | 2001 | 2002 | 2003 | 2004 | 2005 | | | | 2006 | | | | |
					Total	4th qtr	1st qtr	2d qtr	3d qtr	4th qtr	Total
USDA Forest Service[a]	285 665	244 332	190 614	334 180	426 346	99 689	78 856	50 219	88 791	53 590	271 456
U.S. Bureau of Land Management[b]	1 453	602	2 048	206	50	NA	NA	NA	NA	NA	30
State of California	0	NA	NA	NA	NA	NA	NA	NA	NA	NA	NA
Total	287 118	NA	NA	NA	NA	NA	NA	NA	NA	NA	NA

Note: The U.S. Bureau of Indian Affairs land is now privately owned and no longer managed by the BIA. That category has been dropped

NA = not available

[a] Convertible products only. Includes all of the Pacific Southwest Region and the portion of the Pacific Northwest Region in northern California

[b] Does not include cull, log sales or volume given away through free-use permits

Source: Respective agencies listed

Table 84—Average stumpage prices of timber sold on publicly owned or managed lands in California, 2001-2006

(In dollars per thousand board feet)

Agency	2001	2002	2003	2004	2005 Average	2005 4th qtr	2006 1st qtr	2006 2d qtr	2006 3d qtr	2006 4th qtr	2006 Average
USDA Forest Service[a][b]	53 37	69 99	51 89	52 77	65 00	29 62	58 01	82 78	59 11	77 19	66 74
U S Bureau of Land Manage[c]	155 67	59 67	22 80	178 20	129 25	NA	NA	NA	NA	NA	179 06
State of California	—	NA	NA	NA	NA	NA	NA	NA	NA	NA	NA
Average	53 89	NA	NA	NA	NA	NA	NA	NA	NA	NA	NA

Note The U S Bureau of Indian Affairs land is now privately owned and no longer managed by the B A That category has been dropped

NA = not available

[a] Prices received for individual sales may vary significantly from the averages shown in this table because of differences in species mix, quality, road costs, logging and processing costs, size and length of sale, number of bidders, and other related price determinants Prices for stumpage on National Forest lands are high bid value Road costs and an allowance for sale-area betterment are included in the bid

[b] Includes all of the Pacific Southwest Region and the portion of the Pacific Northwest Region in California

[c] Does not include current log sales or volume given away through free-use permits

Source Respective agencies listed

Table 85—Volume of sawtimber sold on National Forests by selected species, Pacific Southwest Region, 1996-2006

(Volume in thousand board feet, Scribner scale)

Year and quarter	Douglas fir	Ponderosa and Jeffrey pines	Sugar pine	Lodgepole pine	Cedars	True firs	All species
1996	47,887	53,449	13,679	2,012	15,541	105,469	287,635
1997	34,499	95,747	15,783	4,038	19,728	116,807	351,297
1998	21,255	45,183	7,232	1,042	12,733	63,310	212,509
1999	31,179	40,018	5,359	484	17,913	71,728	205,286
2000	18,250	33,494	5,946	611	15,411	57,937	141,329
2001	10,566	36,344	4,447	305	6,530	56,223	150,706
2002	5,467	32,750	5,991	2,949	11,632	64,952	150,217
2003	15,970	32,716	3,789	5,399	5,255	31,341	104,603
2004	17,045	46,767	3,433	584	5,813	47,183	174,400
2005:							
1st quarter	2,834	6,137	370	0	995	5,305	23,912
2d quarter	788	11,882	393	15	611	5,436	61,007
3d quarter	10,932	60,616	15,260	144	15,088	35,650	153,142
4th quarter	2,666	45,611	4,308	46	6,475	10,363	77,484
2005 total	17,220	124,246	20,331	205	23,169	56,754	315,545
2006:							
1st quarter	2,189	2,337	132	9	822	5,140	44,346
2d quarter	2,285	6,320	893	29	6,147	13,223	34,407
3d quarter	1,134	6,184	635	1,575	1,228	19,053	65,596
4th quarter	206	2,337	568	47	1,205	5,265	25,874
2006 total	5,815	17,179	2,228	1,659	9,401	42,681	170,223

Source: Forest Service, U.S. Department of Agriculture. Pacific Southwest Region includes California and Hawaii.

Table 86—Average stumpage prices for sawtimber sold on National Forests by selected species, Pacific Southwest Region, 1996-2006

(In dollars per thousand board feet)

Year and quarter	Douglas fir	Ponderosa and Jeffrey pines	Sugar pine	Lodgepole pine	Cedars	True firs	All species
1996	189.36	299.48	318.08	53.61	135.26	182.11	184.12
1997	183.17	237.48	212.37	71.66	114.66	181.90	169.37
1998	172.89	182.66	177.47	47.98	183.87	135.01	134.71
1999	157.97	210.83	224.25	114.12	131.15	138.13	137.39
2000	150.90	155.27	183.04	28.06	97.80	100.87	118.72
2001	129.85	126.54	219.65	50.47	110.68	78.74	87.81
2002	85.83	129.03	131.51	163.43	71.91	65.21	79.68
2003	124.91	86.09	47.77	145.26	39.10	70.87	83.97
2004	165.33	98.95	121.25	66.68	93.53	95.29	86.97
2005:							
1st quarter	150.91	78.69	88.33		231.63	30.38	78.66
2d quarter	155.71	110.08	235.83	28.81	290.59	217.79	113.48
3d quarter	173.02	82.82	108.52	48.16	185.69	73.42	100.14
4th quarter	34.81	26.10	28.20	3.42	42.64	19.07	29.71
2005 average	147.20	64.40	93.59	36.74	150.44	73.30	83.79
2006:							
1st quarter	26.11	45.39	138.94	96.96	72.53	111.23	81.91
2d quarter	40.96	95.12	104.96	36.35	61.02	162.05	115.65
3d quarter	92.72	76.06	192.32	17.14	112.32	96.09	73.59
4th quarter	722.56	106.93	43.01	11.62	139.10	151.59	113.20
2006 average	69.63	83.10	116.09	17.73	78.73	125.19	90.28

[a] Prices received for individual sales may vary significantly from the averages shown in this table because of differences n species mix, quality, road costs, logging and processing costs, size and length of sale, number of bidders, and other related price determinants. Before 1984, prices for stumpage on National Forest lands are statistical high bids. The statistical high bid is defined as the bid price minus credits for road costs; it includes an allowance for sale area betterment (K V funds). Beginning in 1984, prices for stumpage on National Forest lands are high bid value. Road costs and an allowance for sale area betterment are included in the bid.

Source: Forest Service, U.S. Department of Agriculture. Pacific Southwest Region includes California and Hawaii.

Table 87—Volume and average value of timber harvested on the National Forests of the Pacific Southwest Region, 2006

(Volume in million board feet; value in dollars per thousand board feet)

Quarter	Angeles Volume	Angeles Average value	Cleveland Volume	Cleveland Average value	Eldorado Volume	Eldorado Average value	Inyo Volume	Inyo Average value	Klamath [b] Volume	Klamath [b] Average value
1st qtr.	0.2	31.98	0		3.5	31.34	0.3	26.11	7.1	59.36
2d qtr.	.1	77.56	0		23.4	40.26	0.1	52.48	7.7	128.10
3d qtr.	.2	69.89	0		19.4	57.13	0.9	33.81	5.2	9.50
4th qtr.	.1	63.89	.1	53.33	11.8	50.41	1.5	33.87	3.5	85.81
Total	.6	56.97	.1	53.33	58.1	47.42	2.8	33.83	23.5	74.97

Quarter	Lassen Volume	Lassen Average value	Los Padres Volume	Los Padres Average value	Mendocino Volume	Mendocino Average value	Modoc Volume	Modoc Average value	Plumas Volume	Plumas Average value
1st qtr.	a	1,037.90	a	22.86	.2	10.00	1.3	4.39	1.4	53.13
2d qtr.	5.3	53.35	a	28.28	a	10.00	2.6	0.84	10.3	32.68
3d qtr.	23.7	43.75	a	23.64	.5	27.26	4.1	5.61	29.2	52.75
4th qtr.	14.7	33.82	a	22.00	.4	10.00	3.8	9.40	8.0	65.71
Total	43.7	40.62	.2	23.88	1.1	17.93	11.8	5.65	49.0	50.65

Quarter	San Bernardino Volume	San Bernardino Average value	Sequoia Volume	Sequoia Average value	Shasta Trinity Volume	Shasta Trinity Average value	Sierra Volume	Sierra Average value	Six Rivers Volume	Six Rivers Average value
1st qtr.	1.8	13.86	.9	42.19	13.2	130.77	0.8	24.24	.4	24.36
2d qtr.	.4	10.37	1.5	135.84	9.5	178.51	1.6	33.43	.7	16.23
3d qtr.	.5	7.94	3.7	89.05	9.4	116.95	8.3	30.20	2.5	33.65
4th qtr.	.9	14.28	2.2	51.14	20.6	136.11	4.3	25.08	5.2	26.61
Total	3.7	12.70	8.3	82.17	52.7	139.02	14.0	28.75	8.8	27.66

Quarter	Stanislaus Volume	Stanislaus Average value	Tahoe Volume	Tahoe Average value	LTBMU [c] Volume	LTBMU [c] Average value	All Forests Volume	All Forests Average value
1st qtr.	1.3	12.93	5.4	21.37	a	2143.75	38.0	66.88
2d qtr.	2.8	36.33	1.9	68.53	a	11.09	68.2	70.09
3d qtr.	6.2	38.69	13.1	16.13	.1	34.03	127.1	47.55
4th qtr.	8.5	47.52	18.4	21.68	.9	10.65	104.8	57.24
Total	18.8	40.49	38.8	22.10	1.1	14.30	338.1	57.27

[a] Less than 0.1 million board feet.

[b] Includes a small portion of the Forest that lies in southern Oregon.

[c] Lake Tahoe Basin Management Unit.

Source: Forest Service, U.S. Department of Agriculture. Pacific Southwest Region includes California and Hawaii.

Table 88—Monthly stumpage volume and average value of timber sold on National Forest lands in Washington and Oregon, 2004-2006

(Volume in million board feet; average value in dollars per thousand board feet)

Year and month	East side Volume	East side Average value	West side Volume	West side Average value	Pacific Northwest Region Volume	Pacific Northwest Region Average value
2004:						
January	23	78.76	0		23	78.76
February	0		a	525.71	a	525.71
March	0		23	105.17	23	105.17
April	67	37.10	5	119.05	72	42.33
May	77	55.97	12	120.48	89	64.43
June	7	85.50	10	171.96	16	136.97
July	11	56.42	94	51.26	105	51.81
August	1	109.33	42	31.99	42	32.94
September	57	86.06	44	56.97	101	73.30
October	66	74.93	6	125.45	72	79.12
November	23	147.30	20	82.09	43	117.34
December	25	50.54	30	21.45	55	34.45
Total	356	68.44	285	62.38	641	65.75
2005:						
January	42	42.57	4	177.25	46	53.62
February	7	38.70	12	205.71	19	144.52
March	a	44.40	3	210.84	3	209.25
April	1	34.25	2	236.64	3	182.26
May	8	107.33	21	139.40	29	130.63
June	24	115.92	17	153.46	41	131.38
July	29	72.14	0		29	72.14
August	85	79.94	20	128.39	105	89.28
September	7	139.26	34	178.91	42	172.08
October	63	119.00	40	169.53	103	136.77
November	7	50.43	8	109.76	16	82.15
December	a	170.34	16	140.44	16	140.58
Total	273	85.89	179	160.36	452	115.36
2006:						
January	1	53.27	4	54.50	5	54.28
February	9	120.90	7	284.12	16	180.06
March	30	69.06	3	203.28	33	80.58
April	3	117.81	20	128.85	23	127.22
May	5	91.48	3	169.16	8	121.74
June	12	149.32	28	40.00	41	73.27
July	8	72.53	18	94.15	26	87.42
August	46	73.73	30	104.02	76	85.77
September	43	87.15	81	168.45	124	140.21
October	28	87.60	14	100.65	42	91.86
November	24	61.02	14	227.00	38	122.69
December	5	54.32	5	130.77	11	93.94
Total	215	83.11	227	134.98	442	109.73

[a] Less than 1 million board feet.

Note: These figures are preliminary.

Source: Forest Service, U.S. Department of Agriculture.

Table 89—Volume of timber sold on publicly owned or managed lands, Washington and Oregon, 2002-2006

(In thousand board feet, Scribner scale)

Agency	2002	2003	2004	2005		2006				
				Total	4th qtr.	1st qtr.	2d qtr.	3d qtr.	4th qtr.	Total
Western Washington:										
USDA Forest Service[a]	16,335	37,007	43,902	40,897	16,868	902	3,241	2,981	10,489	17,614
U.S. Bur. Land Mgmt.	0	0	0	NA	NA	NA	NA	NA	NA	NA
State of Washington[b]	45,805	374,056	420,515	NA	NA	NA	NA	NA	NA	NA
Total	62,140	411,063	464,417	NA	NA	NA	NA	NA	NA	NA
Eastern Washington:										
USDA Forest Service[a]	59,018	98,043	41,618	84,647	21,157	9,833	20,268	52,759	24,187	107,047
U.S. Bur. Land Mgmt.	138	0	0	NA	NA	NA	NA	NA	NA	NA
State of Washington[b]	b	98,685	79,799	NA	NA	NA	NA	NA	NA	NA
Total	59,156	196,727	121,417	NA	NA	NA	NA	NA	NA	NA
Western Oregon:										
USDA Forest Service[a]	151,224	182,735	173,204	145,534	50,709	22,150	60,902	120,533	19,895	223,480
U.S. Bur. Land Mgmt.	104,936	215,077	171,442	174,100	NA	NA	NA	NA	NA	419
State of Oregon	221,058	237,277	244,358	290,799	47,425	87,600	96,500	54,400	36,100	274,600
Total	477,218	635,089	589,004	610,433	98,134	NA	NA	NA	NA	498,499
Eastern Oregon:										
USDA Forest Service[a]	113,972	101,152	261,315	180,089	59	24,986	26,662	53,472	49,041	154,161
U.S. Bur. Land Mgmt.	107	5,239	2,360	NA	NA	NA	NA	NA	NA	30
State of Oregon	2,692	1,746	8,276	11,275	11,275	0	0	8,000	0	8,000
Total	116,771	108,137	271,951	NA	NA	NA	NA	NA	NA	162,191
All public lands:										
USDA Forest Service[a]	340,549	418,937	520,039	451,167	147,668	58,871	111,073	229,745	103,613	502,302
U.S. Bur. Land Mgmt.	105,182	220,315	173,802	NA	NA	NA	NA	NA	NA	449
State of Washington[b]	45,805	472,741	500,314	NA	NA	NA	NA	NA	NA	NA
State of Oregon	223,750	239,023	252,634	302,074	58,700	87,600	96,500	62,400	36,100	282,600
Total	715,286	1,351,015	1,446,789	NA	NA	NA	NA	NA	NA	NA

Note: The U.S. Bureau of Indian Affairs land is now privately owned and no longer managed by the BIA. That category has been dropped.

NA = not available.

[a] Convertible products only.

[b] Excludes sales under $20,000.

Source: Respective agencies listed.

Table 90—Average stumpage prices of timber sold on publicly owned or managed lands, Washington and Oregon, 2002-2006

(In dollars per thousand board feet)

Agency	2002	2003	2004	2005 Total	2005 4th qtr.	2006 1st qtr.	2006 2d qtr.	2006 3d qtr.	2006 4th qtr.	2006 Total
Western Washington:										
USDA Forest Service[a]	55.32	102.86	76.40	148.61	191.61	15.78	118.05	104.76	26.10	55.80
U.S. Bur. Land Mgmt.				NA	NA	NA	NA	NA	NA	NA
State of Washington[b]	177.89	289.17	327.33	NA	NA	NA	NA	NA	NA	NA
Average	145.67	272.40	303.60	NA	NA	NA	NA	NA	NA	NA
Eastern Washington:										
USDA Forest Service[a]	97.47	71.25	111.42	100.77	98.54	50.20	104.73	79.07	92.10	84.22
U.S. Bur. Land Mgmt.	95.70			NA	NA	NA	NA	NA	NA	NA
State of Washington[b]	b	182.56	298.63	NA	NA	NA	NA	NA	NA	NA
Average	97.47	127.09	234.46	NA	NA	NA	NA	NA	NA	NA
Western Oregon:										
USDA Forest Service[a]	184.74	152.82	119.14	141.41	170.23	133.52	113.65	157.17	220.99	148.65
U.S. Bur. Land Mgmt.	153.93	111.75	125.21	197.51	NA	NA	NA	NA	NA	204.80
State of Oregon	342.63	294.04	340.14	377.40	394.49	415.53	373.06	375.00	368.42	386.38
Average	251.10	191.67	212.59	269.83	278.61	NA	NA	NA	NA	279.65
Eastern Oregon:										
USDA Forest Service[a]	49.49	45.13	80.27	89.78	97.36	73.21	72.08	71.71	45.85	63.82
U.S. Bur. Land Mgmt.	119.44	58.05	107.43	NA	NA	NA	NA	NA	NA	45.40
State of Oregon	196.38	152.32	195.92	259.71	259.71			262.50		262.50
Average	52.94	47.48	84.02	NA	NA	NA	NA	NA	NA	73.62
All public lands:										
USDA Forest Service[a]	118.14	103.32	95.38	113.83	133.32	91.49	102.17	118.68	88.28	105.63
U.S. Bur. Land Mgmt.	153.81	110.48	124.97	NA	NA	NA	NA	NA	NA	NA
State of Washington[b]	177.89	266.92	322.75	NA	NA	NA	NA	NA	NA	NA
State of Oregon	340.87	293.00	335.41	373.01	368.60	415.53	373.06	360.58	368.42	382.87
Average	196.88	195.29	219.48	NA	NA	NA	NA	NA	NA	NA

Note: The U.S. Bureau of Indian Affairs land is now privately owned and no longer managed by the BIA. That category has been dropped.

NA = not available.

[a] Prices received for individual sales may vary significantly from the averages shown in this table because of differences in species mix, quality, road costs, logging and processing costs, size and length of sale, number of bidders, and other related price determinants. Prices for stumpage on National Forest land are high bid value. Road costs and an allowance for sale area betterment are included in the bid.

[b] Excludes sales under $20,000.

Source: Respective agencies listed.

Table 91—Volume of sawtimber sold on National Forests by selected species, Pacific Northwest Region, 1995-2006

(Volume in thousand board feet Scribner scale)

Year and quarter	Douglas-fir West side	Douglas-fir East side	Ponderosa and Jeffrey pines	Sugar pine	White pine	Lodgepole pine	Engelmann spruce	Sitka spruce	Western hemlock	Cedars[a]	Larch	Noble fir and Shasta red fir	Other true firs	All species
1995	161 107	72 291	87 349	2 885	985	31 194	1 568	176	29 358	8 012	7 953	19 606	51 284	499 871
1996	66 447	319 093	89 490	15 443	824	34 968	1 870	279	32 291	3 326	12 484	10 883	128 497	769 512
1997	61 852	179 294	55 173	2 086	2 560	17 884	82	1 186	24 553	2 243	3 374	11 156	50 661	452 332
1998	31 883	115 978	90 082	299	535	41 860	47	937	17 235	2 204	1 142	3 369	89 777	413 415
1999	18 922	92 888	58 382	380	898	33 223	196	7	10 241	1 450	2 375	4 970	36 114	278 439
2000	23	63 493	34 857	157	0	15 880	7	10	182	1 283	38	0	37 894	155 084
2001	12 326	55 614	21 642	19	0	35 418	669	0	7 954	1 093	678	0	28 276	170 771
2002	24 665	110 040	28 268	0	19	23 311	0	1 094	11 408	1 133	4 165	3 339	31 942	257 780
2003	20 523	191 225	32 050	462	25	22 887	958	5	33 855	4 451	11	90	37 639	352 337
2004	8 969	201 727	121 327	3 897	25	13 394	12	294	23 232	2 871	188	272	68 296	456 744
2005														
1st quarter	1 982	43 408	21 921	0	0	1 381	0	0	0	0	0	0	9 736	81 668
2d quarter	1 601	25 265	5 180	0	0	1 741	40	0	10 248	906	64	0	3 136	48 705
3d quarter	0	69 306	25 411	0	24	3 322	0	0	8 555	2 965	4	0	23 302	133 858
4th quarter	0	76 650	14 247	0	0	7 475	780	0	1 520	169	0	0	22 804	123 757
2005 total	3 582	214 629	66 758	0	24	13 919	819	0	20 323	4 040	68	0	58 978	387 988
2006														
1st quarter	0	18 269	11 576	7	0	5 489	595	0	968	0	0	0	12 036	48 946
2d quarter	0	55 145	3 671	0	20	12 217	0	0	8 542	254	5	736	8 288	89 010
3d quarter	0	130 451	25 999	0	97	6 819	646	0	4 486	367	351	0	35 756	204 971
4th quarter	0	33 749	16 876	0	10	9 411	93	0	5 025	1 894	0	0	7 105	74 174
2006 total	0	237 614	58 122	7	127	33 937	1 334	0	19 021	2 514	356	736	63 186	417 101

[a] Includes Port-Orford-cedar, Alaska cedar, incense cedar, and western redcedar.

Source: Forest Service, U.S. Department of Agriculture. Pacific Northwest Region includes Oregon and Washington and a small portion of northern California.

Table 92—Average stumpage prices for sawtimber sold on National Forests by selected species, Pacific Northwest Region, 1995-2006[a]

(In dollars per thousand board feet)

Year and quarter	Douglas-fir West side	Douglas-fir East side	Ponderosa and Jeffrey pines	Sugar pine	White pine	Lodgepole pine	Engelmann spruce	Sitka spruce	Western hemlock	Cedars[b]	Larch	Noble fir and Shasta red fir	Other true firs	All species
1995	453.38	143.57	253.19	433.58	488.33	136.01	146.22	175.10	291.84	86.56	271.48	285.36	217.78	295.34
1996	398.98	267.68	165.67	58.21	328.74	96.62	60.19	107.67	221.28	497.17	217.49	204.30	139.36	231.78
1997	291.26	284.50	164.38	394.16	250.67	144.24	109.56	109.04	191.38	1174.33	156.28	227.50	128.18	240.46
1998	201.64	199.64	122.17	473.97	233.02	82.66	56.07	74.99	101.41	268.01	218.60	165.08	84.17	139.30
1999	393.98	202.87	139.91	127.31	270.75	94.92	62.15	93.23	77.69	196.44	278.23	273.58	127.35	180.67
2000	747.86	123.20	111.36	397.16	—	144.98	84.59	139.46	158.32	560.04	65.16	—	97.38	120.63
2001	255.38	127.66	83.98	177.15	—	101.62	257.05	—	56.14	283.17	156.14	—	62.38	116.31
2002	152.56	189.52	87.75	—	10.00	149.59	—	85.71	64.71	329.65	177.18	24.43	62.63	158.74
2003	236.85	146.15	54.99	75.91	125.86	77.24	79.83	23.85	92.86	170.69	120.00	633.41	47.50	121.36
2004	105.15	138.35	93.47	98.63	274.46	100.18	65.00	173.91	50.52	113.61	86.83	75.29	74.85	107.31
2005														
1st quarter	321.44	125.38	60.09	—	—	75.81	—	—	—	—	—	—	13.48	93.68
2d quarter	344.64	168.41	49.81	—	—	62.56	243.58	—	52.71	340.48	283.65	—	63.10	128.59
3d quarter	—	162.13	74.21	—	206.34	174.81	—	—	81.42	227.55	294.02	—	91.31	129.16
4th quarter	—	177.71	135.57	—	—	84.32	113.39	—	146.37	255.76	—	—	128.18	157.32
2005 average	331.81	161.00	80.77	—	206.34	102.35	119.67	—	71.80	254.08	284.29	—	91.22	130.60
2006														
1st quarter	—	156.41	91.09	40.38	—	127.00	142.90	—	44.35	—	—	—	38.04	106.16
2d quarter	—	124.95	70.17	—	226.90	140.01	—	—	110.64	482.27	11.54	253.00	113.74	124.46
3d quarter	—	153.80	74.64	—	288.92	91.37	218.76	—	79.82	147.80	279.92	—	97.51	130.72
4th quarter	—	146.72	57.71	—	83.12	89.29	191.94	—	45.99	413.66	—	—	75.11	112.35
2006 average	—	146.30	72.72	40.38	262.63	114.07	183.04	—	82.92	381.81	275.99	253.00	85.79	123.24

[a] Prices for individual sales may vary significantly from the averages shown in this table because of differences in species mix, quality, road costs, logging and processing costs, size and length of sale, number of bidders, and other related price-determinants. Before 1984 prices for stumpage on National Forest lands are stated as high bids. The stated stumpage high bid is defined as the bid price minus credits for road costs to include an allowance for sale-area betterment (K-V funds). Beginning in 1984 prices for stumpage on National Forest lands are high bid value. Road costs and an allowance for sale-area betterment are included in the bid.

[b] includes Port-Orford-cedar, Alaska cedar, incense cedar, and western redcedar.

Source: Forest Service, U.S. Department of Agriculture, Pacific Northwest Region, includes Oregon and Washington and a small portion of northern California.

Figure 7—Average stumpage prices for sawtimber sold on National Forests, Pacific Northwest Region, in dollars per thousand board feet

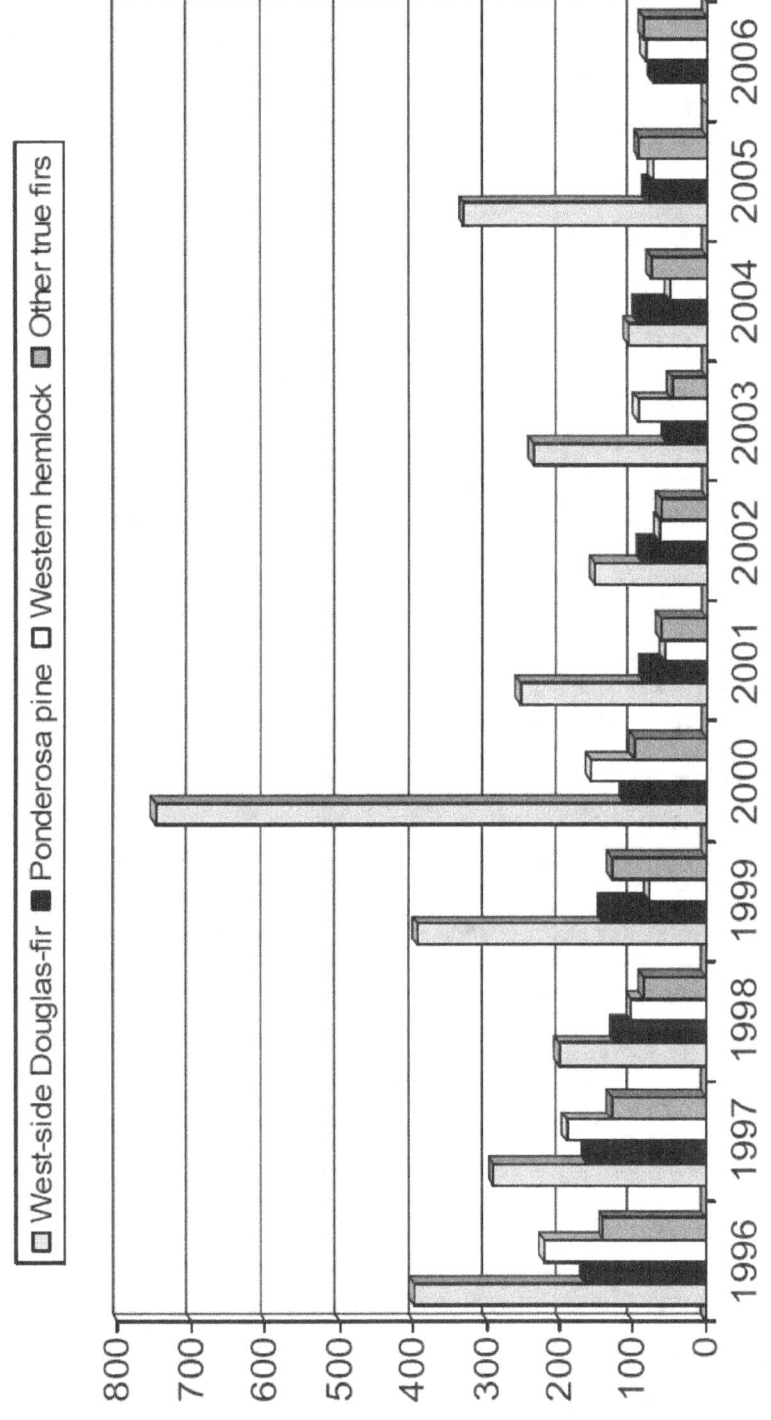

Table 93—Volume and average value of timber harvested on the National Forests of the Pacific Northwest Region, 2006

(Volume in million board feet; value in dollars per thousand board feet)

Quarter	Colville Volume	Colville Average value	Deschutes Volume	Deschutes Average value	Fremont Volume	Fremont Average value	Gifford Pinchot Volume	Gifford Pinchot Average value	Malheur Volume	Malheur Average value
1st qtr.	4.9	138.27	16.0	53.74	.7	21.81	2.3	202.60	4.6	85.29
2d qtr.	1.7	151.23	16.5	53.38	.2	12.22	2.7	2,088.19	3.1	122.47
3d qtr.	9.6	92.65	7.8	72.17	3.9	24.48	1.9	92.68	.7	118.23
4th qtr.	11.8	87.44	14.4	23.15	9.3	4.78	3.2	75.17	5.9	35.69
Total	28.0	101.92	54.7	48.23	14.1	11.25	10.1	644.22	14.3	62.07

Quarter	Mount Baker Snoqualmie Volume	Mount Baker Snoqualmie Average value	Mount Hood Volume	Mount Hood Average value	Ochoco Volume	Ochoco Average value	Okanogan Volume	Okanogan Average value	Olympic Volume	Olympic Average value
1st qtr.	.1	24.70	1.7	97.26	1.8	45.48	7.4	111.98	6.5	130.82
2d qtr.	.1	55.42	4.6	85.40	.6	14.35	1.9	73.29	5.6	101.09
3d qtr.	.5	45.40	8.8	64.61	1.9	21.05	1.6	40.27	2.5	276.66
4th qtr.	1.9	101.11	4.0	5.58	2.1	18.71	3.3	88.34	3.1	141.22
Total	2.5	87.62	19.1	60.24	6.5	26.60	14.3	93.07	17.7	143.83

Quarter	Rogue River [a] Volume	Rogue River [a] Average value	Siskiyou [a] Volume	Siskiyou [a] Average value	Siuslaw Volume	Siuslaw Average value	Umatilla Volume	Umatilla Average value	Umpqua Volume	Umpqua Average value
1st qtr.	.1	92.38	.8	278.97	8.9	160.45	1.5	41.85	.1	94.63
2d qtr.	.7	10.76	6.5	218.82	2.2	117.77	4.3	53.77	.3	33.83
3d qtr.	1.8	227.04	10.4	186.31	7.0	131.03	8.4	75.09	3.5	141.41
4th qtr.	1.0	232.51	8.2	189.15	10.2	110.98	10.9	11.60	5.2	79.92
Total	3.5	174.69	26.0	198.11	28.3	132.08	12.1	58.43	9.1	102.52

Quarter	Wallowa Whitman Volume	Wallowa Whitman Average value	Wenatchee Volume	Wenatchee Average value	Willamette Volume	Willamette Average value	Winema Volume	Winema Average value	Western Oregon Volume	Western Oregon Average value
1st qtr.	2.0	177.05	8.0	105.03	9.4	165.86	6.1	72.41	21.0	160.12
2d qtr.	1.1	64.82	9.0	68.55	5.1	259.72	2.5	116.94	19.4	176.78
3d qtr.	6.6	37.28	5.9	46.10	13.1	204.66	5.2	101.97	44.5	156.90
4th qtr.	6.3	15.74	1.9	28.11	12.2	152.53	10.0	72.90	40.8	128.08
Total	16.1	47.91	24.9	71.90	39.8	186.65	23.8	83.74	125.7	151.16

Quarter	Eastern Oregon Volume	Eastern Oregon Average value	Western Washington Volume	Western Washington Average value	Eastern Washington Volume	Eastern Washington Average value	All Forests Volume	All Forests Average value
1st qtr.	32.4	67.08	8.8	149.02	20.8	115.16	82.9	111.35
2d qtr.	26.8	66.35	8.4	734.85	14.2	77.62	68.8	181.47
3d qtr.	32.8	58.11	4.9	182.65	19.1	70.49	101.3	109.83
4th qtr.	49.7	29.73	8.2	105.93	26.2	62.37	124.9	73.69
Total	141.7	51.76	30.3	305.44	80.3	80.66	378.0	111.26

[a] Includes a small portion of the Forest that lies in northern California.

Source: Forest Service, U.S. Department of Agriculture. Pacific Northwest Region includes Oregon and Washington and a small portion of northern California.

Table 94—Volume and average stumpage price of selected species sold on the National Forests of the Pacific Northwest Region, 2006 [a][b]

(Volume in thousand board feet, Scribner scale; value in dollars per thousand board feet)

National Forest	Douglas-fir West side Volume	Value	Douglas-fir East side Volume	Value	Ponderosa and Jeffrey pines Volume	Value	Western hemlock Volume	Value	True firs[c] Volume	Value	All species Volume	Value
Western Oregon:												
Mount Hood--												
1st quarter	2,461	73.80	1,018	305.52	697	105.85	891	48.20	0	--	6,944	114.72
2d quarter	2,470	188.72	0	--	0	--	0	--	0	--	3,205	145.95
3d quarter	8,088	291.58	1,362	131.61	947	204.55	776	225.87	0	--	15,491	194.77
4th quarter	3,875	290.58	0	--	0	--	0	--	0	--	3,983	282.73
Total and average	16,894	244.59	2,380	206.00	1,644	162.70	1,667	130.91	0	--	29,623	182.55
Rogue River--												
1st quarter	0	--	0	--	0	--	0	--	0	--	0	--
2d quarter	0	--	0	--	0	--	0	--	0	--	0	--
3d quarter	12,142	223.50	0	--	692	192.52	0	--	5,961	183.76	18,795	209.76
4th quarter	0	--	0	--	0	--	0	--	0	--	0	--
Total and average	12,142	223.50	0	--	692	192.52	0	--	5,961	183.76	18,795	209.76
Siskiyou--												
1st quarter	771	295.39	0	--	0	--	0	--	0	--	771	295.39
2d quarter	14,618	20.53	0	--	0	--	0	--	0	--	14,918	20.56
3d quarter	15,107	110.79	0	--	0	--	0	--	0	--	15,107	110.79
4th quarter	0	--	0	--	0	--	0	--	0	--	0	--
Total and average	30,496	72.19	0	--	0	--	0	--	0	--	30,796	71.70
Siuslaw--												
1st quarter	5,783	282.62	0	--	0	--	0	--	0	--	5,783	282.62
2d quarter	10,229	223.08	0	--	0	--	3,704	44.11	0	--	14,012	174.62
3d quarter	0	--	0	--	0	--	0	--	0	--	0	--
4th quarter	6,120	170.78	0	--	0	--	0	--	0	--	6,120	170.78
Total and average	22,132	224.18	0	--	0	--	3,704	44.11	0	--	25,915	197.81
Umpqua--												
1st quarter	0	--	0	--	0	--	0	--	0	--	0	--
2d quarter	5,715	77.75	0	--	262	61.36	0	--	2,211	54.91	8,218	70.80
3d quarter	35,052	164.14	0	--	1,287	139.51	3,359	40.05	1,194	142.21	41,592	149.98
4th quarter	8,403	258.60	0	--	1,381	170.33	1,062	173.80	0	--	10,846	239.06
Total and average	49,170	170.24	0	--	2,930	147.04	4,421	72.18	3,405	85.52	60,656	155,18
Willamette--												
1st quarter	0	--	0	--	0	--	0	--	0	--	0	--
2d quarter	10,448	24.56	0	--	0	--	0	--	0	--	10,448	24.56
3d quarter	34,944	94.28	0	--	0	--	0	--	0	--	35,113	93.83
4th quarter	0	--	0	--	0	--	0	--	0	--	0	--
Total and average	45,392	78.23	0	--	0	--	0	--	0	--	45,561	77.94
All western Oregon:												
1st quarter	9,015	226.71	1,018	305.52	697	105.85	891	48.20	0	--	13,498	196.98
2d quarter	43,480	86.23	0	--	262	61.36	3,704	44.11	2,211	54.91	50,801	79.91
3d quarter	105,333	149.94	1,362	131.61	2,926	173.10	4,135	74.92	7,155	176.83	126,098	144.06
4th quarter	18,398	236.12	0	--	1,381	170.33	1,062	173.80	0	--	20,949	227.41
Total and average	176,226	147.14	2,380	206.00	5,266	157.91	9,792	71.56	9,366	148.05	211,346	140.28
Western Washington:												
Gifford Pinchot--												
1st quarter	0	--	0	--	0	--	0	--	0	--	0	--
2d quarter	280	399.98	0	--	0	--	0	--	0	--	280	399.98
3d quarter	284	95.98	0	--	0	--	22	30.27	0	--	306	91.26
4th quarter	5,875	37.19	0	--	0	--	3,963	11.74	0	--	9,838	26.94
Total and average	6,439	55.56	0	--	0	--	3,985	11.84	0	--	10,424	38.85
Mount Baker-Snoqualmie--												
1st quarter	0	--	0	--	0	--	0	--	0	--	0	--
2d quarter	0	--	0	--	0	--	0	--	0	--	0	--
3d quarter	0	--	0	--	0	--	0	--	0	--	0	--
4th quarter	0	--	0	--	0	--	0	--	0	--	0	--
Total and average	0	--	0	--	0	--	0	--	0	--	0	--
Olympic--												
1st quarter	0	--	0	--	0	--	0	--	0	--	0	--
2d quarter	0	--	0	--	0	--	0	--	0	--	19	1,105.26
3d quarter	1,979	125.23	0	--	0	--	479	19.34	0	--	2,458	104.59
4th quarter	314	184.90	0	--	0	--	1,905	82.86	0	--	2,747	112.02
Total and average	2,293	133.40	0	--	0	--	2,384	70.10	0	--	5,224	112.14

(Volume in thousand board feet, Scribner scale; value in dollars per thousand board feet)

National Forest	Douglas-fir West side Volume	Value	Douglas-fir East side Volume	Value	Ponderosa and Jeffrey pines Volume	Value	Western hemlock Volume	Value	True firs[c] Volume	Value	All species Volume	Value
All western Washington:												
1st quarter	0	--	0	--	0	--	0	--	0	--	0	--
2d quarter	280	399.98	0	--	0	--	0	--	0	--	299	444.80
3d quarter	2,263	121.56	0	--	0	--	501	19.82	0	--	2,764	103.12
4th quarter	6,189	44.68	0	--	0	--	5,868	34.83	0	--	12,585	45.51
Total and average	8,732	76.00	0	--	0	--	6,369	33.65	0	--	15,648	63.31
All western Oregon and western Washington:												
1st quarter	9,015	226.71	1,018	305.52	697	105.85	891	48.20	0	--	13,498	196.98
2d quarter	43,760	88.23	0	--	262	61.36	3,704	44.11	2,211	54.91	51,100	82.05
3d quarter	107,596	149.34	1,362	131.61	2,926	173.10	4,636	68.97	7,155	176.83	128,862	143.18
4th quarter	24,587	187.93	0	--	1,381	170.33	6,930	56.13	0	--	33,534	159.15
Total and average	184,958	143.79	2,380	206.00	5,266	157.91	16,161	56.61	9,366	148.05	226,994	134.98
Eastern Oregon:												
Deschutes--												
1st quarter	0	--	0	--	697	245.24	0	--	0	--	3,848	101.75
2d quarter	0	--	167	95.16	276	297.02	0	--	492	202.85	7,483	122.59
3d quarter	0	--	201	86.50	401	91.72	0	--	3,066	59.64	5,773	71.16
4th quarter	0	--	8,347	38.65	287	207.47	0	--	204	168.38	11,542	52.54
Total and average	0	--	8,715	40.84	1,661	210.25	0	--	3,762	84.26	28,646	81.20
Fremont--												
1st quarter	0	--	0	--	746	77.31	0	--	3,359	151.60	5,188	121.17
2d quarter	0	--	0	--	2,404	50.60	0	--	507	99.31	2,911	59.09
3d quarter	0	--	0	--	7,913	39.36	0	--	517	84.08	8,533	42.85
4th quarter	0	--	0	--	1,790	138.16	0	--	0	--	8,026	87.32
Total and average	0	--	0	--	12,853	57.43	0	--	4,383	137.59	24,658	75.72
Malheur--												
1st quarter	0	--	0	--	0	--	992	12.42	3,927	6.56	4,919	7.74
2d quarter	0	--	428	85.95	898	65.39	0	--	1,271	110.87	3,608	84.65
3d quarter	0	--	1,655	159.99	5,852	100.29	0	--	2,191	155.01	10,747	112.90
4th quarter	0	--	871	67.27	1,999	33.82	0	--	2,867	46.43	6,932	37.75
Total and average	0	--	2,954	121.93	8,749	81.52	992	12.42	10,256	62.35	26,206	69.39
Ochoco--												
1st quarter	0	--	0	--	0	--	0	--	0	--	0	--
2d quarter	0	--	0	--	151	26.28	0	--	0	--	151	26.28
3d quarter	0	--	264	6.55	823	37.47	0	--	0	--	1,127	28.91
4th quarter	0	--	1,669	58.98	5,225	32.88	0	--	488	94.19	7,397	42.77
Total and average	0	--	1,933	51.82	6,199	33.33	0	--	488	94.19	8,675	40.68
Umatilla--												
1st quarter	0	--	0	--	0	--	0	--	0	--	0	--
2d quarter	0	--	38	156.38	0	12.75	0	--	60	86.92	131	88.39
3d quarter	0	--	11,098	65.88	6,157	12.81	0	--	10,870	31.70	29,025	43.10
4th quarter	0	--	0	--	0	--	0	--	1,860	188.23	3,646	113.17
Total and average	0	--	11,136	66.19	6,190	12.81	0	--	12,790	54.72	32,802	51.07
Wallowa-Whitman--												
1st quarter	0	--	0	--	0	--	0	--	0	--	0	--
2d quarter	0	--	36	163.00	0	--	0	--	0	--	36	163.00
3d quarter	0	--	2,836	75.74	2,104	65.29	0	--	4,711	79.20	14,051	65.66
4th quarter	0	--	92	88.19	0	--	0	--	216	78.01	355	70.57
Total and average	0	--	2,964	77.19	2,104	65.29	0	--	4,927	79.15	14,442	66.02
Winema--												
1st quarter	0	--	14	286.19	4,106	126.50	0	--	151	71.13	6,610	139.18
2d quarter	0	--	0	--	0	--	0	--	0	--	0	--
3d quarter	0	--	0	--	1,271	145.69	0	--	2,500	135.52	5,906	103.86
4th quarter	0	--	0	--	0	--	0	--	0	--	0	--
Total and average	0	--	14	286.19	5,377	131.03	0	--	2,651	131.85	12,516	122.51
All eastern Oregon:												
1st quarter	0	--	14	286.19	5,549	134.80	992	12.42	7,437	73.38	20,565	96.19
2d quarter	0	--	669	96.40	3,762	70.90	0	--	2,330	127.16	14,320	98.89
3d quarter	0	--	16,054	76.61	24,521	55.76	0	--	23,855	68.01	75,162	63.99
4th quarter	0	--	10,979	44.43	9,301	58.73	0	--	5,635	103.00	37,898	61.29
Total and average	0	--	27,716	64.44	43,133	67.89	992	12.42	39,257	77.56	147,945	71.15

Table 94--Volume and average stumpage price of selected species sold on the National Forests of the Pacific Northwest Region, 2006[a][b] (continued)

(Volume in thousand board feet, Scribner scale; value in dollars per thousand board feet)

National Forest	Douglas-fir West side Volume	Value	Douglas-fir East side Volume	Value	Ponderosa and Jeffrey pines Volume	Value	Western hemlock Volume	Value	True firs[c] Volume	Value	All species Volume	Value
Eastern Washington:												
Colville--												
1st quarter	0	--	8,087	57.24	88	78.86	0	--	0	--	10,316	76.79
2d quarter	0	--	2,701	197.45	0	--	0	--	532	126.62	6,441	200.29
3d quarter	0	--	4,814	123.07	0	--	587	0.98	1,121	134.63	7,982	143.68
4th quarter	0	--	10,120	47.60	550	115.60	0	--	1,955	65.62	16,300	102.74
Total and average	0	--	25,722	80.49	638	110.53	587	0.98	3,608	96.06	41,039	119.49
Okanogan --												
1st quarter	0	--	0	--	0	--	0	--	0	--	0	--
2d quarter	0	--	5,328	36.39	145	12.78	0	--	0	--	6,867	41.00
3d quarter	0	--	26	78.50	0	--	0	--	0	--	133	20.89
4th quarter	0	--	1,458	103.45	1,303	25.26	0	--	0	--	3,375	72.19
Total and average	0	--	6,812	50.90	1,448	24.01	0	--	0	--	10,375	50.89
Wenatchee --												
1st quarter	0	--	824	50.90	823	65.53	0	--	780	128.32	2,454	79.86
2d quarter	0	--	0	--	0	--	0	--	0	--	0	--
3d quarter	0	--	5,750	159.87	1,141	121.20	0	--	5,810	111.63	13,432	129.59
4th quarter	0	--	0	--	0	--	0	--	0	--	91	9.74
Total and average	0	--	6,574	146.21	1,964	97.87	0	--	6,590	113.61	15,977	121.27
All eastern Washington:												
1st quarter	0	--	8,911	56.66	911	66.82	0	--	780	128.32	12,770	77.38
2d quarter	0	--	8,029	90.57	145	12.78	0	--	532	126.62	13,308	118.10
3d quarter	0	--	10,590	142.94	1,141	121.20	587	0.98	6,931	115.35	21,547	134.14
4th quarter	0	--	11,578	54.64	1,853	52.07	0	--	1,955	65.62	19,766	97.09
Total and average	0	--	39,108	86.39	4,050	73.46	587	0.98	10,198	107.40	67,391	109.35
All eastern Oregon and eastern Washington:												
1st quarter	0	--	8,925	57.02	6,460	125.21	992	12.42	8,217	78.60	33,335	88.99
2d quarter	0	--	8,698	91.02	3,907	68.75	0	--	2,862	127.06	27,628	108.14
3d quarter	0	--	26,644	102.97	25,662	58.67	587	0.98	30,786	78.67	96,709	79.62
4th quarter	0	--	22,557	49.67	11,154	57.62	0	--	7,590	93.37	57,664	73.57
Total and average	0	--	66,824	77.28	47,183	68.37	1,579	8.17	49,455	83.71	215,336	83.11
Pacific Northwest Region:												
1st quarter	9,015	226.71	9,943	82.46	7,157	123.33	1,883	29.35	8,217	78.60	46,833	120.11
2d quarter	43,760	88.23	8,698	91.02	4,169	68.28	3,704	44.11	5,073	95.61	78,728	91.21
3d quarter	107,596	149.34	28,006	104.37	28,588	70.38	5,223	61.33	37,941	97.18	225,571	115.93
4th quarter	24,587	187.93	22,557	49.67	12,535	70.04	6,930	56.13	7,590	93.37	91,198	105.03
Total and average	184,958	143.79	69,204	81.71	52,449	77.36	17,740	52.31	58,821	93.96	442,330	109.73
All of Oregon:												
1st quarter	9,015	226.71	1,032	305.25	6,246	131.57	1,883	29.35	7,437	73.38	34,063	136.13
2d quarter	43,480	86.23	669	96.40	4,024	70.28	3,704	44.11	4,541	91.98	65,121	84.09
3d quarter	105,333	149.94	17,416	80.91	27,447	68.27	4,135	74.92	31,010	93.12	201,260	114.16
4th quarter	18,398	236.12	10,979	44.43	10,682	73.16	1,062	173.80	5,635	103.00	58,847	120.43
Total and average	176,226	147.14	30,096	75.64	48,399	77.69	10,784	66.12	48,623	91,14	359,291	111.82
All of Washington:												
1st quarter	0	--	8,911	56.66	911	66.82	0	--	780	128.32	12,770	77.38
2d quarter	280	399.98	8,029	90.57	145	12.78	0	--	532	126.62	13,607	125.27
3d quarter	2,263	121.56	10,590	142.94	1,141	121.20	1,088	9.66	6,931	115.35	24,311	130.61
4th quarter	6,189	44.68	11,578	54.64	1,853	52.07	5,868	34.84	1,955	65.62	32,351	77.03
Total and average	8,732	76.00	39,108	86.39	4,050	73.46	6,956	30.89	10,198	107.40	83,039	100.68

[a] Preliminary.

[b] Prices for individual sales may vary from the averages shown in this table because of differences in species mix, quality, road costs, logging and processing costs, size and length of sale, number of bidders, and other related price determinants. Prices for stumpage in National Forest lands are high bid value. Road costs and an allowance for sale-area betterment are included in the bid.

[c] Does not include noble fir or Shasta red fir.

Source: Forest Service, U.S. Department of Agriculture. Pacific Northwest Region includes Oregon and Washington and a small portion of northern California.

Table 95—Volume of timber sold on publicly owned or managed lands in Alaska, 2001-2006

(in thousand board feet Scribner scale)

Agency	2001	2002	2003	2004	2005			2006				
					Total	4th qtr	1st qtr	2d qtr	3d qtr	4th qtr	Total
USDA Forest Service[a]	52 838	23 669	56 094	88 858	81 815	41 664	6 290	16 967	20 110	3 320	46 687
US Bureau of Land Management[b]	0	336	0	0	NA	NA	NA	NA	NA	NA	NA
State of Alaska	NA	NA	18 605	NA	NA	NA	NA	NA	NA	NA	NA
Total	NA	NA	74 699	NA	NA	NA	NA	NA	NA	NA	NA

Note: The U.S. Bureau of Indian Affairs land is now privately owned and no longer managed by the BIA. That category has been dropped.

NA = not available.

[a] Convertible products only.

[b] Does not include cull, log sales, or volume given away through free use permits.

Source: Respective agencies listed.

Table 96—Average stumpage prices of timber sold on publicly owned or managed lands in Alaska, 2001-2006

(In dollars per thousand board feet)

Agency	2001	2002	2003	2004	2005		2006				
					Average	4th qtr	1st qtr	2d qtr	3d qtr	4th qtr	Average
USDA Forest Service[a]	34 70	41 65	23 05	10 45	14 67	14 27	10 05	9 88	10 02	26 97	11 18
U S Bureau of Land Manage[b]	--	33 33	--	--	NA	NA	NA	NA	NA	NA	NA
State of Alaska	NA	NA	NA	NA	14 95	NA	NA	NA	NA	NA	NA
Average	NA	NA	NA	NA	NA	NA	NA	NA	NA	NA	NA

Note: The U.S. Bureau of Indian Affairs land is now privately owned and no longer managed by the BIA. That category has been dropped.

NA = not available

[a] Prices received for individual sales may vary significantly from the averages shown in this table because of differences in species mix, quality, road costs, logging and processing costs, size and length of sale, number of bidders, and other related price determinants. Prices for stumpage on National Forest lands are higher in bid value. Road costs are not included in the bid.

[b] Does not include cull, log sales or volume given away through free use permits.

Source: Respective agencies listed.

153

Table 97—Volume of sawtimber sold on National Forests by selected species, Alaska Region, 1995-2006

(Volume in thousand board feet, Scribner scale)

Year and quarter	Sitka spruce	Western hemlock	Cedars	Other softwoods	All species
1995	10,560	41,131	1,548	1,229	54,468
1996	17,767	40,556	7,453	1,786	67,563
1997	31,844	87,704	20,790	4,583	144,922
1998	3,615	9,443	3,458	0	16,517
1999	26,358	70,913	18,501	238	116,008
2000	12,620	48,247	16,641	170	77,684
2001	11,935	27,243	8,396	590	48,164
2002	6,491	11,532	3,707	9	21,738
2003	20,459	18,136	8,450	0	47,062
2004	18,909	34,147	15,697	0	68,752
2005:					
1st qtr.	2,099	2,414	2,520	0	7,041
2d qtr.	12,521	3,082	467	19	16,093
3d qtr.	2,887	3,084	3,654	0	9,625
4th qtr.	10,186	21,335	3,682	0	35,203
2005 total	27,693	29,915	10,323	19	67,962
2006:					
1st qtr.	992	3,071	1,176	0	5,239
2d qtr.	3,134	8,576	2,758	0	14,468
3d qtr.	3,439	9,205	4,662	0	17,305
4th qtr.	684	1,410	753	0	2,847
2006 total	8,249	22,262	9,349	0	39,859

Source: Forest Service, U.S. Department of Agriculture. Alaska Region is the State of Alaska.

Table 98—Average stumpage prices for sawtimber sold on National Forests by selected species, Alaska Region, 1995-2006[a]

(In dollars per thousand board feet)

Year and quarter	Sitka spruce	Western hemlock	Cedars	Other softwoods	All species
1995	278.05	14.75	945.53	25.63	92.50
1996	551.87	1.27	668.55	43.04	220.78
1997	100.37	15.27	675.55	8.81	128.48
1998	123.88	7.34	195.63		70.54
1999	27.90	4.07	91.68	21.73	23.49
2000	96.85	3.20	139.98	25.31	47.77
2001	49.88	4.52	130.23	1.78	37.64
2002	97.75	1.62	85.30	19.57	44.60
2003	31.01	3.50	68.08		27.06
2004	17.27	2.66	29.71		12.86
2005:					
1st quarter	18.95	2.89	37.43		20.04
2d quarter	15.54	2.97	37.67	5.32	13.76
3d quarter	35.64	2.11	31.71		23.40
4th quarter	35.99	2.38	44.47		16.51
2005 average	25.42	2.45	37.93	5.32	17.20
2006:					
1st quarter	15.87	2.98	30.50		11.60
2d quarter	29.13	2.01	19.57		11.23
3d quarter	14.46	2.67	25.53		11.17
4th quarter	32.97	5.66	71.99		29.77
2006 average	21.74	2.65	28.14		12.58

[a] Prices received for individual sales may vary significantly from the averages shown in this table because of differences in species mix, quality, road costs, logging and processing costs, size and length of sale, number of bidders, and other related price determinants.

Source: Forest Service, U.S. Department of Agriculture. Alaska Region is the State of Alaska.

Table 99—Volume and average value of all species of all timber products sold from the USDA Forest Service Regions of the Western United States, 1995-2006[a]

(Volume in million board feet Scribner scale value in dollars per thousand board feet)

Year	Northern Region Volume	Northern Region Value	Rocky Mountain Region Volume	Rocky Mountain Region Value	Southwestern Region Volume	Southwestern Region Value	Intermountain Region Volume	Intermountain Region Value	Pacific Southwest Region Volume	Pacific Southwest Region Value	Pacific Northwest Region—eastside Volume	Pacific Northwest Region—eastside Value	Pacific Northwest Region—westside Volume	Pacific Northwest Region—westside Value	Alaska Region[b] Volume	Alaska Region[b] Value
1995	258.6	149.05	130.5	165.68	76.1	35.36	203.3	121.28	453.1	109.20	431.7	108.43	327.4	349.41	63.9	35.47
1996	478.6	127.50	94.8	96.36	37.8	23.68	299.4	61.34	480.2	117.08	595.8	86.11	532.0	235.86	74.5	165.54
1997	328.7	158.65	217.4	117.81	110.8	79.58	155.0	126.83	538.8	105.58	289.2	75.26	330.6	249.04	170.5	64.71
1998	246.4	121.97	148.9	74.96	87.0	38.04	131.7	113.76	400.4	81.51	392.1	70.42	160.4	162.68	19.6	47.68
1999	200.4	162.73	153.9	99.51	65.1	34.45	73.1	72.46	314.1	87.84	248.6	83.61	132.6	210.14	133.6	17.26
2000	145.8	144.05	53.0	55.25	67.7	17.05	50.9	89.88	213.1	85.43	223.5	80.95	10.5	133.26	92.4	40.56
2001	262.0	112.03	85.1	80.45	89.4	17.33	116.1	73.88	285.7	53.37	213.9	62.05	56.9	136.07	52.8	34.70
2002	195.3	65.49	91.4	89.93	66.2	17.06	66.1	67.55	244.4	55.18	173.0	65.86	167.6	171.58	23.7	41.65
2003	140.7	114.04	117.1	70.16	99.9	12.49	58.0	42.06	190.7	51.86	199.2	57.99	219.7	144.41	56.2	23.01
2004	210.0	126.98	151.8	63.71	109.9	8.35	125.9	77.22	334.2	52.77	302.9	84.55	217.1	110.50	88.9	10.45
2005																
1st qtr	84.0	96.74	29.0	67.02	15.0	27.05	11.8	107.36	36.0	59.18	35.2	77.86	52.1	95.66	8.8	16.57
2d qtr	35.0	136.40	40.3	91.87	24.6	19.24	9.6	44.41	107.0	66.59	32.3	54.73	32.5	146.21	20.7	11.28
3d qtr	65.7	93.80	43.2	69.09	48.0	11.32	31.8	67.65	183.7	84.42	117.2	105.55	34.2	147.68	10.7	21.22
4th qtr	38.9	125.12	28.1	65.62	33.6	14.19	27.2	83.12	99.7	29.62	80.1	97.67	67.6	175.57	41.7	14.27
Total and average	223.7	118.22	140.6	74.50	121.2	15.67	80.4	75.96	426.3	65.00	264.7	93.29	186.4	142.99	81.8	14.67
2006																
1st qtr	43.2	58.01	57.2	66.78	16.9	27.15	9.6	79.12	78.9	58.01	34.8	66.71	23.1	128.91	6.3	10.05
2d qtr	23.1	78.08	19.9	56.41	38.5	12.51	17.9	78.78	50.2	82.78	46.9	86.18	64.1	113.87	17.0	9.88
3d qtr	88.6	139.44	95.0	65.12	41.1	12.18	53.3	57.56	88.8	59.11	106.2	75.41	123.5	155.90	20.1	10.02
4th qtr	17.0	54.77	29.4	41.95	21.6	10.42	29.0	45.75	53.6	77.19	73.2	61.13	30.4	153.71	3.3	26.97
Total and average	171.9	102.29	201.6	61.35	118.2	14.11	109.8	59.79	271.5	66.74	261.2	72.18	241.1	141.86	46.7	11.18

[a] Northern Region includes Montana northeastern Washington northern Idaho North Dakota and northwestern South Dakota Rocky Mountain Region includes Colorado Kansas Nebraska remainder of South Dakota and eastern Wyoming Southwestern Region includes Arizona and New Mexico Intermountain Region includes southern Idaho Nevada Utah and western Wyoming Pacific Southwest Region includes California and Hawaii Pacific Northwest Region includes Oregon and Washington Alaska Region is all of Alaska

[b] Does not include long-term timber contracts

Source Respective Regions of the Forest Service U S Department of Agriculture

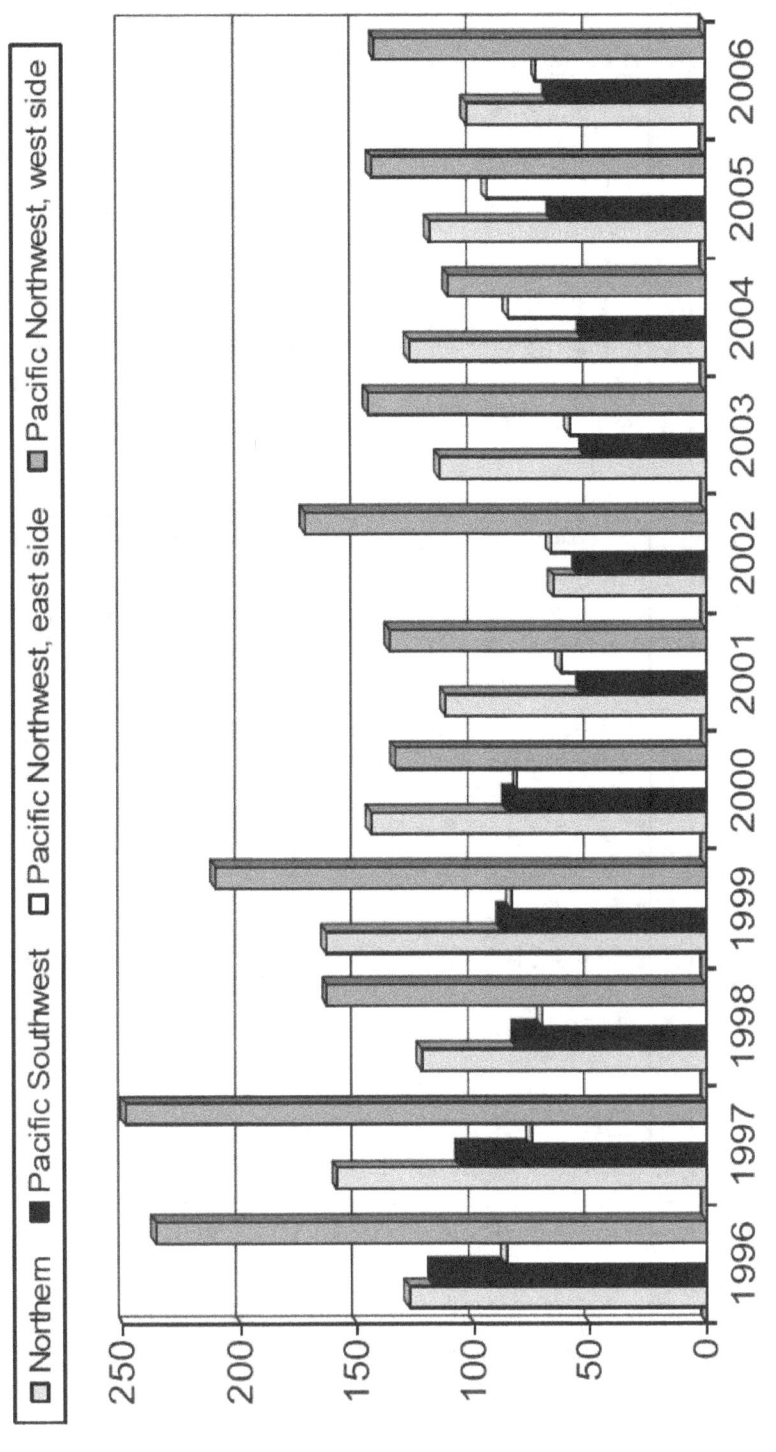

Figure 8—Average value of all timber products sold from Forest Service Regions of the Western United States, in dollars per thousand board feet

157

Table 100—Volume and average value of all species of timber harvested from the USDA Forest Service Regions of the Western United States, 1995-2006[a]

(Volume in million board feet. Scribner scale value in dollars per thousand board feet)

Year	Northern Region		Rocky Mountain Region		Southwestern Region		Intermountain Region		Pacific Southwest Region		Pacific Northwest Region—east side		Pacific Northwest Region—west side		Alaska Region	
	Volume	Value	Volume	Value	Volume	Value	Volume	Value	Volume	Value	Volume	Value	Volume	Value	Volume	Value
1995	325.6	184.72	184.8	120.51	78.0	66.30	215.9	122.72	544.1	209.44	489.3	183.37	320.5	349.66	199.7	66.34
1996	340.1	181.92	134.4	144.78	45.7	53.12	262.0	134.06	457.5	137.68	442.1	109.61	294.7	370.63	97.9	104.14
1997	352.1	161.91	129.1	169.16	97.4	76.26	200.1	154.35	548.0	125.84	474.8	123.58	334.8	336.93	124.6	16.41
1998	330.4	152.86	147.4	143.12	96.1	36.04	169.9	98.00	452.9	106.64	358.5	64.49	267.0	292.93	121.5	43.50
1999	265.4	149.76	139.9	118.51	75.7	49.79	133.1	96.64	441.4	93.54	316.2	76.70	217.2	230.04	153.6	37.69
2000	234.6	148.96	125.8	101.38	64.8	37.80	107.0	103.53	367.6	87.37	230.3	63.30	154.1	238.88	119.5	39.35
2001	171.5	125.00	140.6	70.76	72.8	35.08	80.6	92.71	297.2	46.45	210.0	59.11	52.0	166.46	44.4	37.50
2002	251.2	102.11	125.0	99.37	72.6	19.21	84.4	71.97	298.5	63.24	221.4	72.86	77.1	145.12	32.1	29.88
2003	233.1	99.11	113.3	80.66	71.7	15.05	69.8	63.90	284.1	50.79	229.4	58.89	91.5	135.21	48.2	31.01
2004	238.7	130.15	141.1	126.03	75.4	11.95	66.8	73.82	263.6	50.67	331.9	86.77	175.0	218.60	49.2	15.18
2005																
1st qtr	53.8	113.42	34.4	131.01	10.9	12.66	9.4	37.55	30.0	43.98	73.9	81.25	34.1	136.42	9.4	17.22
2d qtr	38.2	129.96	18.4	98.14	19.7	12.16	5.5	85.23	61.4	105.67	51.9	80.62	54.5	97.35	23.1	10.82
3d qtr	78.1	108.38	49.0	80.60	27.8	12.13	22.8	68.56	125.9	70.10	61.0	71.46	77.4	168.81	7.8	5.92
4th qtr	66.2	113.58	49.3	88.05	31.8	18.69	38.0	59.69	156.6	54.23	74.7	85.62	54.4	149.70	6.3	27.30
Total and average	236.3	114.47	151.1	96.67	90.3	14.51	75.7	61.47	374.0	67.20	261.5	80.09	220.3	141.41	46.6	13.53
2006																
1st qtr	41.5	120.87	38.7	108.71	22.2	22.21	8.6	59.00	38.0	66.88	53.2	85.87	29.8	156.85	10.5	13.10
2d qtr	17.0	111.04	24.6	83.59	19.2	20.30	4.4	76.02	68.2	70.09	41.0	70.25	27.8	345.29	9.0	27.59
3d qtr	46.2	133.64	40.4	66.19	16.5	13.65	29.1	65.63	127.1	47.55	52.0	62.67	49.4	159.45	17.4	12.34
4th qtr	48.0	40.68	59.7	51.51	36.4	11.85	34.1	44.56	104.7	57.24	75.9	40.99	49.0	124.38	3.2	16.12
Total and average	152.7	98.40	163.4	73.52	94.2	16.32	76.2	56.06	338.0	57.27	222.1	62.21	156.0	181.09	40.1	16.25

Note Negative stumpage value caused by emergency rate redeterminations.

[a] Northern Region includes Montana, northeastern Washington, northern Idaho, North Dakota and northwestern South Dakota. Rocky Mountain Region includes Colorado, Kansas, Nebraska, remainder of South Dakota and eastern Wyoming. Southwestern region includes Arizona and New Mexico. Intermountain Region includes southern Idaho, Nevada, Utah and western Wyoming. Pacific Southwest Region includes California and Hawaii. Pacific Northwest Region includes Oregon and Washington. Alaska Region is all of Alaska.

Source Respective Regions of the Forest Service. U.S. Department of Agriculture.

Table 101—Uncut volume under contract on National Forest lands in Montana, Idaho, California, Oregon, and Washington, 1996-2006[a]

(In million board feet, Scribner log rule)

| Year | California[b] | Montana | Idaho | | Oregon | Washington |
			Northern	Southern		
1996	519.5	323.7	249.2	375.7	503.4	209.7
1997	585.0	386.8	343.7	[c]282.5	1,176.4	342.5
1998	569.4	[c]291.6	[c]284.9	211.5	1,023.5	295.2
1999	467.6	294.7	247.5	162.9	929.4	240.3
2000	359.5	243.3	222.9	165.8	792.5	216.5
2001	278.6	196.5	196.7	187.1	682.9	197.5
2002	336.3	264.1	217.5	165.9	695.5	201.8
2003	305.4	234.9	142.0	106.9	741.6	150.8
2004	254.6	159.3	132.1	140.2	707.9	183.4
2005	353.5	196.1	118.6	162.1	667.0	162.0
2006	341.6	[d]182.5	[d]135.9	157.1	648.3	185.5

[a] As of June 30 unless otherwise noted.

[b] This figure is sawtimber volume only.

[c] As of September 30.

[d] As of December 31.

Source: Forest Service, U.S. Department of Agriculture; and Timber Data Company, Eugene, Oregon.

Table 102—Sale quantity and unyarded volume under contract on Bureau of Land Management lands in Western Oregon, 1996-2006

(In million board feet, Scribner scale)

Year	Sale quantity	Unyarded volume under contract	Ratio
1996	190	239	1.3
1997	212	275	1.3
1998	258	258	1.0
1999	62	214	3.4
2000	69	100	1.5
2001	56	113	2.0
2002	163	164	1.0
2003	163	207	1.3
2004	140	252	1.8
2005	174	285	1.6
2006	196	237	1.2

Source: Bureau of Land Management.

Table 103—Allowable annual cut and uncut volume under contract on Oregon State lands, 1996-2006[a]

(In million board feet, Scribner scale)

Year	Allowable cut	Uncut volume under contract	Ratio
1996	177	241	1.4
1997	177	267	1.5
1998	182	362	2.0
1999	225	339	1.5
2000	272	326	1.2
2001	226	301	1.3
2002	238	309	1.3
2003	254	268	1.1
2004	259	357	1.4
2005	298	294	1.0
2006	307	315	1.0

[a] As of December 31.

Source: State of Oregon, Department of Forestry.

Table 104—Sustainable harvest and uncut volume under contract on Washington State lands, 1996-2006[a]

(In million board feet, Scribner scale)

Year	Sustainable harvest	Uncut volume under contract	Ratio
1996	b	1,088	NA
1997	655	1,005	1.5
1998	655	1,034	1.6
1999	560	935	1.7
2000	560	806	1.4
2001	560	737	1.3
2002	560	731	1.3
2003	560	773	1.2
2004	560	680	1.2
2005	NA	NA	NA
2006	NA	NA	NA

NA = not available.

[a] As of June 30.

[b] Figure does not reflect environmental constraints; permitted or "sustainable" harvest is unknown.

Source: State of Washington, Department of Natural Resources.

Table 105—Small business set-aside sales and total sales on the National Forests, Pacific Northwest Region, 2001-2006

(Number of sales)

Quarter	Colville Set-aside sales	Colville Total sales	Deschutes Set-aside sales	Deschutes Total sales	Fremont Set-aside sales	Fremont Total sales	Gifford Pinchot Set-aside sales	Gifford Pinchot Total sales	Malheur Set-aside sales	Malheur Total sales
2001	1	8	0	22	1	4	1	1	0	9
2002	0	9	0	19	0	3	5	6	0	4
2003	0	12	0	15	0	6	2	8	0	8
2004	0	7	0	11	0	11	6	9	0	9
2005	0	10	0	12	0	7	1	6	0	5
2006:										
1st qtr.	0	1	2	2	0	1	0	0	0	1
2d qtr.	0	2	2	5	0	3	1	1	0	2
3d qtr.	0	2	1	4	1	3	0	1	0	5
4th qtr.	0	2	2	7	1	2	1	1	0	2
2006 total	0	7	7	18	2	9	2	3	0	10

Quarter	Mount Baker-Snoqualmie Set-aside sales	Mount Baker-Snoqualmie Total sales	Mount Hood Set-aside sales	Mount Hood Total sales	Ochoco Set-aside sales	Ochoco Total sales	Okanogan/Wenatchee Set-aside sales	Okanogan/Wenatchee Total sales	Olympic Set-aside sales	Olympic Total sales
2001	0	2	0	3	0	6	0	4	0	3
2002	0	2	1	9	0	1	2	4	0	0
2003	0	1	5	13	0	2	2	10	1	3
2004	3	3	1	2	0	5	2	7	3	3
2005	0	2	2	10	0	7	0	4	4	5
2006:										
1st qtr.	0	0	0	3	0	0	0	2	0	0
2d qtr.	0	0	0	3	0	1	0	0	0	1
3d qtr.	0	0	0	6	0	4	0	3	0	1
4th qtr.	0	0	0	1	0	2	0	6	0	1
2006 total	0	0	0	13	0	7	0	11	0	3

Quarter	Rogue River Set-aside sales	Rogue River Total sales	Siskiyou Set-aside sales	Siskiyou Total sales	Siuslaw Set-aside sales	Siuslaw Total sales	Umatilla Set-aside sales	Umatilla Total sales	Umpqua Set-aside sales	Umpqua Total sales
2001	0	0	0	3	0	8	0	9	0	1
2002	0	5	0	12	0	18	0	7	0	6
2003	0	3	0	15	2	8	0	3	0	4
2004	0	0	0	14	3	7	2	11	0	11
2005	1	3	1	8	1	7	2	18	1	4
2006:										
1st qtr.	0	0	0	1	0	1	0	0	0	0
2d qtr.	0	0	0	3	1	4	0	2	1	2
3d qtr.	3	6	0	1	0	0	0	3	0	7
4th qtr.	0	0	0	0	1	2	0	3	0	1
2006 total	3	6	0	5	2	7	0	8	1	10

Quarter	Wallowa-Whitman Set-aside sales	Wallowa-Whitman Total sales	Wenatchee Set-aside sales	Wenatchee Total sales	Willamette Set-aside sales	Willamette Total sales	Winema Set-aside sales	Winema Total sales	All forests Set-aside sales	All forests Total sales
2001	1	8	0	6	4	5	0	1	8	99
2002	0	6	0	6	4	30	0	7	12	154
2003	0	7	a	a	10	27	3	7	25	152
2004	0	7	a	a	0	17	2	4	22	138
2005	2	9	0	8	1	16	0	6	16	147
2006:										
1st qtr.	0	0	0	3	0	0	0	3	2	18
2d qtr.	0	1	0	0	0	3	0	0	5	33
3d qtr.	1	12	1	3	0	8	1	3	8	72
4th qtr.	0	1	0	2	0	0	0	0	5	33
2006 total	1	14	1	8	0	11	1	6	20	156

ª In 2003 and 2004, the Wenatchee National Forest was combined with the Okanogan National Forest.

Source: Forest Service, U.S. Department of Agriculture. Pacific Northwest Region includes Oregon and Washington and a small portion of northern California.

Table 106—Volume and average value of timber sold on set-aside sales on the National Forests, Pacific Northwest Region, 2001-2006

(Volume in thousand board feet; value in dollars per thousand board feet)

Quarter	Colville Volume	Colville Average value	Deschutes Volume	Deschutes Average value	Fremont Volume	Fremont Average value	Gifford Pinchot Volume	Gifford Pinchot Average value	Malheur Volume	Malheur Average value
2001	2,007	155.82	0	--	7,020	50.09	382	174.67	0	--
2002	0	--	0	--	0	--	10,898	60.23	0	--
2003	0	--	0	--	0	--	4,413	103.11	0	--
2004	0	--	0	--	0	--	14,685	126.13	0	--
2005	0	--	0	--	0	--	4,214	244.44	0	--
2006:										
1st qtr.	0	-	3,848	101.75	0	--	0	--	0	--
2d qtr.	0	--	2,823	164.21	0	--	280	399.98	0	--
3d qtr.	0	--	1,936	121.86	4,721	32.76	0	--	0	--
4th qtr.	0	--	2,010	128.74	6,669	78.80	9,838	26.94	0	--
2006 total	0	--	10,617	127.13	11,390	59.72	10,118	37.26	0	--

Quarter	Mount Baker-Snoqualmie Volume	Mount Baker-Snoqualmie Average value	Mount Hood Volume	Mount Hood Average value	Ochoco Volume	Ochoco Average value	Okanogan/Wenatchee Volume	Okanogan/Wenatchee Average value	Olympic Volume	Olympic Average value
2001	0	--	0	--	0	--	0	--	0	--
2002	0	--	4,792	85.16	0	--	571	77.91	0	--
2003	0	--	14,246	104.04	0	--	8,898	103.34	8,381	105.17
2004	3,878	33.42	2,772	213.67	0	--	7,108	152.08	13,754	76.36
2005	0	--	0	--	0	--	0	--	15,351	151.31
2006:										
1st qtr.	0	--	0	--	0	--	0	--	0	--
2d qtr.	0	--	0	--	0	--	0	--	0	--
3d qtr.	0	--	0	--	0	--	0	--	0	--
4th qtr.	0	--	0	--	0	--	0	--	0	--
2006 total	0	--	0	--	0	--	0	--	0	--

Quarter	Rogue River Volume	Rogue River Average value	Siskiyou Volume	Siskiyou Average value	Siuslaw Volume	Siuslaw Average value	Umatilla Volume	Umatilla Average value	Umpqua Volume	Umpqua Average value
2001	0	--	0	--	0	--	0	--	0	--
2002	0	--	0	--	0	--	0	--	0	--
2003	0	--	0	--	7,928	125.88	0	--	0	--
2004	0	--	0	--	7,029	158.82	1,335	126.91	0	--
2005	416	166.31	2	511.00	299	107.52	442	22.41	8,876	189.92
2006:										
1st qtr.	0	--	0	--	0	--	0	--	0	--
2d qtr.	0	--	0	--	1,004	188.87	0	--	2,148	163.53
3d qtr.	11,054	192.42	0	--	0	--	0	--	0	--
4th qtr.	0	--	0	--	2,751	149.49	0	--	0	--
2006 total	11,054	192.42	0	--	3,755	160.02	0	--	2,148	163.53

Quarter	Wallowa-Whitman Volume	Wallowa-Whitman Average value	Wenatchee Volume	Wenatchee Average value	Willamette Volume	Willamette Average value	Winema Volume	Winema Average value	All forests Volume	All forests Average value
2001	2,701	39.33	0	--	367	270.66	0	--	12,477	75.07
2002	0	--	0	--	4,880	51.09	0	--	21,141	64.24
2003	0	--	a	a	20,069	279.68	7,381	46.03	71,316	149.88
2004	0	--	a	a	0	--	11,476	93.10	62,037	113.80
2005	985	30.72	0	--	2,573	137.21	0	--	38,659	164.15
2006:										
1st qtr.	0	--	0	--	0	--	0	--	3,848	101.75
2d qtr.	0	--	0	--	0	--	0	--	6,255	178.49
3d qtr.	1,619	49.63	560	175.43	0	--	2,510	80.72	22,400	129.41
4th qtr.	0	--	0	--	0	--	0	--	21,268	68.67
2006 total	1,619	49.63	560	175.43	0	--	2,510	80.72	53,771	109.12

ᵃ In 2003 and 2004, the Wenatchee National Forest was combined with the Okanogan National Forest.

Source: Forest Service, U.S. Department of Agriculture. Pacific Northwest Region includes Oregon and Washington and a small portion of northern California.